First World War
and Army of Occupation
War Diary
France, Belgium and Germany

29 DIVISION
Headquarters, Branches and Services
General Staff
1 September 1916 - 31 December 1916

WO95/2281/1

The Naval & Military Press Ltd
www.nmarchive.com
Published in association with The National Archives

Published by

The Naval & Military Press Ltd

Unit 10 Ridgewood Industrial Park,

Uckfield, East Sussex,

TN22 5QE England

Tel: +44 (0) 1825 749494

www.naval-military-press.com

www.nmarchive.com

This diary has been reprinted in facsimile from the original. Any imperfections are inevitably reproduced and the quality may fall short of modern type and cartographic standards.

© **Crown Copyright**
Images reproduced by permission of The National Archives, London, England, 2015.

Contents

Document type	Place/Title	Date From	Date To
Heading	War Diary General Staff 29th Division Sept 1916 Apr 1917		
Heading	War Diary General Staff 29th Division 1st To 30th September 1916. Volume XVIII		
War Diary		01/09/1916	30/09/1916
Miscellaneous	Headquarters, VIIIth Corps.	01/09/1916	01/09/1916
Miscellaneous	Report on Gas Discharge on 29th Division Front on Night of 31st August/1st September.	31/08/1916	31/08/1916
Miscellaneous	Appendices.		
Diagram etc	Reliefs in 29th Division Area for September 1916. Appendix 1 (a)		
Miscellaneous	General Idea. Appendix 1 (b)		
Miscellaneous	29th Division. C.G.S. 149.	12/09/1916	12/09/1916
Miscellaneous	87th Inf. Bde. A/821.	14/09/1916	14/09/1916
Operation(al) Order(s)	87th Infantry Brigade Operation Order No. 000		
Miscellaneous	87th Inf. Bde. A/821/1.	15/09/1916	15/09/1916
Miscellaneous	Remarks By The G.O.C. 29th Division.		
Operation(al) Order(s)	29th Division Order No. 59. Appendix 2 (a)	07/09/1916	07/09/1916
Miscellaneous	Moves Table.		
Miscellaneous	Relief Of Brigades-Time Table.	07/09/1916	07/09/1916
Miscellaneous	Notes On The Attack.	12/09/1916	12/09/1916
Operation(al) Order(s)	29th Division Operation Order No. 60. Appendix 2 (b)	16/09/1916	16/09/1916
Miscellaneous	Table Of Moves.		
Operation(al) Order(s)	29th Division Order No. 61	17/09/1916	17/09/1916
Operation(al) Order(s)	29th Division Order No. 62	20/09/1916	20/09/1916
Operation(al) Order(s)	29th Division Order No. 63.	20/09/1916	20/09/1916
Operation(al) Order(s)	29th Division Order No. 64. Appendix 2 (c)	26/09/1916	26/09/1916
Miscellaneous	Moves Table.		
Miscellaneous	A Form. Messages And Signals.		
Miscellaneous	86th Brigade. Appendix 3 (a)	14/09/1916	14/09/1916
Miscellaneous	Arrangements For Raid To Be Carried Out By 29th Division.		
Miscellaneous	Report On Raid Carried Out By The 29th Division On Night 15/16th September 1916. Appendix 3 (b)	15/09/1916	15/09/1916
Miscellaneous	Report On Raid Carried Out By 2nd Royal Fusiliers. Appendix 3 (c)	20/09/1916	20/09/1916
Miscellaneous	Report on Raid made by 1st Border Regiment on night 30th Sept. 1916. Appendix 3 (d)		
Miscellaneous	Report On Raid Carried Out By 1st Lancashire Fusiliers On The Night Of/30th Sept. 1916 Appendix 3 (e)	30/09/1916	30/09/1916
Miscellaneous	C Form (Duplicate). Messages And Signals. Appendix 3 (b)		
Miscellaneous	C Form (Duplicate). Messages And Signals. Appendix 3 (f)		
Operation(al) Order(s)	29th Division Order No. 62 Appendix 4 (a)	20/09/1916	20/09/1916
Operation(al) Order(s)	29th Division Order No. 63. Appendix 4 (b)	20/09/1916	20/09/1916
Miscellaneous	29th Division Daily Summary. From 10 a.m. 31.8.16. to 10 a.m. 1.9.16. Appendix 5	31/08/1916	31/08/1916
Miscellaneous	29th Division Daily Summary. From 10 a.m. 1.9.16. to 10 a.m. 2.9.16.	01/09/1916	01/09/1916

Miscellaneous	29th Division Daily Summary. From 10 a.m. 2.9.16. to 10 a.m. 3.9.16.	02/09/1916	02/09/1916
Miscellaneous	29th Division Daily Summary. From 10 a.m. 3.9.16. to 10 a.m. 4.9.16.	03/09/1916	03/09/1916
Miscellaneous	29th Division Daily Summary. From 10 a.m. 4.9.16. to 10 a.m. 5.9.16.	04/09/1916	04/09/1916
Miscellaneous	29th Division Daily Summary. From 10 a.m. 3.9.16. to 10 a.m. 6.9.16.	05/09/1916	05/09/1916
Miscellaneous	29th Division Daily Intelligence Summary from 10.O a.m. 6/9/1916 to 10.O a.m. 7/9/1916.	06/09/1916	06/09/1916
Miscellaneous	29th Division Daily Summary. From 10 a.m. 7.9.16. to 10 a.m. 8.9.16.	07/09/1916	07/09/1916
Miscellaneous	29th Division Daily Summary. From 10 a.m. 8.9.16. to 10 a.m. 9.9.16.	08/09/1916	08/09/1916
Miscellaneous	29th Division Daily Summary. From 10 a.m. 9.9.16. to 10 a.m. 10.9.16.	09/09/1916	09/09/1916
Miscellaneous	29th Division Daily Summary. From 10 a.m. 10.9.16. to 10 a.m. 11.9.16.	10/09/1916	10/09/1916
Miscellaneous	29th Division Daily Summary. From 10 a.m. 11.9.16. to 10 a.m. 12.9.16.	11/09/1916	11/09/1916
Miscellaneous	29th Division Daily Summary. From 10 a.m. 12.9.16. to 10 a.m. 13.9.16.	12/09/1916	12/09/1916
Miscellaneous	29th Division Daily Summary. From 10 a.m. 13.9.16. to 10 a.m. 14.9.16.	13/09/1916	13/09/1916
Miscellaneous	29th Division Daily Summary. From 10 a.m. 14.9.16. to 10 a.m. 15.9.16.	14/09/1916	14/09/1916
Miscellaneous	29th Division Daily Summary. From 10 a.m. 15.9.16. to 10 a.m. 16.9.16.	15/09/1916	15/09/1916
Miscellaneous	29th Division Daily Summary. From 10 a.m. 16.9.16. to 10 a.m. 17.9.16.	16/09/1916	16/09/1916
Miscellaneous	29th Division Daily Summary. From 10 a.m. 17.9.16. to 10 a.m. 18.9.16.	17/09/1916	17/09/1916
Miscellaneous	29th Division Daily Summary. From 10 a.m. 18.9.16. to 10 a.m. 19.9.16.	18/09/1916	18/09/1916
Miscellaneous	29th Division Daily Summary. From 10 a.m. 19.9.16. to 10 a.m. 20.9.16.	19/09/1916	19/09/1916
Miscellaneous	29th Division Daily Summary. From 10 a.m. 20.9.16. to 10 a.m. 21.9.16.	20/09/1916	20/09/1916
Miscellaneous	29th Division Daily Summary. From 10 a.m. 21.9.16. to 10 a.m. 22.9.16.	21/09/1916	21/09/1916
Miscellaneous	29th Division Daily Summary. From 10 a.m. 22.9.16. to 10 a.m. 23.9.16.	22/09/1916	22/09/1916
Miscellaneous	29th Division Daily Summary. From 10 a.m. 23.9.16. to 10 a.m. 24.9.16.	23/09/1916	23/09/1916
Miscellaneous	29th Division Daily Summary. From 10 a.m. 24.9.16 to 10 a.m. 25.9.16.	24/09/1916	24/09/1916
Miscellaneous	29th Division Daily Summary. From 10 a.m. 25.9.16. to 10 a.m. 26.9.16.	25/09/1916	25/09/1916
Miscellaneous	29th Division Daily Summary. From 10 a.m. 26.9.16. to 10 a.m. 27.9.16.	26/09/1916	26/09/1916
Miscellaneous	29th Division Daily Summary. From 10 a.m. 27.9.16. to 10 a.m. 28.9.16.	27/09/1916	27/09/1916
Miscellaneous	29th Division Daily Summary. From 10 a.m. 28.9.16. to 10 a.m. 29.9.16.	28/09/1916	28/09/1916
Miscellaneous	29th Division Daily Summary. From 10 a.m. 29.9.16. to 10 a.m. 30.9.16.	29/09/1916	29/09/1916

Miscellaneous	29th Division Weekly Operation Report. From 10 a.m. 21.9.16. to 10 a.m. 28.9.16. Appendix 6	21/09/1916	21/09/1916
Miscellaneous	Casualties from 12 noon 21st to 12 noon 28th September 1916	28/09/1916	28/09/1916
Miscellaneous	29th Division Weekly Operation Report. From 10 a.m. 14.9.16. to 10 a.m. 21.9.16.	14/09/1916	14/09/1916
Miscellaneous	Weekly Strength, Week ending 23rd Sept. 1916	23/09/1916	23/09/1916
Miscellaneous	Casualties from 12 noon 14th to 12 noon 21st Septr.	21/09/1916	21/09/1916
Miscellaneous	29th Division Weekly Operation Report. From 6 p.m. 7.9.16. to 6 p.m. 14.9.16.	07/09/1916	07/09/1916
Miscellaneous	Strength Return W.E. Saturday 16th Septr, 1916	16/09/1916	16/09/1916
Miscellaneous	29th Division Weekly Operation Report. From 6 p.m. 31.8.16. to 6 p.m. 7.9.16.	31/08/1916	31/08/1916
Miscellaneous	Casualties From 12 noon 30th Aug. to 12 noon 7th Sept.	30/08/1916	30/08/1916
Heading	War Diary General Staff 29th Division October 1916		
Heading	War Diary General Staff 29th. Division. For The Period 1st.-31st. October, 1916. Volume XX.		
Miscellaneous	Headquarters, 29th Division.	09/11/1916	09/11/1916
Map	Plan 6 shewing Trenches in XV Corps Area.		
Miscellaneous		09/11/1916	09/11/1916
Operation(al) Order(s)	29th Division Order No. 65 Appendix 1 (a)	01/10/1916	01/10/1916
Miscellaneous	Movements Of 29th Division.		
Miscellaneous	Movements Of 29th Division. Positions on nights of		
Miscellaneous	Movements Of 55th Division.		
Miscellaneous	Amendment to 29th Division Order No. 65	01/10/1916	01/10/1916
Miscellaneous	C Form (Duplicate). Messages And Signals.		
Miscellaneous	C Form (Duplicate). Messages And Signals.	03/10/1916	03/10/1916
Miscellaneous	86th Brigade.	03/10/1916	03/10/1916
Miscellaneous	O.C., 2nd Royal Fusiliers.	02/10/1916	02/10/1916
Operation(al) Order(s)	29th Division Order No. 66 Appendix 1 (b)	09/10/1916	09/10/1916
Miscellaneous	A Form. Messages And Signals.		
Miscellaneous	March Table of Infantry Moves to accompany 29th Division Order No. 67		
Operation(al) Order(s)	29th Division Order No. 67 Appendix 1 (C)	12/10/1916	12/10/1916
Operation(al) Order(s)	29th Division Order No. 68. Appendix 1 (d)	17/10/1916	17/10/1916
Operation(al) Order(s)	29th Division Order No. 69. Appendix 1 (e)	18/10/1916	18/10/1916
Miscellaneous	March Table.		
Operation(al) Order(s)	29th Division Order No. 70. Appendix 1 (f)	23/10/1916	23/10/1916
Miscellaneous	Appendix "A".		
Map	Plan Shewing Trenches in XV Corps Area.		
Miscellaneous	86th Brigade. Appendix 1 (8)	24/10/1916	24/10/1916
Miscellaneous	86th Brigade. Appendix 1 (b)	26/10/1916	26/10/1916
Miscellaneous	C.G.S. 125. Appendix 1 (i)	28/10/1916	28/10/1916
Operation(al) Order(s)	29th Division Order No. 71. Appendix 1 (j)	26/10/1916	26/10/1916
Operation(al) Order(s)	29th Division Order No. 72. Appendix 1 (K)	28/10/1916	28/10/1916
Miscellaneous	Movements Of 29th Division.		
Miscellaneous	Movements Of 1st Australian Division.		
Miscellaneous	Movements Of 29th Division.		
Operation(al) Order(s)	29th Division Order No. 73. Appendix 1 (L)	29/10/1916	29/10/1916
Operation(al) Order(s)	29th Division Order No. 74. Appendix 1 (m)	30/10/1916	30/10/1916
Miscellaneous	Movements Of 29th Division.		
Miscellaneous	Appendices.		
Miscellaneous	Headquarters, XVth Corps. Appendix 1 (b)		
War Diary		29/10/1916	31/10/1916
War Diary		27/10/1916	28/10/1916

War Diary		25/10/1916	26/10/1916
War Diary		23/10/1916	24/10/1916
War Diary		21/10/1916	22/10/1916
War Diary		19/10/1916	20/10/1916
War Diary		17/10/1916	18/10/1916
War Diary		15/10/1916	16/10/1916
War Diary		13/10/1916	14/10/1916
War Diary		11/10/1916	12/10/1916
War Diary		09/10/1916	10/10/1916
War Diary		07/10/1916	08/10/1916
War Diary		05/10/1916	06/10/1916
War Diary		03/10/1916	04/10/1916
War Diary		01/10/1916	02/10/1916
Miscellaneous	Appendices.		
Heading	War Diary General Staff 29th. Division For The Month Of October 1916. Volume XX.		
Miscellaneous	Position Oct. 30th & Oct. 31st	30/10/1916	30/10/1916
Miscellaneous	Report On Raid Carried Out By The 1st Lancashire Fusiliers On 30th September.	30/09/1916	30/09/1916
Map	WO95/2281		
Diagram etc			
Miscellaneous	HQ 29 Divn.	30/09/1916	30/09/1916
Miscellaneous	HQ 29 Divn Appendix 2 (a)	20/10/1916	20/10/1916
Map	References. 7		
Miscellaneous		02/10/1916	02/10/1916
Miscellaneous	Headquarters, VIIIth Corps.	01/10/1916	01/10/1916
Miscellaneous	Report on Raid made by 1st Border Regiment on night 30th Sept. 1916.	30/09/1916	30/09/1916
Miscellaneous	29th Div. Lt Qrs. "G" 564	01/10/1916	01/10/1916
Miscellaneous	Report on Raid made by 1st Battn Regt. on night 30th Sept. 1916	30/09/1916	30/09/1916
Miscellaneous	Disposition Of Units Of 29th Division On Morning 5th October. Appendix 3 (a)	05/10/1916	05/10/1916
Miscellaneous	Disposition Of Units Of 29th Division On Night 5th/6th October. Appendix 3 (g)	05/10/1916	05/10/1916
Miscellaneous			
Miscellaneous	Locations-29th Division-10th October 1916 Appendix 3 (c)	10/10/1916	10/10/1916
Miscellaneous	Locations-29th Division-13th October 1916. Appendix 3 (d)	13/10/1916	13/10/1916
Miscellaneous	Dispositions. Appendix 3 (e)	20/10/1916	20/10/1916
Miscellaneous	Dispositions Of The 29th Division-26th October 1916 Appendix 3 (f)	26/10/1916	26/10/1916
Miscellaneous	Dispositions Of 29th Division On 28th October 1916 Appendix 3 (g)	28/10/1916	28/10/1916
Miscellaneous	Dispositions Of The 29th Division-29th October, 1916. Appendix 3 (h)	29/10/1916	29/10/1916
Miscellaneous	Locations-29th Division-Night 30/31st October 1916 Appendix 3 (i)	30/10/1916	30/10/1916
Miscellaneous	29th Division Daily Summary. From 12 Noon 28.10.16. to 12 Noon 29.10.16. Appendix 4	28/10/1916	28/10/1916
Miscellaneous	29th Division Daily Summary. From 12 Noon 27.10.16. to 12 Noon 28.10.16.	27/10/1916	27/10/1916
Miscellaneous	29th Division Daily Summary. From 12 Noon 25.10.16. to 12 Noon 27.10.16.	25/10/1916	25/10/1916

Miscellaneous	29th Division Daily Summary. From 12 Noon 25.10.16. to 12 Noon 26.10.16.	25/10/1916	25/10/1916
Miscellaneous	29th Division Daily Summary. From 12 Noon 24.10.16. to 12 Noon 25.10.16.	24/10/1916	24/10/1916
Miscellaneous	29th Division Daily Summary. From 12 Noon 23.10.16. to 12 Noon 24.10.16.	23/10/1916	23/10/1916
Miscellaneous	29th Division Daily Summary. From 12 Noon 22.10.16. to 12 Noon 23.10.16.	22/10/1916	22/10/1916
Miscellaneous	29th Division Daily Summary. From 12 Noon 21.10.16. to 12 Noon 22.10.16.	21/10/1916	21/10/1916
Miscellaneous	Appendix 5		
Map	Plan shewing Trenches in 29th Divl. Area. Appendix 5		
Heading	War Diary. General Staff 29th Division. For The Month Of November 1916. Volume XXI.		
War Diary		01/11/1916	30/11/1916
Miscellaneous	List Of Appendices.		
Miscellaneous	Programme Of 86th Brigade Inspection And-Attack. Appendix 1 (a)		
Miscellaneous	Form Messages And Signals.	03/10/1916	03/10/1916
Operation(al) Order(s)	Operation Order No. 41 By Brigadier General D.E. Cayley, C.M.G. Commanding 88th Brigade. Appendix 1 (c)	12/11/1916	12/11/1916
Miscellaneous	O.C., 2nd Royal Fusiliers. Appendix 1 (d)	13/11/1916	13/11/1916
Map	Rough Trench Map		
Miscellaneous	Agenda for 29th Division Conference No. 13 to be held at Corbie at 5 p.m. on 14th Nov. 1916. Appendix 2 (a)	14/11/1916	14/11/1916
Operation(al) Order(s)	29th Division Order No. 75 Appendix 3 (a)	12/11/1916	12/11/1916
Miscellaneous	March Table "A".		
Miscellaneous	A Form Messages And Signals.	14/11/1916	14/11/1916
Operation(al) Order(s)	29th Division Order No. 76. Appendix 3 (b)	13/11/1916	13/11/1916
Operation(al) Order(s)	29th Division Order No. 77. Appendix 3 (c)	17/11/1916	17/11/1916
Miscellaneous	29th Division Warning Order. Appendix 3 (d)	25/11/1916	25/11/1916
Miscellaneous	Amendment to 29th Division No. C.G.S. 71	25/11/1916	25/11/1916
Operation(al) Order(s)	29th Division Order No. 78. Appendix 3 (e)	27/11/1916	27/11/1916
Miscellaneous	29th Division Daily Summary. From 8.30 a.m. 17.11.16. to 8.30 a.m. 18.11.16. Appendix 4	17/11/1916	17/11/1916
Miscellaneous	29th Division Daily Summary. From 8.30 a.m. 18.11.16. to 8.30 a.m. 19.11.16.	18/11/1916	18/11/1916
Miscellaneous	29th Division Daily Summary. From 8.30 a.m. 19.11.16. to 8.30 a.m. 20.11.16.	19/11/1916	19/11/1916
Miscellaneous	29th Division Daily Summary. From 8.30 a.m. 20.11.16. to 8.30 a.m. 21.11.16.	20/11/1916	20/11/1916
Miscellaneous	29th Division Daily Summary. From 8.30 a.m. 21.11.16. to 8.30 a.m. 22.11.16.	21/11/1916	21/11/1916
Miscellaneous	29th Division Daily Summary. From 8.30 a.m. 22.11.16. to 8.30 a.m. 23.11.16.	22/11/1916	22/11/1916
Miscellaneous	29th Division Daily Summary. From 8.30 a.m. 23.11.16. to 8.30 a.m. 24.11.16.	23/11/1916	23/11/1916
Miscellaneous	29th Division Daily Summary. From 8.30 a.m. 24.11.16. to 8.30 a.m. 25.11.16.	24/11/1916	24/11/1916
Miscellaneous	29th Division Daily Summary. From 8.30 a.m. 25.11.16. to 8.30 a.m. 26.11.16.	25/11/1916	25/11/1916
Miscellaneous	29th Division Daily Summary. From 8.30 a.m. 26.11.16. to 8.30 a.m. 27.11.16.	26/11/1916	26/11/1916
Miscellaneous	29th Division Daily Summary. From 8.30 a.m. 27.11.16. to 8.30 a.m. 28.11.16.	27/11/1916	27/11/1916

Miscellaneous	29th Division Daily Summary. From 8.30 a.m. 28.11.16. to 8.30 a.m. 29.11.16.	28/11/1916	28/11/1916
Miscellaneous	29th Division Daily Summary. From 8.30 a.m. 29.11.16. to 8.30 a.m. 30.11.16.	29/11/1916	29/11/1916
Miscellaneous	29th Division Daily Disposition Report. Appendix 5	19/11/1916	19/11/1916
Miscellaneous	29th Division Daily Disposition Report.	21/11/1916	21/11/1916
Miscellaneous	29th Division Daily Disposition Report.	22/11/1916	22/11/1916
Miscellaneous	29th Division Daily Disposition Report.	24/11/1916	24/11/1916
Miscellaneous	29th Division Daily Disposition Report.	25/11/1916	25/11/1916
Miscellaneous	29th Division Daily Disposition Report.	27/11/1916	27/11/1916
Miscellaneous	29th Division Daily Disposition Report.	28/11/1916	28/11/1916
Miscellaneous	29th Division Daily Disposition Report.	29/11/1916	29/11/1916
Miscellaneous	29th Division No. I.G. 39.	30/11/1916	30/11/1916
Miscellaneous	March Table "A".		
Miscellaneous	March Table "B".		
Miscellaneous	29th Division Daily Disposition Report.	19/11/1916	19/11/1916
Miscellaneous	29th Division Daily Disposition Report.	21/11/1916	21/11/1916
Miscellaneous	29th Division Daily Disposition Report.	22/11/1916	22/11/1916
Miscellaneous	29th Division Daily Disposition Report.	24/11/1916	24/11/1916
Miscellaneous	29th Division Daily Disposition Report.	25/11/1916	25/11/1916
Miscellaneous	29th Division Daily Disposition Report.	27/11/1916	27/11/1916
Miscellaneous	29th Division Daily Disposition Report.	28/11/1916	28/11/1916
Miscellaneous	29th Division Daily Disposition Report.	29/11/1916	29/11/1916
Miscellaneous	29th Division No. I.G. 39.	30/11/1916	30/11/1916
Heading	War Diary of General Staff, 29th Division. from 1st December, 1916-31st December, 1916. Volume XXII		
War Diary		01/12/1916	31/12/1916
Heading	War Diary, General Staff, 29th Division. December, 1916 Appendix I Comprises. (a) Trench Map, 1/20,000, dated 6th December.		
Miscellaneous	War Diary, General Staff, 29th Division. December, 1916	00/12/1916	00/12/1916
Miscellaneous	War Diary, General Staff, 29th Division. December 1916.	00/12/1916	00/12/1916
Miscellaneous	War Diary, General Staff, 29th Division. December, 1916	00/12/1916	00/12/1916
Map	Trench Map 29th Div. Area Scale-1.20,000 6th Dec 1916 No 6. Appendix 1 (a)		
Operation(al) Order(s)	29th Division Order No. 79. Appendix 2 (a)	06/12/1916	06/12/1916
Miscellaneous	Locations Table.		
Miscellaneous	March Table.		
Miscellaneous	Amendment to 29th Division Order No. 79. Appendix 2 (b)	07/12/1916	07/12/1916
Operation(al) Order(s)	29th Division Order No. 80. Appendix 2 (c)	10/12/1916	10/12/1916
Miscellaneous	Table "A".		
Miscellaneous	Table "B".		
Miscellaneous	Table "C". Billeting List.		
Miscellaneous	Divisional Conference No. 14 held at Cavillon, December 15th, 1916, Brigadiers and Battalion Commanders attending. Appendix 3 (a)	15/12/1916	15/12/1916
Miscellaneous	C.R.A. Appendix 3 (b)	19/12/1916	19/12/1916
Miscellaneous	Minutes of Conferences held at each Brigade Commanding Officers attending, on 30th December, 1916. Appendix 3 (c)	30/12/1916	30/12/1916

Miscellaneous	29th Division Weekly Operation Report. From 8.30 a.m. 30th November to 8.30 a.m. 7th December, 1916. Appendix (4)	07/12/1916	07/12/1916
Miscellaneous	29th Division Daily Summary. From 8.30 a.m. 30.11.16. to 8.30 a.m. 1.12.16. Appendix 5	30/11/1916	30/11/1916
Miscellaneous	29th Division Daily Summary. From 8.30 a.m. 3.12.16. to 8.30 a.m. 4.12.16.	03/12/1916	03/12/1916
Miscellaneous	29th Division Daily Summary. From 8.30 a.m. 4.12.16. to 8.30 a.m. 5.12.16.	04/12/1916	04/12/1916
Miscellaneous	29th Division Daily Summary. From 8.30 a.m. 5.12.16. to 8.30 a.m. 6.12.16.	05/12/1916	05/12/1916
Miscellaneous	29th Division Daily Summary. From 8.30 a.m. 8.12.16. to 8.30 a.m. 9.12.16.	08/12/1916	08/12/1916
Miscellaneous	29th Division Daily Summary. From 8.30 a.m. 9.12.16. to 8.30 a.m. 10.12.16	09/12/1916	09/12/1916
Miscellaneous	29th Division Daily Summary. From 8.30 a.m. 10.12.16 to 8.30 a.m. 11.12.16.	10/12/1916	10/12/1916

Index..............

SUBJECT.

WAR DIARY

No.	Contents.	Date.

GENERAL STAFF
29 21st DIVISION

Sept 1916
—
Apr 1917

CONFIDENTIAL.

WAR DIARY

GENERAL STAFF 29TH DIVISION

1ST TO 30TH SEPTEMBER 1916.

VOLUME ~~XVIII~~

Army Form C. 2118.

WAR DIARY – GENERAL STAFF, 29TH DIVISION.

INTELLIGENCE SUMMARY

(Erase heading not required.)

SEPTEMBER 1916.

Instructions regarding War Diaries and Intelligence Summaries are contained in F. S. Regs., Part II. and the Staff Manual respectively. Title pages will be prepared in manuscript.

Place	Date	Hour	Summary of Events and Information	Remarks and references to Appendices
	Sept. 1st		G.O.C. visited the trenches in the morning. The G.S.O.III visited all the O.Ps. on the Division front and noted positions for others. G.S.O.II went to see 400 men of 86th (Reserve) Brigade digging cable trenches at ST. JEAN, in order to investigate the arrangements and report on result of the work. GAS was to have been emitted at 2.30 a.m. night 1/2nd but the wind died down and it was cancelled. Tables showing reliefs in 29th Division Area attached (App. 1a)	App. 1a.
	Sept. 2nd		The G.S.O.I visited the trenches early. The G.O.C. inspected the classes at the Divisional School on termination of the course. Capt. CARDEN-ROE, Royal Irish Fusiliers, joined the Division as G.S.O.III. A false gas alarm took place at 11 p.m., Strombos horns being heard to the South.	

Army Form C. 2118.

WAR DIARY – GENERAL STAFF, 29TH DIVISION.

INTELLIGENCE SUMMARY.

(Erase heading not required.)

Instructions regarding War Diaries and Intelligence Summaries are contained in F. S. Regs., Part II. and the Staff Manual respectively. Title pages will be prepared in manuscript.

Place	Date	Hour	Summary of Events and Information	Remarks and references to Appendices
	Sept. 3rd		The G.S.O.III went round the trenches with Major CLARKE. A quiet day. It was not possible to emit gas on the night 3rd/4th.	
	Sept. 4th		The G.O.C. visited the right sector early, and the G.S.O.I visited the left sector in the morning. The G.S.O.II and Major CLARKE went to trenches in the afternoon. The 2nd West Riding Regiment (4th Division) commenced digging cable trenches along the ST. JEAN Road, this Battalion was billeted in POPERINGHE.	

Army Form C. 2118.

WAR DIARY - GENERAL STAFF, 29TH DIVISION.

INTELLIGENCE SUMMARY

(Erase heading not required.)

Instructions regarding War Diaries and Intelligence Summaries are contained in F. S. Regs., Part II. and the Staff Manual respectively. Title pages will be prepared in manuscript.

Place	Date	Hour	Summary of Events and Information	Remarks and references to Appendices
	Sept. 5th		Heavy rain most of the day. The G.S.O.II visited trenches of the right Battalion of the left Brigade early. G.S.O.III and Major CLARKE went to the same sector in the afternoon. The cable burying was cancelled owing to the wet. It was decided not to attempt to let off gas during the night 5th/6th.	
	Sept. 6th		The G.O.C. visited the right sector trenches early. A misty morning. A Corps Conference was held at 5 p.m. at Corps H.Q. to discuss the method of carrying out forthcoming raids, the G.O.C., G.S.O.I and C.R.As. of 20th and 4th Divisions attended. The 4th Division Artillery commenced taking over from the 20th Division Artillery. A new course commenced at the Divisional School.	

WAR DIARY - GENERAL STAFF, 29TH DIVISION.

Army Form C. 2118.

Instructions regarding War Diaries and Intelligence Summaries are contained in F. S. Regs., Part II. and the Staff Manual respectively. Title pages will be prepared in manuscript.

404.

Place	Date	Hour	Summary of Events and Information	Remarks and references to Appendices
	Sept 7th		G.S.O.I visited left sector trenches early. A fine dry day. G.O.C. visited C. Camp in morning. A quiet day. 4th Division Artillery finally took over from 20th Division Artillery.	
	Sept 8th		G.O.C. visited right sector trenches early, and had a conference at 88th Brigade H.Q. G.S.O.III arranged about signal from trenches to Artillery for fire after the camouflet opposite 2A Crater was blown. This was successfully done at 4 p.m. and our artillery effectively bombarded enemy's trenches opposite RAILWAY WOOD. Very little hostile retaliation. 20th Division Artillery moved out of our area. A fine dry day. The G.S.O.II visited the right sector trenches in afternoon. 2 Battalions of 86th Brigade moved from Reserve in Camp C. to YPRES and CANAL BANK in relief of 2 Battalions of 87th Brigade. Bombing Demonstration was held at Camp C, under Divisional Grenadier Officer. G.S.O.I. attended it	

T.2134. Wt. W708—776. 500000. 4/15. Sir J. C. & S.

Army Form C. 2118.

WAR DIARY - GENERAL STAFF, 29TH DIVISION.

~~INTELLIGENCE SUMMARY~~

(Erase heading not required.)

Instructions regarding War Diaries and Intelligence Summaries are contained in F. S. Regs., Part II. and the Staff Manual respectively. Title pages will be prepared in manuscript.

Place	Date	Hour	Summary of Events and Information	Remarks and references to Appendices
	Sept. 9th		The G.S.O.I and G.S.O.II visited the right and left sectors respectively early. The G.O.C. visited the 2nd Army Bombing School at TERDEGHEM. Major CLARKE and the O.C. Signals witnessed the contact aeroplane practice by 86th Brigade and 5th Squadron R.F.C. In the evening 2 Battalions of 86th Brigade moved from Reserve (Camp C) to YPRES and CANAL BANK. 2 Battalions of 86th Brigade from YPRES and CANAL BANK relieved 2 Battalions 87th Brigade in trenches, who came back into Reserve.(App. 2a) GAS ALERT ON. A fine and dry day. Enemy was active with Trench Mortars in the morning against WIELTJE and the left Battalion front trenches.	App. 2a
	Sept. 10th		A quiet day. G.S.O.III visited the trenches at night. 4th Division supplied 600 more men to dig cable trenches, they began at WHITE CHATEAU and dug the trench along MENIN ROAD.	

405

WAR DIARY - GENERAL STAFF, 29TH DIVISION.   Army Form C. 2118.

App. 1b   406.

Place	Date	Hour	Summary of Events and Information	Remarks and references to Appendices
	Sept. 11th		G.O.C. visited trenches early. G.S.O.II visited the Machine Gun emplacements along RAMPARTS with O.C. 88th Machine Gun Company. G.S.O.I and CRE visited POTIJZE and KRUIE Salient Or 2!" A.Yorks Pioneers. Rain during night 11th/12th, the day was fine.	
	Sept. 12th		The G.S.O.I/visited the right sector trenches early, and inspected position for a strong point near WITTE POORT FARM. G.S.O.II and Major CLARKE visited the site of northern O.P. and front trenches in the centre of our line. Enemy fired 30 5.9" shells into PICCADILLY about 11 a.m. and we retaliated energetically with about 60 H.E. shells and our Divisional Artillery. Fine day. ↓CRE. Special idea for recapture of WIELTJE in case of occupation by the enemy issued to the 87th Brigade on this date. Orders issued by Brigade concerned with criticisms by G.O.C. 29th Division attached. (App. 1b)	App. 1b

Army Form C. 2118.

WAR DIARY - GENERAL STAFF, 29TH DIVISION.

INTELLIGENCE SUMMARY.

(Erase heading not required.)

Instructions regarding War Diaries and Intelligence Summaries are contained in F. S. Regs., Part II. and the Staff Manual respectively. Title pages will be prepared in manuscript.

407

Place	Date	Hour	Summary of Events and Information	Remarks and references to Appendices
	Sept. 13th		The G.O.C. visited the right sector trenches early. The G.S.O.I and G.S.O.II visited the works at P.1 and REIGERSBERG in the afternoon. Slight rain during the day. Wind still unfavourable for our discharge of gas.	
	Sept. 14th		The G.S.O.I and Major CLARKE visited the centre and right of the line, in the morning. The G.S.O.II visited a part of the 5th Australian Brigade trenches on our right, during the afternoon. It rained a good deal in the evening. The 4th Divisional Artillery commenced wire cutting at 5 different places on the enemy's front; orders having been received during the afternoon that to-morrow is to be "Z" Day, on the night of "Z" Day a raid is to be carried out by the 29th and 38th Divisions respectively. (App. 3a)	App. 3a

T.I134. Wt. W708-776. 500000. 4/15. Sir J. C. & S.

Army Form C. 2118.

WAR DIARY - GENERAL STAFF, 29TH DIVISION.

INTELLIGENCE SUMMARY.

(Erase heading not required.)

Instructions regarding War Diaries and Intelligence Summaries are contained in F. S. Regs., Part II. and the Staff Manual respectively. Title pages will be prepared in manuscript.

408.

Place	Date	Hour	Summary of Events and Information	Remarks and references to Appendices
	Sept. 15th		The G.O.C. visited the trenches early. The G.S.O.I visited the 2 forward Brigade H.Q. ascertaining that they understood the details of the operations to be carried out tonight. A fine day, westerly and northwesterly winds. At 11 p.m. an artillery bombardment took place on the 5 places mentioned above, also on I.11.b.95.70, on which point the raid took place at 11.30 p.m. 1 German prisoner was secured and 1 German was killed and 1 wounded. Many dugouts were bombed. An account of the raid is attached to App.3b. Gas was successfully discharged by us from trenches A.5.a. to A.7 at 11 p.m. there was very little hostile retaliation.	App. 3b
	Sept. 16th		The G.S.O.I visited the left sector trenches in the morning. Some damage had been done south of WIELTJE by the enemy's retaliation with Trench Mortars, and a few casualties had been caused. The G.S.O.II supervised a tactical exercise undertaken by the officers of the 87th Machine Gun Coy. between VLAMERTINGHE and BRIELEN, in the morning. G.S.O.III and Major CLARKE went to the O.Ps. in the afternoon. The 29th Divisional Artillery took over guns from the 4th Divisional Artillery. Orders were received from VIIIth Corps for a further raid to be carried out either to-morrow 17th or 18th instant.	

Army Form C. 2118.

WAR DIARY - GENERAL STAFF, 29TH DIVISION.

INTELLIGENCE SUMMARY

(Erase heading not required.)

Instructions regarding War Diaries and Intelligence Summaries are contained in F. S. Regs., Part II. and the Staff Manual respectively. Title pages will be prepared in manuscript.

Place	Date	Hour	Summary of Events and Information	Remarks and references to Appendices
	Sept. 17th		A quiet day.	
	Sept. 18th		The G.O.C. visited the right sector trenches with the Brigadier 86th Brigade early. [The enemy severely bombarded RAILWAY WOOD, and the vicinity at 8 a.m. for half an hour, causing 40 casualties (of whom 15 were killed) and badly damaging our trenches in several places. Our Heavy Artillery retaliated but suffered rather from shortage of ammunition.) Heavy rain all day but fine evening. G.S.O.1 and 2 visited Elverdinghe and h.3 wks in the afternoon. The first moves of the double relief took place at night (18th/19th) vide Division Order No. 60 After the relief the whole Division front was held by the 86th Brigade, 2 Battalions 87th Brigade being in reserve to left sector under G.O.C. 86th Brigade, and 2 Battalions of 88th Brigade being in reserve to right sector under G.O.C. 88th Brigade.	App. 2b 409.

Captain G.A.N. Robertson 2/S. W. Borderers was attached to the General Staff at Div H.Q. for 6 day

Army Form C. 2118.

WAR DIARY - GENERAL STAFF, 29TH DIVISION.

~~INTELLIGENCE~~ SUMMARY

(Erase heading not required.)

Instructions regarding War Diaries and Intelligence Summaries are contained in F.S. Regs., Part II. and the Staff Manual respectively. Title pages will be prepared in manuscript.

410.

Place	Date	Hour	Summary of Events and Information	Remarks and references to Appendices
	Sept. 19th		G.S.O.I and G.S.O.II visited RAILWAY WOOD trenches, and inspected damage done by yesterday's bombardment: several portions of the trenches had been blown in, more especially the new works under construction, but the damage was being repaired rapidly. During the night 19th/20th the 2nd stage of the double relief was carried out and the G.O.C. 86th Brigade assumed command of the right sector and the G.O.C. 87th Brigade the left sector. At 2 a.m. an attempt was made to raid the German trenches at C.29.d.4.3 by a party from the 86th Brigade (Royal Fusiliers) but it failed. Casualties were 1 Sergeant killed and 5 other ranks wounded, vide report. There were heavy showers throughout the day, and night of 19th/20th.	App.2b App.3c
	Sept. 20th		The G.S.O.I went to England on 10 days leave. The G.O.C. visited the 2 Brigade H.Q. in YPRES, in the morning. Weather still bad, heavy showers all day. Gas cylinders were removed from the left sector during night 20th/21st. Vide Order No. 62 (App. 4a)	App.4a

WAR DIARY – GENERAL STAFF, 29TH DIVISION, Army Form C. 2118.

~~INTELLIGENCE SUMMARY~~

(Erase heading not required.)

Instructions regarding War Diaries and Intelligence Summaries are contained in F. S. Regs., Part II. and the Staff Manual respectively. Title pages will be prepared in manuscript.

411.

Place	Date	Hour	Summary of Events and Information	Remarks and references to Appendices
	Sept. 21st		Quiet day. The first official intimation of the forthcoming move of the Division to the South was received, but no dates were given. The Division is to be relieved by the 55th Division. The gas cylinders (except 8) were removed from the right sector during the night 21st/22nd. (Vide Order No. 63) Fine day. Capt. ROBERTSON visited left sector trenches in afternoon.	App. 4b
	Sept. 22nd		Quiet day. G.O.C. held a conference of Brigadiers, C.R.A. and Bombing Officer at 86th Brigade Headquarters in morning to discuss points regarding handing over to incoming Division, forthcoming raids, and establishment of Battalion bombers. At 3.30 p.m. the Army Commander inspected the Essex Regiment and Hampshire Regiment at C. Camp, the G.O.C. was present; the G.O.C. afterwards went round the transport camps. The remainder of the gas cylinders were removed from the right sector during the night 22nd/23rd.	

Army Form C. 2118.

WAR DIARY - GENERAL STAFF, 29TH DIVISION.

INTELLIGENCE SUMMARY

(Erase heading not required.)

Instructions regarding War Diaries and Intelligence Summaries are contained in F.S. Regs., Part II. and the Staff Manual respectively. Title pages will be prepared in manuscript.

412.

Place	Date	Hour	Summary of Events and Information	Remarks and references to Appendices
	Sept. 23rd		The G.O.C. went round the right and centre trenches early, accompanied by the Corps Commander. The Artillery fired 400 rounds on the enemy's back and communication trenches, a prisoner having recently stated that a Battalion relief was taking place during the night 23rd/24th, the result is unknown. A fine day. Quiet. G.S.O.II visited the Aerodrome of the 5th Squadron R.F.C. during the afternoon. G.S.O.III returned from bombing course at TERDEGHEM, which commenced on 17th inst	
	Sept. 24th		A quiet uneventful day.	

T.2134. Wt. W708-776. 500000. 4/15. Sir J.C. & S.

Army Form C. 2118.

WAR DIARY - GENERAL STAFF, 29TH DIVISION.

INTELLIGENCE SUMMARY.

(Erase heading not required.)

Instructions regarding War Diaries and Intelligence Summaries are contained in F. S. Regs., Part II. and the Staff Manual respectively. Title pages will be prepared in manuscript.

413.

Place	Date	Hour	Summary of Events and Information	Remarks and references to Appendices
	Sept. 25th		G.S.O.II accompanied Major BAKER CARR, Commandant Machine Gun School, round the trenches early.	
	Sept. 26th		G.O.C. inspected the Divisional School on completion of 6th Course. The Corps Commander was present. G.S.O.II arranged about forthcoming raid by 87th Brigade, date to be 30th/1st October night. A fine uneventful day.	

T.I34. Wt. W708—776. 500000. 4/15. Sir J. C. & S.

WAR DIARY – GENERAL STAFF, 29TH DIVISION.

Army Form C. 2118.

~~INTELLIGENCE SUMMARY~~

(Erase heading not required.)

Instructions regarding War Diaries and Intelligence Summaries are contained in F. S. Regs., Part II. and the Staff Manual respectively. Title pages will be prepared in manuscript.

414

Place	Date	Hour	Summary of Events and Information	Remarks and references to Appendices
	Sept. 27th		The G.O.C. went round the left sector trenches accompanied by the Corps Commander, early in the morning. A very quiet day, little artillery activity on either side. Report on position of Strombos horns and rockets was sent to Corps, also statement to effect that they were in good working order.	
	Sept. 28th		G.O.C. visited forward Brigade Headquarters to discuss the details of a new raid to be undertaken against RAILWAY WOOD on 30th Sept./1st Oct. night, in conjunction with the one being arranged against point C.29.a.30.95. A quiet day. Orders were received from Corps regarding the relief of 29th Division by 55th Division, the latter to arrive in VIIIth Corps area on 2nd October, 29th Division to entrain on October 6th. The King of the Belgians and the Corps Commander visited our trenches and expressed their entire satisfaction. The King of the Belgians presented the Division with several boxes of cigarettes.	

T2134. Wt. W708 –776. 500000. 4/15. Sir J. C. & S.

Army Form C. 2118.

WAR DIARY - GENERAL STAFF, 29TH DIVISION.

INTELLIGENCE SUMMARY

(Erase heading not required.)

Instructions regarding War Diaries and Intelligence Summaries are contained in F. S. Regs., Part II. and the Staff Manual respectively. Title pages will be prepared in manuscript.

Place	Date	Hour	Summary of Events and Information	Remarks and references to Appendices
	Sept. 29th		The G.O.C. visited left sector and Northern O.P. early. Capt. ROBERTSON also visited the Northern O.P. to make a visibility sketch. The G.S.O.I returned from leave.	App. 2c.
			On the nights 28th/29th and 29th/30th the 88th Brigade relieved 86th Brigade in the Right Sector, vide Operation Order No. 64 (App. 2o).	
	Sept. 30th		The G.O.C. inspected the D.A.C. lines in the morning. At 8 p.m. a successful raid was carried out by the 1st Border Regiment (87th Brigade) opposite WIELTJE, 8 prisoners being taken. Another successful raid was carried out by the 1st Lancashire Fusiliers (86th Brigade) opposite RAILWAY WOOD, the enemy's trenches being entered and several kits and rifles being taken. No Germans were encountered in the trench but one was seen running away. Identifications proved the enemy's dispositions to be normal. The feature of the RAILWAY WOOD raid was the use of 24 Stokes Mortars besides 2" Mortars and Artillery. A full account of both raids is attached to App. 3d and 3e. Congratulatory wires were received from the Corps and Army Commanders.	App. 3d. App. 3e. App. 3f.
			Daily Intelligence Summaries from 1st to 30th September attached (App. 5).	App. 5
			Weekly Operation Reports from 1st to 30th September attached (App. 6).	App. 6

Headquarters,
    VIIIth Corps.

[HEADQUARTERS, 29th DIVISION. GENERAL STAFF. No. G.S.35/15 Date 1/9/16]

S E C R E T.

[GENERAL STAFF, HEADQUARTERS, 8th CORPS. No. G2987 Date ...]

    I forward herewith report on the gas discharge from our Right Sector, which was carried out last night.

    It is proposed, if the wind is favourable, to discharge the gas from the Left Sector to-night at 2.30 a.m.

1st September, 1916.

C. Fuller,
Major-General,
Commanding 29th Division.

Report on Gas Discharge on 29th Division Front
on night of 31st August/1st September.
----

1.   A satisfactory gas discharge took place at 1.30 a.m. in the Right Sector of this Division front (from H.14 to No.4 Crater), the wind being S.W. and from 6 to 7 miles per hour. 83% of the 160 cylinders installed were discharged, the non-discharge of the remainder being due to defects in the apparatus etc.

2.   It had been intended to discharge simultaneously 200 cylinders in the Left Sector on the front A.5.a. to A.7., but at the time detailed for the attack, the wind had not steadied down on this portion of the front and was veering between S. and S.W., so it was decided not to discharge the gas in this section.

3.   According to the Battalion in the trenches from H.14 to Crater No.4, the enemy detected the gas from the hissing, and immediately sent up flares, followed almost/at once by a red rocket bursting into white balls. The Germans also opened a heavy machine gun and rifle fire, directed principally against Craters 2 and 2.A, and along the Railway line. The enemy likewise retaliated with Trench Mortar bombs, which fell behind the firing line, and blew in the parapet in MUDDY LANE. Their artillery fire was however not heavy, and both their gun and Trench Mortar fire are reported as erratic.

4.   Our artillery bombardment, which had been limited to the guns bearing on the Right Sector, opened at 1.40 a.m., and continued till 2.10 a.m. About 2 a.m. the enemy's rifle and machine gun fire dwindled and gradually ceased.

5.   At 2.30 a.m., patrols went out towards I.12.a.0.4 and I.6.c.11.

The Newfoundland patrol on the right was unable to get through the hostile wire, but they heard the enemy coughing, running about on duck-boards, and flapping dugouts.

The Essex patrol reached the German wire, but could not penetrate it. The enemy were sending up flares from every second bay, and the patrol heard no noises in their trenches.

6. In the opinion of the Special Brigade Officer, the gas *in front of the Left Bn* reached the Germans before they knew anything about it. The Patrols reported that there was a strong smell of gas on the ground.

7. There were no casualties among the Battalions in the Right Sector, but 2 men in a Trench Mortar Battery in this locality were wounded. The casualties in the Left Sector were also slight, 4 men of the Special Brigade being hit by shell fire.

APPENDICES.

Appendix 1. Comprises (a) Reliefs in 29th Division Area for September, 1916.

(b) Special Idea for recapture of WIELTJE, in case of enemy occupation.

Appendix 2. Comprises (a) Relief of 87th Brigade by the 86th Brigade. Order No. 59.

(b) Relief of 86th Brigade by the 87th Brigade and relief of 88th Brigade by 86th Brigade. Order No. 60.

(c) Relief of 86th Brigade by 88th Brigade. Order No. 64.

Appendix 3. Comprises (a) Arrangements for raid carried out on the night 15th/16th September, 1916.

(b) Report on raid carried out by 4th Worcester Regiment on above night.

(c) Report on raid carried out by 2nd Royal Fusiliers on night of 19th/20th September.

(d) Report on raid carried out by 1st Border Regiment on night of 30th September.

(e) Report on raid carried out by 1st Lancashire Fusiliers on night of 30th September.

(f) Telegram from VIIIth Corps repeating Army Commanders message of congratulations on the successful results of the raids carried out on the night of 30th September. Corps Commanders congratulations on above.

Appendix 4. Comprises (a) Removal of full and empty gas cylinders from the front line on night of 20th/21st September. Order No. 62.

(b) Removal of full and empty gas cylinders from the front line on night of 21st/22nd September. Order No. 63.

Appendix 5. Comprises 29th Division Daily Summaries 1st to 30th September inclusive.

Appendix 6. Comprises 29th Division Weekly Operation Reports for month of September.

Appendix 1(a)

RELIEFS in 29th Division Area for September 1916.

Brigade / Unit	1	2	3	4	5	6	7	8	9	10	11	12	13	14	15	16	17	18	19	20	21	22	23	24	25	26	27	28	29	30	31	Reliefs days
86th Brigade.																																
2nd R. Fus.											L.S.	L.S.	R.								R.	S.	R.			R.	S.	R.				9/10, 14/15, 19/20, 24/25, 29/30
1st Lanc. Fus.				Corps Reserve												L.S.	L.S.	L.			R.	S.	R.			R.	S.	L.				14/15, 19/20, 24/25, 29/30
16th Middlesex Regt.																																do. do. do.
1st R. Dub. Fus.										L.S.	L.S.	S.	L.								R.	S.	L.									9/10, 14/15, 19/20, 24/25
87th Brigade.																																
1st K.O.S.B.																				L.S.	L.	L.S.	L.			L.	S.	R.		L.S.L		19/20, 24/25, 30
2nd S.W.B.															Divisional Reserve					L.S.	L.	L.S.	R.			L.	S.	R.		L.S.R		do. do. do.
1st R. Inniskillings					L.S.	L.S.	R.																									9/10, 14/15, 29/30
1st Border Regt.					L.S.	L.S.	L.																									do. do. do.
88th Brigade.																																
4th Worcester Regt.														R.	S.	R.														R.S.R		9/10, 14/15, 19/20
2nd Hants.														R.	S.	L.									Divisional Reserve					R.S.L		do. do. do.
1st Essex.							R.	S.	L.																							3/1, 9/10
Newfoundland Regt.							R.	S.	R.																							do. do.

Reference.

R.S.R. Right Sector Right sub-sector.
R.S.L. " " Left "
L.S.R. Left " Right "
L.S.L. " " Left "

Appendix 1 (6).
(1) 417

GENERAL IDEA.

The 29th Division is holding its present line with the 38th Division on its northern Flank and the 2nd Australian Division on its southern Flank.

The enemy, after a severe bombardment of our trenches in the YPRES SALIENT, has attacked the left of the 29th Divisional Front and captured WIELTJE.

SPECIAL IDEA.

The 29th Divisional Front is held by two Brigades, with one Brigade in Reserve West of YPRES. The 87th Brigade is holding the left sector with two Battalions in the line and two in support in the vicinity of YPRES and CANAL BANK. The enemy has succeeded in penetrating the left sub-sector as far as NEW JOHN STREET - S.10.a. - B.11 - B.12; he has established bombing posts in S.12, and at the junction of S.12.a. with GARDEN STREET. Grenade fighting can also be heard in B.9. The rest of the front line is intact. One support Company of the Battalion holding the right sub-sector has been moved up and holds the STRAND and FLEET STREET (facing North). A local counter-attack made by the Officer Commanding the Battalion holding the left sub-sector failed, and his support Companies are lying out in the open astride the ST. JEAN - WIELTJE ROAD about PARADISE ALLEY where they came under heavy Machine gun fire. Both Battalions holding the left sector have suffered severe casualties.

The G.O.C. 29th Division has ordered the Brigadier-General Commanding 87th Brigade to immediately organize a counter-attack and endeavour to re-establish his original line.

Note by G.O.C. The Brigadier-General Commanding 87th Brigade to give notes to his Brigade Major showing his place of attack. The Brigade Major to write orders to enable this plan to be carried out.

29th Division.
C.G.S.149.

Headquarters,
    87th Brigade.

      With reference to the attached General and Special Ideas, the G.O.C. directs that the Brigadier-General Commanding 87th Brigade will give his notes shewing the plan of counter-attack to his Brigade Major, who will write the necessary orders.

      Orders for counter-attack to reach this office by Noon 15th instant.

                          (Signed) C. G. FULLER,
                              Lieut-Colonel, G.S.,

12th September, 1916.   29th Division.

87th Inf. Bde. A/821.

29th Division "G".

      Forwarded in reference to your C.G.S.149 dated 12.9.16.

                            (Signed) C. H. TINBALL LUCAS,
                                    Brigade General,

14.9.16.   Commanding 87th Infantry Brigade.

(2) continued.

Notes by Brigadier-General Commanding 87th Brigade
to his Brigade Major.
----

(1) <u>Note.</u> Dispositions of Brigade as in defence scheme
K.O.S.Bs. right and S.W.Bs. left subsectors firing line.
Inniskillings in the Prison in Divisional Reserve and Borders
on the Canal Bank in Brigade Reserve.
Time 8.30 a.m.

(2) (i) Wire O.C. Battalions firing line to stop all further
local counter-attacks and prepare for counter-attack by
reserve battalion at midday after intense bombardment.
They must verify actual area in occupation of enemy.

(ii) Report situation to Division, Left Group and Brigades
on both flanks. Ask for intense bombardment 12.30 - 1 p.m.
preparatory to counter-attack at 1 p.m.

(iii) Send for O.C. R.I.F. and Borders, T.M.B. and M.G. Coy.
to Brigade Headquarters.

(3) On arrival of O.Cs. the plan for the counter-attack
will be explained.
The plan is that the Border Regiment will move up,
3 companies into X.8 and CONGREVE WALK, one company in support
at ST. JEAN (in low ground S. of it). The 3 companies will
counter-attack across the open against WIELTJE, right coy.
up both sides of NEW JOHN STREET and occupy firing line at
junction of B.9 and B.10. Centre company between GARDEN
STREET and WIELTJE ROAD through B.11 and WIELTJE and occupy
B.10. This Coy. will pick up the men of the S.W.Bs. lying
out near PARADISE ALLEY en route and take them forward.
Left coy. to occupy B.12 and work up B.10.a. These companies
will move forward into the open at 12.50 p.m. and form up
ready for assault at 1 p.m. As soon as they evacuate the
X line the reserve coy. will move up into it.
2 Stokes mortars from S.8 with the platoon of the
K.O.S.Bs. in S.8 and 2 K.O.S.B. bombing squads will move along
the firing line to the point in B.9 where the trench is
blocked, and be ready to bomb up B.9 and clear the trench
simultaneously with the assault.
The one remaining Stokes mortar in the ST. JEAN sector
(i.e. the one in X.8), and 2 bombing squads of the S.W.Bs.
will similarly move up GARDEN STREET to point where trench
is blocked and be prepared to clear GARDEN STREET at 1 p.m.
The platoon of K.O.S.Bs. in Garden of Eden will move up to
S.8.
The company of K.O.S.Bs. in the STRAND will cover the
assault with rifle and Lewis gun fire.
The S.W.Bs. to hold on to their present positions and
prevent enemy extending their gains.
The Brigade on the left to be asked to assist by
Stokes mortars and bombing squads clearing S.12 and B.12
and by covering the assault with machine gun fire along N.
face of the WIELTJE Salient.
When the assault takes place the artillery barrage
will lift at the rate of 100^x every 2 minutes.
The Machine Gun Coy. will cover the advance with direct
fire from all guns suitably placed, the remaining guns to
fire indirect on their night targets.

The Royal Inniskilling Fusiliers and section Machine Gun
Company in reserve to man the RAMPARTS - KAAIE - and
CANAL Defences.

(2) continued.

Copy No.1.

87th INFANTRY BRIGADE.
OPERATION ORDER NO. 000.

Ref. Map.
Trench Diagram
1/10,000 No.2.

X/X/16.

1. The enemy has penetrated the left sub-sector as far as NEW JOHN STREET - S.10.a. - B.11 - B.12; he has established Bombing Posts in S.12 and at junction of S.12.a. and GARDEN STREET. Grenade fighting is also going on in B.9.
The remainder of our front is intact.
One support Company 1st K.O.S.Bs. is holding the STRAND - FLEET STREET. (facing North).
A local counter-attack by the O.C. 2nd South Wales Borderers has failed and the support companies are lying astride the ST. JEAN - WIELTJE ROAD about PARADISE ALLEY.

2. The 2nd South Wales Borderers will at all costs hold on to their present position and prevent the enemy extending his gains.

3. The 1st Border Regiment will counter-attack at 1 p.m. to-day and re-establish the line.
The O.C. 1st Border Regiment will at once move up three Companies into X.8 and CONGREVE WALK, and one in support to the Low Ground South of ST. JEAN.
The three leading Companies will counter-attack across the open against WIELTJE with the following objectives :-
(a) Right Company. Along both sides of NEW JOHN ST. and occupy the firing line at junction of B.9 and B.10.
(b) Centre Company. Between GARDEN STREET and WIELTJE ROAD through B.11 and WIELTJE and occupy B.10.
This Company will pick up the men of the 2nd South Wales Borderers lying out near PARADISE ALLEY and take them forward.
(c) Left Company. To occupy B.12 and work up B.10.a.
These Companies will move forward from the X.8 - CONGREVE WALK LINE into the open at 12.45 p.m. and form up ready for the assault at 1 p.m.
As soon as they evacuate the X Line the Reserve Company will occupy it.

4. The Artillery will open an intense bombardment of the area in occupation of the enemy from 12.30 p.m. to 1 p.m.
At 1 p.m., the hour for the assault, the barrage will lift at the rate of 100 yards every two minutes.

5. (a) The two Stokes Mortars from S.8 with the platoon of the 1st K.O.S.B. in S.8, together with two bombing squads from the 1st K.O.S.B. will move along the firing line to the point in B.9 where the trench is blocked, and be ready to bomb up B.9 and clear the trench simultaneously with the assault.
(b) The one Stokes Mortar in X.8 with two bombing squads 2nd South Wales Borderers will similarly move up GARDEN STREET to the point where the trench is blocked and be prepared to clear GARDEN STREET.
The Stokes Mortars will open fire at 12.57 p.m.
(c) The 114th Brigade have been asked to cooperate with Stokes Mortars and bombing squads clearing S.12 and B.12, and by covering the assault with machine gun fire along the North face of the WIELTJE SALIENT.
(d) The Company of the 1st K.O.S.B. in the STRAND will cover the assault with rifle and Lewis gun fire.
(e) The one platoon of the 1st K.O.S.Bs. in the GARDEN of EDEN will move up into S.8
(f) The Machine Gun Coy. will cover the advance with direct
/ fire

- 2 -

fire from those guns suitably placed; the remaining guns will fire indirect on their night lines.

6. The 1st Royal Inniskilling Fusiliers and the Reserve Section Machine Gun Company will man the RAMPARTS - KAAIE SALIENT - CANAL DEFENCES.

7. The O.C. 1st R. Innis. Fus. will furnish a carrying party as demanded by the O.C. 87th Trench Mortar Battery to assist carrying Stokes Mortar ammunition to where required.

8. Brigade Headquarters will not move.

(Signed) J. C. BRAND, Captain,

Brigade Major,

87th INFANTRY BRIGADE.

Issued at 9 a.m.

Copies to :-
2nd S.W.B.
1st K.O.S.B.
1st R. Innis. Fus.
1st Border Regt.
87th M.G. Coy.
87th T.M.B.
29th Division.
88th Bde.
114th Bde.
Left Group R.A.
Staff.

SECRET

(3)

87th Inf. Bde. A/821/1.

29th Division "G".

428

      Reference my A/821 of the 14th inst. forwarding Operation Order under your C.G.S.149 dated 14.9.16.

Please note the following assumptions are made :-

(i) The 2nd South Wales Borderers and the 1st Kings Own Scottish Borderers were holding the left and right sub-sectors respectively.

(ii) The 1st Royal Inniskilling Fusiliers and the 1st Border Regiment were in Reserve at the PRISON and CANAL BANK respectively.

(iii) The situation described in the above letter was timed at 8.30 a.m.

                                  (Signed) C. W. H. COX, Capt.,

                                        for Brigade General,

15th Sept. 1916.   Commanding 87th Infantry Brigade.

(4)

REMARKS BY THE G.O.C. 29TH DIVISION.

429

(1) The task set is one that might occur at any time to a Brigade holding the line. It was purposely expressed in an indefinite way to test the Staff work of the Brigade.
    The Brigadier has to ask himself :-
  (i) Is it possible to retake WIELTJE with one Battalion by day.
  (ii) If not, Division must decide whether both Battalions may be used for the purpose. This would leave the 2nd Line (CONGREVE WALK) and the CANAL without defenders until the arrival of part of the Brigade in Divisional Reserve - evidently unsound.

If 1 Battalion is not sufficient to make a certainty of recovering the line it would be better to pospone the attack until 9 p.m.

An immediate counter-attack usually succeeds. If 1 hour has elapsed it is better to wait till all the circumstances are favourable and then make a certainty of it. It would take at least 4 hours to interview C.Os. then Draft Orders and ensure everyone getting them. To write orders between 8.30 and 9 a.m. is "eyewash". It could not be done by the best staff officer. This appears to be a case for Field Messages rather than an Operation Order.

(2) The situation is critical, yet the Brigade on hearing about it at 8.30 a.m. have not immediately wired the Border Regiment to send up three Companies to hold the line CONGREVE WALK - X.8, but wait until 9 a.m. to issue written orders to this effect.

(3) Brigade orders give the time for the attack as 1 p.m., while B.M.0830 says midday. This may lead to confusion.

(4) Para. 3 of Operation Order is not sound and could not be carried out. The route from YPRES to ST. JEAN is not indicated. How could the left Company reach B.12 ?

(5) Brigade Headquarters in the RAMPARTS cannot control the fight. They should move up immediately to POTIJZE.

(6) The Heavy Artillery must co-operate in the bombardment. This point is not mentioned.

(7) The fight as arranged is likely to develop into a bombing match. Arrangements should be made to send up supplies of bombs and Mortar ammunition.

Appendix 2(a)

SECRET.   Copy No. 3

29TH DIVISION ORDER NO. 59.

September 7th, 1916.

1. The 86th Brigade will relieve the 87th Brigade in the left sector on the 8th and 9th September in accordance with the attached "Moves Table".

2. On relief the 87th Brigade will be in Divisional Reserve.

3. Details of reliefs will be arranged direct between Brigades concerned.

4. The 86th Machine Gun Coy. and 86th Trench Mortar Battery will relieve the 87th Machine Gun Coy. and 87th Trench Mortar Battery on the night of the 8th/9th September, the latter leaving a proportion of their detachments in the line until the night of the 9th/10th September to assist the incoming units.

5. (a) The 86th Machine Gun Coy., the 86th Trench Mortar Battery and the 2 Battalions of 86th Brigade which move to YPRES and CANAL BANK on the 8th/9th night will come under the command of the G.O.C. 87th Brigade.
   (b) The 2 Battalions of the 87th Brigade, the 87th Machine Gun Coy. and 87th Trench Mortar Battery which move from YPRES and CANAL BANK on the 8th/9th night will on arrival come under the command of the G.O.C. 86th Brigade as Corps Reserve.

6. The G.O.C. 86th Brigade will take over command of the left sector on completion of the relief on the 9th/10th night.

7. The time table of train services will be issued later by the A.A. & Q.M.G.

8. The Brigade Signal Section in the line will not be relieved.

9. Completion of moves and reliefs will be reported to these Headquarters. The new dispositions will be forwarded to these Headquarters by 9 a.m. on 10th instant.

10. Acknowledge by wire.

C.J. Fuller
Lieut-Colonel, G.S.,
29th Division.

Issued at 4.0.p.m.

Copies 1 - 5	General Staff.	11	Officer i/c Signals.
6	86th Brigade.	12	1/2nd Monmouth Regiment.
7	87th Brigade.	13 - 17	A.A. & Q.M.G.
8	88th Brigade.	18	VIIIth Corps.
9	C.R.A.	19	4th Division.
10	C.R.E.	20	38th Division.

MOVES TABLE.

Date.	Unit.	From.	To.	Remarks.
Night 8th/9th Sept.	2 Bns. 86th Bde.	Camps A.B.C.O.	YPRES (left sector) and CANAL BANK.	Train.
	86th M.Gun Coy.	H.7.a.	Trenches.	March.
	86th T.M. Battery.	A.30.d.	"	"
	87th M.Gun Coy.	Trenches.	H.7.a.	"
	87th T.M. Battery.	"	A.30.d.	"
Night 9th/10th Sept.	2 Bns. 86th Bde.	YPRES (left sector) and CANAL BANK.	Trenches.	March.
	H.Q. 86th Bde.	Camp C.	YPRES (left sector)	Train.
	2 Bns. 87th Bde.	Trenches.	Camps A.B.C.O.	"
	2 Bns. 86th Bde.	Camps A.B.C.O.	YPRES (left sector) and CANAL BANK.	"
	H.Q. 87th Bde.	YPRES (left sector)	Camp C.	"

86 Brigade.

RELIEF OF BRIGADES — TIME TABLE.

Date.	Train.	Place of Entrainment.	Time of Departure.	Place of Detrainment.	Units to Entrain	Strength of Units. Off.	Men.
8/9th	1st	G.6.d.	8.00 p.m.	ASYLUM	Royal Fusrs.	31	683
8/9th	2nd	G.6.d.	8.30 p.m.	ASYLUM	Dublin Fusrs.	28	582
8/9th	1st	ASYLUM	11.15 p.m.	G.6.d.	K.O.S.B.	25	475
8/9th	2nd	ASYLUM	11.45 p.m.	G.6.d.	S.W.Bs.	32	501
9/10th	1st	H.8.a.	8.00 p.m.	ASYLUM	Lancs.Fusrs.	23	510
9/10th	2nd	G.6.d.	8.30 p.m.	ASYLUM	M'sex Regt.	27	492
9/10th	1st	ASYLUM	11.15 p.m.	H.8.a.	Borders	30	553
9/10th	2nd	ASYLUM	11.45 p.m.	G.6.d.	R.Innis:Fus.	24	396

7th September, 1916.

P. Fraser.
Major,
D.A.Q.M.G., 29th Division.

To all Units

S E C R E T.

RELIEF OF BRIGADES - TIME TABLE.

Date.	Train.	Place of entrainment.	Time of Departure	Place of detrainment.	Units to entrain	Strength of units. Off.	N.C.O.
8th/9th	1st	G.S.J.	8.00 p.m.	ASKERN	Royal Fusiliers	31	635
8th/9th	2nd	G.S.J.	8.30 p.m.	ASKERN	Dublin Fusiliers	29	533
9th/10th	1st	H.S.J.	8.00 p.m.	ASKERN	Lancs.Fusiliers	25	519
9th/10th	2nd	G.S.J.	8.30 p.m.	ASKERN	M'ches Regt.	27	492

The 86th Machine Gun Company and 86th Trench Mortar Battery will proceed by march route.

7th September, 1916.

Staff Captain, 86th Brigade.

S E C R E T.

II Corps G.1266.

12/9/16.

NOTES ON THE ATTACK.

The Corps Commander wishes the following elementary lessons of the SOMME Battle to be so thoroughly rubbed into all ranks down to the lowest, by means of conferences, lectures, rehearsals, drills or any other measures, that they become common knowledge, unlikely to be forgotten in the excitement of an attack.

1. Every individual must be perfectly clear about his own particular task before he starts. So clear as to be practically independent of any further orders after the attack has started. Once the noise and confusion of the fight begins the issue of further orders and instructions becomes at least problematical until the objectives have all been gained, consolidated and linked with the rear - a matter of several hours or even a whole day.

2. Generally speaking there are eight main tasks for the assaulting troops, each requiring men to be specially detailed to carry them out -

    (1) The trench clearers, who bayonet, shoot or bomb any Germans found in the trench when we first enter it under our barrage.

    (ii) The moppers up, who capture or kill those Germans remaining in their dug-outs.

    (iii) The consolidators, who set to work at once to deepen and clear the captured trench and form fire-steps and parapets facing the right way. One special party is required to begin at once to clear and clean all captured dug-outs. Failing enemy dug-outs, work to begin at once upon bomb-proof shelters or shell slits.

    (iv) The carriers, who carry forward essential stores (bombs, ammunition, tools, etc), rapidly form and organise new dumps; collect spares from the killed and wounded.

    (v) The communication openers, who begin at once to dig back towards the rear.

    (vi) The signallers, who with flags, flares, etc. signal back the progress, both to ground observers in rear and to our aeroplanes.

    (vii) The coverers, who by their fire protect from hostile rifle or machine gun fire the parties working at (ii) - (vi) above.

    (viii) The exploiterers, who bomb down the enemy's lines of retreat or to the flanks of the captured trench and erect bomb stops in all approaches.

N.B. Although separate parties should be told off for the execution of these different duties every man should understand what all

/ the

the duties are. The officer in command can then, if the necessity arises (e.g. unduly heavy casualties in one particular party), rapidly re-allot the duties with the minimum of explanation.

3. The chief and best protection for our infantry during their advance upon their objectives is our own artillery barrage. Before the infantry are asked to attack the ground, maps and aeroplane photographs are thoroughly studied and every point whence the enemy might bring rifle and machine gun fire to bear upon No Man's Land are either completely demolished or carefully registered and ranged. The trenches about to be attacked are not demolished, or there would be nothing left for our infantry to occupy. These and all danger points whence fire might be opened are, directly our advance begins, put under such a heavy shrapnel fire that no German could put his head up and live. Simultaneously, all the known guns of the enemy's artillery are engaged by our long range guns. Such an intensely heavy fire can only be maintained for a limited period. Our Infantry must take full advantage of it while it lasts.

4. The barrage on the actual objectives is calculated to last just long enough to enable our infantry to walk at a steady pace from their starting points to within 50 yards of the trenches they intend to take.

Up to within this 50 yards, little is therefore to be gained by going too fast - haste may lead to loss of direction, bunching or confusion in the ranks.

Much, on the other hand, will be lost by failing to start exactly at Zero (the outburst of our guns) or by going too slow. Because (a) unless the objective is rushed immediately our barrage lifts, the trench will be manned by German rifles and machine guns (b) within a few minutes of Zero (in practice averaging 6 to 8 minutes) the German artillery barrage, which can never be completely neutralised by our guns, will open on No Man's Land.

Although the German barrage will open comparatively quickly upon our starting points, upon trenches in rear of our starting points and upon that portion of No Man's Land nearest to our starting points, no hostile artillery fire need be anticipated upon the trenches actually captured until after a considerable interval; because not until a considerable time can the German gunners know, definitely, which trenches, if any, are lost, and which are held. Nor will his initial artillery fire upon his lost trenches be accurate, as a rule, because only rarely are the Germans able thoroughly to register, beforehand on their own trenches.

Consequently, for quite a considerable period after its capture a captured trench will be practically immune from artillery fire - long enough to enable consolidating parties to make a thoroughly good start. In fact the captured trench, once captured, is for a time the least shelled trench in the whole battle area; and all ranks should therefore realise that, other reasons apart, their personal safety depends upon their hanging on.

Conversely, the region immediately in rear of the captured trench is, for a time, the most shelled area. Therefore (a) nothing could be more fatal for the assaulting troops than to attempt to retire, and (b) they must realise that until communications are dug back, or until night falls, or until the hostile fire dies down they must hold their own and expect little support from the rear.

5.	Generally speaking, the enemy holds his front line weakly, a few rifles with comparatively many machine guns; supports are echelonned behind in depth; well in rear is a comparatively large reserve. Two kinds of counter-attacks may, therefore be expected -

(a) Immediate i.e. within five to thirty minutes, by the local supports who have very strict orders XXXX to rush forward at once to reinforce their first line when attacked. This immediate attack would generally be spasmodic, flurried and easily repulsed if expected and laid for by our coverers. It is more likely to be an attack by bombers than an attack overland, as all ground beyond our objectives will be swept by our artillery barrages during the first five to thirty minutes. Counter-attacks by bombers have rarely been successful <u>except</u> when our men have run out of bombs. Until the captured <u>trench</u> is linked with the starting points all supplies are somewhat precarious. Therefore the expenditure of grenades during our initial attack must be <u>most economical</u> - practically all the fighting in the first rush <u>being with the bayonet or rifle</u>. The two bombs carried by each man must be retained as a reserve and the temptation to throw them indiscriminately down dug-outs most XXX sternly checked. If each individual retains his two bombs, and if the carriers establish their dumps and collect from the casualties, the total available supply will be sufficient to beat back a dozen bombing attacks.

(b) <u>Deliberate</u>, i.e. after several hours (seldom less than six) and <u>preceded by</u> an artillery bombardment. Against this, protection principally depends upon the progress made in our consolidation and in opening up communications with the rear. Even if no counter-attack takes place at all, heavy hostile shelling <u>is certain</u>, sooner or later, so that the ultimate safety of all ranks <u>depends largely</u> upon the intensity with which they dig.

6.	If the above few facts are fully realised, if the plan is simple and well prepared, if the objectives are clearly indicated and really exist (i.e. have been reconnoitred, can be observed, are shown on aeroplane photographs as well as on the map), if each individual knows his job and does it, if the advance is <u>resolute</u> and if the position once gained is <u>really</u> dug down into, <u>it is</u>, with the help of our artillery, practically impossible for the infantry attack to fail.

(Sd) P. HOWELL,

B.G.G.S.

SECRET

Appendix 2 (6)

4/20

Copy No. 2

29th DIVISION OPERATION ORDER NO.60.

16th September 1916.

1. The 87th Brigade will relieve the 86th Brigade in the Left Sector of the line and the 86th Brigade on relief from the Left Sector will take over the Right Sector from the 88th Brigade on the nights 18th/19th and 19th/20th September in accordance with the attached Moves Table.

2. The 88th Brigade on relief will be in Corps Reserve.

3. Details of moves will be arranged direct between Brigades concerned.

4.(a) The two Battalions 86th Brigade that move from YPRES to the trenches Right Sector on the night of the 18th/19th September will on arrival come under the command of the G.O.C. 88th Brigade.
  (b) The two Battalions 87th Brigade that move up to YPRES on the night of the 18th/19th September will on arrival come under the command of the G.O.C. 86th Brigade as Brigade Reserve Left Sector, & Divl.Res.respectively.
  (c) The two Battalions 88th Brigade that move from YPRES to Camps A,B,C,O on the night of the 18th/19th September will on arrival come under the command of the G.O.C. 87th Brigade as Corps Reserve.

5. The 88th and 86th Machine Gun Companies and Trench Mortar Batteries will be relieved by corresponding units of the 86th and 87th Brigades respectively on the night of the 18th/19th September, but a proportion of the detachments of the 88th and 86th Machine Guns and Trench Mortars will remain in the line until the night of the 19th/20th September to assist the incoming units. The relief by the 87th Machine Guns and Trench Mortars will be completed by 10-30p.m. on the 19th September.

6. The G.O.Cs. 86th and 87th Brigades will take over the commands of the Right and Left Sectors respectively on completion of the reliefs on the night of the 19th/20th September.

7. No. 2 Section Divisional Signal Company will relieve No. 4 Section Divisional Signal Company in the Right Sector on the 19th September.

8. The time table of the train service will be issued later by the A.A. & Q.M.G.

9. Completion of all moves and reliefs will be reported to these Headquarters. The new dispositions will be forwarded to these Headquarters by 9 a.m. on the 19th and 20th instant.

10. Acknowledge by wire.

C.J. Fuller
Lieut-Colonel, G.S.,
29th Division.

Issued at ..11 p.m....
Copies 1 - 5 General Staff.
       6 86th Brigade.
       7 87th Brigade.
       8 88th Brigade.
       9 C. R. A.
      10 C. R. E.
      11 Off. i/c Signals.
      12 O.C. 1/2nd Monmouth Regiment.
      13 - 17 A.A. & Q.M.G.
      18 VIIIth Corps.
      19 38th Division.
      20 2nd Australian Division.

TABLE OF MOVES.

Date.	UNIT.	From.	To.	Remarks.
Night of 18th/19th September.	2 Battalions 87th Bde.	Camps A.B.C.O.	YPRES, Left Sector	Train.
	87th Machine Gun Coy.	H.7.a.	Trenches, Left Sector	March.
	87th Trench Mortar Batty.	A.30.d.	Trenches, Left Sector	March.
	2 Battalions 86th Bde.	YPRES, Left Sector.	Trenches, Right Sector	March.
	86th Machine Gun Coy.	Trenches, Left Sector.	Trenches, Right Sector	March.
	86th Trench Mortar Batty.	Trenches, Left Sector.	Trenches, Right Sector	March.
	2 Battalions 88th Bde.	Trenches, Right Sector.	Camps A.B.C.O.	Train.
	88th Machine Gun Coy.	Trenches, Right Sector.	H.7.a.	March.
	88th Trench Mortar Batty.	Trenches, Right Sector.	A.30.d.	March.
Night of 19th/20th September.	Headquarters, 87th Bde.	Camp C.	YPRES, Left Sector	Train.
	2 Battalions, 87th Bde.	Camps A.B.C.C.	YPRES, Left Sector	Train.
	2 Battalions 87th Bde.	YPRES, Left Sector.	Trenches, Left Sector	March.
	Headquarters, 86th Bde.	YPRES, Left Sector.	YPRES, Right Sector	March.
	2 Battalions 86th Ble.	Trenches, Left Sector.	YPRES, Right Sector	March.
	Headquarters, 88th Bde.	YPRES, Right Sector.	Camp C.	Train.
	2 Battalions, 88th Bde.	YPRES, Right Sector.	Camps A.B.C.O.	Train.
	No.2 Section Div. Signals	Camp C.	YPRES, Right Sector	March.
	No.4 Section Div. Signals	YPRES, Right Sector.	Camp C.	March.

SECRET.   Copy No. 6

29TH DIVISION ORDER NO. 61.

17th September, 1916.

1.   The Brigade in Divisional Reserve will form Corps Reserve from 10 a.m. 17th instant.

This Brigade will find one battalion for work on and defence of ELVERDINGHE, and the "L" Works. The battalion will be disposed as follows :-

H.Q. and 2 Companies	ELVERDINGHE.
2 platoons	L.4.
1 Company (including 2 platoons for defence of L.3)	L.8.
2 platoons	L.2.

The battalion will move to the above positions on evening of the 17th instant, taking over from the details of the 4th Division left in charge of the above defences. The battalion detailed will be one of the two battalions moving into support on the night of the 19th/20th September.

2.   One section of a Field Company R.E. will be placed at the disposal of the Chief Engineer, VIIIth Corps, for work on New Camps at ST. JAN TER BIEZEN. This section will proceed to ST. JAN TER BIEZEN on September 17th.

3.   A working party of 400 men each night will be found from the Brigade in Corps Reserve for work on the buried cable system under A.D.A.S. VIIIth Corps, commencing 18th instant.

4.   Acknowledge.

C.J. Fuller.
Lieut-Colonel, G.S.,
29th Division.

Issued at 12 noon.

Copies	1 - 5	General Staff.	11. Off. i/c Signals.
	6	86th Brigade.	12. O.C. 1/2nd Monmouth Regt.
	7	87th Brigade.	13 - 17. A.A. & Q.M.G.
	8	88th Brigade.	18 VIIIth Corps.
	9	C.R.A.	19 38th Division.
	10	C.R.E.	20 2nd Australian Division.

SECRET.   Copy No...........

29TH DIVISION ORDER NO. 62.

20th Sept. 1916.

1. A total of 45 full and 155 empty gas cylinders will be removed from the left sector (A.5.a, A.6, A.7) front line on the night 20th/21st September.

2. The 87th Brigade will detail carrying parties in the following order :-

First party.   - 1 officer, 4 N.C.Os., 120 men.

Second party.   - 1 officer, 4 N.C.Os., 120 men.

Third party.   - 1 officer, 4 N.C.Os., 90 men.

Fourth party.   - 1 officer, 4 N.C.Os., 80 men.

Fifth party.   - 1 officer, 4 N.C.Os., 80 men.

3. These parties will report at the junction of POTIJZE ROAD and the FRONT LINE TRENCH (A.6), where each party will be met by a guide from "J" Coy. R.E. at the following times :-

    1st party - 8.30 p.m.   (to carry 30 full cylinders).
    2nd   "   - 9.0 p.m.   (to carry 15 full and 30 empty cylinders).
    3rd   "   - 9.30 p.m.   (to carry 45 empty cylinders).
    4th   "   - 10.0 p.m.   ("   " 40   "   ").
    5th   "   - 10.30 p.m. ("   " 40   "   ").

Four men will be detailed to each full cylinder, 2 carrying and 2 in relief, and 2 men will carry each empty cylinder.

4. Parties will leave trench by DUKE STREET and proceed along HAYMARKET and POTIJZE ROAD to the dump at I.4.c.2.9 (POTIJZE) where the cylinders will be loaded into lorries.
    Carrying parties will wear Box or P.H.G. Helmets in "Alert" position.
    DUKE STREET and HAYMARKET will be kept clear of all traffic between the hours of 8 p.m. and 1 a.m. or until such time as the last carrying party reaches POTIJZE ROAD. Wounded men even will not be moved, but will be attended to on the spot, and medical arrangements will be made accordingly.
    Sentries will be stationed at junction of DUKE STREET and A.5.a and at junction of HAYMARKET and POTIJZE ROAD to enforce this order.

5. "J" Company R.E. will get cylinders out of the boxes and attend to the poling of such as may require it; they will also assist in the loading of the lorries at I.4.c.2.9 (POTIJZE).

6. The full cylinders to be carried by the first two parties will be prepared and placed ready in A.5.a North of DUKE STREET by "J" Coy. R.E. during the day.

7. Parties should be sized and numbered before arrival at A.6 and each man supplied with a sandbag to act as a shoulder pad.

8. Smoking will on no account be permitted.

- 2 -

9. It is important that silence be maintained during the operation.

10. All reference to these arrangements on the telephone is prohibited.

11. Acknowledge by wire.

for Lieut-Colonel, G.S.,
29th Division.

```
Copies 1 - 5  General Staff.
        6     86th Brigade.
        7     87th Brigade.
        8     88th Brigade.
        9     VIII Corps.
       10     A.D.M.S.
       11     A.A. & Q.M.G.
       12     "J" Coy. Spec. Bde. R.E.
```

SECRET.   Copy No. 6.

29TH DIVISION ORDER NO. 63.

20th September, 1916.

1. A total of 40 full and 120 empty gas cylinders will be removed from the right sector front line trenches (between H.14 and No.4 Crater) on the night 21st/22nd September.

2. The 86th Brigade will detail the carrying parties in the following order :-

First party.   - 1 Officer, 4 N.C.Os., 80 men.

Second party. - 1 Officer, 4 N.C.Os., 80 men.

Third party.   - 1 Officer, 4 N.C.Os., 80 men.

Fourth party. - 1 Officer, 4 N.C.Os., 80 men.

Fifth party.   - 1 Officer, 4 N.C.Os., 80 men.

3. Carrying parties will proceed by the following route :- WEST LANE - F.12 - F.11 - MUD LANE to the junction of MUD LANE and FRONT LINE TRENCH (H.15), where each party will be met by a guide from "J" Coy. R.E., at the following times :-

First party.   - 8.30 p.m.   (to carry 20 full cylinders).

Second party. - 9.0 p.m.   (to carry 20 full cylinders).

Third party.   - 9.30 p.m.   (to carry 40 empty cylinders).

Fourth party. - 10.0 p.m.   (to carry 40 empty cylinders).

Fifth party.   - 10.30 p.m. (to carry 40 empty cylinders).

Four men will be detailed to carry each full cylinder; two carrying and two in relief, and two men will carry each empty cylinder

4. Carrying parties will leave the trench by the DUCK WALK proceeding along F.12 to the point where it crosses the RAILWAY TRACK. They will then proceed along RAILWAY TRACK and MENIN ROAD to a point due south of the WHITE CHATEAU where cylinders will be placed on lorries.

Carrying parties will wear BOX or P.H.G. helmets in the "ALERT" position.

DUCK WALK and F.12 will be kept clear of all traffic between the hours of 8 p.m. and 1 a.m. or until such time as the last carrying party reaches the RAILWAY TRACK. Not even wounded men will be moved, but will be attended to on the spot, and medical arrangements will be made accordingly. Sentries will be stationed at junction of F.12 and RAILWAY TRACK to enforce this order.

5. "J" Coy. R.E. will, during the day, prepare the cylinders for removal and attend to the poling of such as may require it; the full cylinders being placed in one spot ready to be carried out by the first two parties. They will also assist in loading the lorries at the MENIN DUMP on the MENIN ROAD, South of WHITE CHATEAU (I.10.c.1.4

6. Parties should be numbered and sized before arrival at junction of MUD LANE and H.15, and each man supplied with a sandbag to act as a shoulder pad.

7. Smoking will on no account be permitted.

8. It is important that silence be maintained during the operations.

/ 9.

- 2 -

9. Any reference to these arrangements on the telephone is prohibited.

10. Acknowledge by wire.

                                        Major, G.S.,

                             for Lieut-Colonel, G.S.,

                                  29th Division.

Issued at .... 11.45 pm

```
Copies 1 - 5  General Staff.
       6      86th Brigade.
       7      87th Brigade.
       8      88th Brigade.
       9      A.D.M.S.
      10      A.A. & Q.M.G.
      11      "J" Coy. Special Brigade, R.E.
      12      VIIIth Corps.
```

Appendix 2 (c).

SECRET.   Copy No. 1

29TH DIVISION ORDER NO. 64.

432

September 26th, 1916.

1. The 88th Brigade will relieve the 86th Brigade in the Right Sector on the 28th and 29th September in accordance with the attached "Moves Table".

2. On relief the 86th Brigade, less 1 Battalion at ELVERDINGHE, will be in Divisional Reserve.

3. Details of reliefs will be arranged direct between Brigades concerned.

4. The 88th Machine Gun Coy. and 88th Trench Mortar Battery will relieve the 86th Machine Gun Coy. and 86th Trench Mortar Battery on the night of the 28th/29th September, the latter leaving a proportion of their detachments in the line until the night of 29th/30th September to assist the incoming units.

5.(a) The 88th Machine Gun Coy., the 88th Trench Mortar Battery, which move to the trenches, and the 2 Battalions 88th Brigade which move to YPRES on the 28th/29th September, will come under the command of the G.O.C. 86th Brigade.

(b) The 2 Battalions of the 86th Brigade, the 86th Machine Gun Coy. and the 86th Trench Mortar Battery, which move from YPRES and the trenches to Camps B.C.O. and ELVERDINGHE on the 28th/29th night will on arrival come under the command of the G.O.C. 88th Brigade.

6. The G.O.C. 88th Brigade will take over command of the Right Sector on completion of the relief on the 29th/30th night.

7. The time table of the train services will be issued later by the A.A. & Q.M.G.

8. The Brigade Signal Section in the line will not be relieved.

9. Completion of moves and reliefs will be reported to these Headquarters. The new dispositions will be forwarded to these Headquarters by 9 a.m. on 30th instant.

10. Acknowledge by wire.

Major, G.S.,
for Lieut-Colonel, G.S.,
29th Division.

Issued at 12-30 pm

Copies 1 - 5 General Staff.   11 Officer i/c Signals.
       6 86th Brigade.   12 1/2nd Monmouth Regt.
       7 87th Brigade.   13 - 17 A.A. & Q.M.G.
       8 88th Brigade.   18 VIIIth Corps.
       9 C.R.A.   19 2nd Australian Division.
      10 C.R.E.   20 38th Division.

MOVES TABLE.

Date.	Unit.	From.	To.	Remarks.
Night of 28th/29th September.	2 Batts. 88th Bde.	Camps B.C.O.	YPRES (Right Sector).	Train.
	2 Batts. 86th Bde.	YPRES (Right Sector).	Camps/B.C.O. A.	Train.
	88th M.G. Coy.	BRANDHOEK.	Trenches.	March.
	88th T.M. Battery.	Camp C.	Trenches.	March.
	86th M.G. Coy.	Trenches.	BRANDHOEK.	March.
	86th T.M. Battery.	Trenches.	Camp C.	March.
Night of 29th/30th September.	2 Batts. 88th Bde.	YPRES (Right Sector).	Trenches.	March.
	H.Q. 88th Bde.	Camp C.	YPRES (Right Sector).	Train.
	1 Battn. 86th Bde.	Trenches.	Camps/B.C.O. A.	Train.
	1 Battn. 86th Bde.	Trenches.	ELVERDINGHE.	March.
	1 Battn. 88th Bde.	Camps B.C.O.	YPRES (Right Sector).	Train.
	1 Battn. 88th Bde.	ELVERDINGHE.	YPRES (Right Sector).	March.
	H.Q. 86th Bde.	YPRES (Right Sector).	Camp C.	Train.

"A" Form. Army Form C. 2121.
MESSAGES AND SIGNALS.   No. of Message ....

Prefix .... Code .... m. Words Charge   This message is on a/c of: Recd. at .... m.
Office of Origin and Service Instructions.
                                                                            Date ....
                        Sent
                       At .... m.   ....Service.   From ....
                       To
                       By ....   (Signature of "Franking Officer.")   By ....

TO   114 Bde.   427

Sender's Number.   Day of Month.   In reply to Number.
* B.M.0835   X   A A A

Ref.	my	B.M.0834	AAA	Can
you	co-operate	in	counter	attack,
at	1 p.m.	with	Stokes	Mortars
and	bombing	squads	clearing	S.12
and	S.12	and	by	covering
assault	with	M.G.	fire	along
North	face	of	WIELTJE	Salient.

From   Z.7   (Signed) J. C. BRAND,
Place   Captain,
Time   Brigade Major.

The above may be forwarded as now corrected.   (Z)
                                    Censor.   Signature of Addressor or person authorised to telegraph in his name.
* This line should be erased if not required.

"A" Form. Army Form
MESSAGES AND SIGNALS. No. of Message..........

Prefix....Code......m.	Words	Charge	This message is on a/c of:	Recd. at.........m.
Office of Origin and Service Instructions.	Sent		............Service.	Date..........
	At............m.			From..........
	To........			
	By..........		(Signature of "Franking Officer.")	By..........

TO — 2/S.W.B.   1/K.O.S.B.   4m

Sender's Number.	Day of Month.	In reply to Number.	
* B.M. 0830	X		A A A

Stop	all	further	local	counter
attacks	AAA	Prepare	for	counter
attack.	by	1/Border	Regt.	at
midday	after	intense	bombardment	AAA
Verify	actual	area	in	occupation
of	enemy	and	report	at
once	any	change	in	situation

no time given

(Signed) J. C. BRAND,
Captain,
Brigade Major.

From   Z.7
Place
Time

The above may be forwarded as now corrected.   (Z)

....
*Censor.   Signature of Addressee or person authorised to telegraph in his name.
* This line should be erased if not required.
225,000 W 14042—M 44. H. W & V., Ld. 12/15.

"A" Form.
MESSAGES AND SIGNALS.
Army Form C. 2121.

| TO | 1/Borders | 1/R. Innis. Fus. | 423 |

| Sender's Number. | Day of Month. | In reply to Number. | |
| B.M.0831 | X | | A A A |

Be prepared to move forward on receipt of further orders

(Signed) J.C. BRAND,
Captain,
Brigade Major.

From Z.7

"A" Form.
Army Form C. 2121.

MESSAGES AND SIGNALS.

No. of Message ....

Prefix .... Code .... m.	Words	Charge	*This message is on a/c of:*	Recd. at .... m.
Office of Origin and Service Instructions.	Sent			Date ....
	At .... m.		.... Service.	From
	To			424
	By		(Signature of "Franking Officer.")	By

TO — 29th Division Left Group R.A. 88th Bde.
114 Bde.

Sender's Number.	Day of Month.	In reply to Number.	A A A
* B.M.0832	X		

Situation appears to be ~~as~~
follows AAA Enemy has penetrated
left subsector as far as
NEW JOHN STREET S.10.a. B.11
B.12 and has established bombing
posts in S.12 and at
junction of S.12.a. with GARDEN
STREET AAA Grenade fighting also
taking place in B.9 AAA
Remainder of front intact ~~AAA~~
Local counter attack has ~~failed~~
AAA Am organizing ~~counter~~ ~~attack~~
with Reserve Battalion

(Signed) J.C. BRAND,
Captain,
Brigade Major.

From Z.7
Place
Time

The above may be forwarded as now corrected. (Z)

Censor. Signature of Addressor or person authorised to telegraph in his name.

* This line should be erased if not required.

"A" Form.
Army Form C. 2121.
MESSAGES AND SIGNALS.
No. of Message ....

Prefix ...... Code ...... m.	Words	Charge	This message is on a/c of :	Recd. at .... m.
Office of Origin and Service Instructions.	Sent		..................Service.	Date ....
....	At .... m.			From ....
....	To		(Signature of "Franking Officer.")	By ....
	By			

TO { 29th Divn.   Left Group R.A.   4.35

Sender's Number.	Day of Month.	In reply to Number.	
* B.M.0833	X		A A A

Please	arrange	for	intense	bombard-
ment	of	area	in	possession
of	enemy	from	12.30 p.m.	to
1 p.m.	preparatory	to	counter	attack
at	1 p.m.	AAA	Addressed	29th
Divn.	repeated	Left	Group	

(Signed) J.C. BRAND,
Captain,
~~Brigade Major.~~

From   Z.7
Place
Time

The above may be forwarded as now corrected.   (Z)

....
Censor.   Signature of Addressee or person authorised to telegraph in his name.
* This line should be erased if not required.

"A" Form. Army Form C. 2121.
MESSAGES AND SIGNALS.

TO: 1/Borders 1/R. Innis. Fus. M.G. Coy. T.M.B.

AAA

~~B.M.0834~~ X

| G.O.C. | will | see | C.Os. | at |
| B.H.Q. | at | once | | |

From Place: Z.7
Time:

(Signed) J. C. BRAND,
Captain,
Brigade Major.

SECRET

Appendix 3(a).

HEADQUARTERS,
29th DIVISION.
GENERAL STAFF.
No. C.G.S.53/10
Date 14.9.16

86th Brigade.
88th Brigade.
C.R.A.

434

1. Unexpected orders have been received from Second Army to the effect that the raid, detailed in my C.G.S.53/10 of 9th instant, will take place tomorrow, September 15th.

2. Wirecutting will take place all day tomorrow together with the bombardment ordered for "Z" day in the letter above quoted.

3. The actual hour of ZERO will be notified later.

Lieut.Colonel, G.S.,
29th Division.

14th September, 1916.

ARRANGEMENTS FOR RAID TO BE CARRIED OUT BY 29TH DIVISION.

"X" Day.

Wirecutting by 18-prs. on following points:-
I.12.c.67.
North of OSCAR FARM.
I.5.b.54.
KAISER BILL.
C.29.a.66.

"X" Night.

Machine Guns and Lewis Guns on gaps made in wire.
Patrols to these points at intervals during night.

"Y" Day.

Wirecutting by 18-prs. on same points as on "X" Day.

"Y" Night.

Machine Guns and Lewis Guns on gaps made in wire.
Patrols to these points at intervals during night.

"Z" Morning.

Continue wirecutting on same points. Bombard two Northern points KAISER BILL and C.29.a.66 by Divisional and all Heavy Artillery if sufficient ammunition available for Heavy Artillery.

"Z" Night.

0 - 0.30 Heavy bombardment by Divisional and Corps Heavy Artillery on point of entry and on five places where wire has been previously cut

0.30 Raiders enter point of entry I.12.a.08.

0.30 Divisional Artillery lifts to form pockets round point of entry and at points where wire has been cut. Heavy Artillery remains on same targets.

1.15 Raiders return.

1.20 Artillery bombardment gradually dies down. Barrage does not return to front line trench. If raiders have not returned by that hour barrage continues by orders to be conveyed to Artillery by telephone.

2.30   ) 5 minutes burst of
3.15   ) shrapnel on points
4.15   ) where wire has
5.0 (if foggy morning)) been cut.

Strength of Raiding Party.

3 officers.
30 other ranks.

Allotment of Heavy Artillery.

"Z" Morning.

Bombardment by whole of Heavy Artillery if ammunition available.

"Z" Night.

        2 - 9.2" Hows.
        4 - 6" Hows.
        4 - 60-prs.

Estimate of ammunition requirements.

		Extra amount required for bombardment on "Z" Morning.
9.2" Hows.	50	160
6" hows.	240	350
60-prs.	200	200
4.7" gun.	Nil	100
13-prs.	8000	
4.5" Hows.	1200	720
2" T.M.	as required.	

It is proposed that ZERO shall be 11 p.m.

REPORT ON RAID CARRIED OUT BY THE 29th DIVISION
ON NIGHT 15/16th SEPTEMBER 1916.

Reference. Maps.

1/10000 ST. JULIEN
1/10000 ZONNEBEKE.

GENERAL IDEA.   At 11.0 pm. on the night 15/16th September an intense bombardment was to be directed against the German trenches at I.12.a. Under cover of this bombardment a raiding party of the 4th Worcester Regt. were to creep out into NO MAN'S LAND, and when the artillery bombardment lifted at 11.30 pm. on to the enemy's support line and communication trenches, were to penetrate into the enemy's front line at I.12.a.0.8. In co-operation with this enterprise, at 11.0 pm. gas was to be discharged from our trenches from pt. I.5.b.1.5. to C.29.c.6.4.

During the day of the 15th September the enemy wire had been cut at various points.

The wire at the point of entry was to be cut by artillery and trench mortar fire during the bombardment commencing at 11.0 pm.

OBJECT.   The objects of the raid were to obtain identification of the enemy's troops opposite, to inflict loss on the enemy, and to shake his moral.

COMPOSITION OF PARTY.   Lieut DAW, 2/Lieuts. TRENLETT and WYATT with 30 Other Ranks of the 4th Worcester Regt.

ACCOUNT OF OPERATIONS.   1. At 11.15 pm. the raiding party left our trenches and moved forward to a point to the immediate right of our bombing post on the YPRES - ROULERS Railway. 2/Lieut. WYATT with a Bangalore torpedo party leading. The leading party laid a tape for about 20 yards, where it became caught in loose wire and stopped short. Owing to the extreme darkness of the night and the driving rain, the party lost direction and led in the direction of No. 3 Crater. Lieut. DAW (in charge

(2).

of the raiding party) realised this and ordered the whole party to turn about. This order did not reach the Bangalore torpedo party or the left blocking party who continued on their way.

The main party then proceeded towards the point of entry arranged, but could not find a gap in the enemy wire. A Bangalore torpedo was sent for but as the fuses and detonators were with the forward party they were unable to use it, and so failed to enter the enemy trench. This party threw bombs into the smaall salient at I.12.a.0.8. and withdrew to our own line.

In the meantime 2/Lieut WYATT and Bangalore Torpedo party passed through Crater No. 3 and found a gap about 20 yards wide in the enemy's wire on the South Side of the Railway line. They entered the enemy's trench where they were fired at from a dug-out, 2/Lieut WYATT Being wounded. 18 bombs were thrown into the dug-out and the party then returned. 2/Lieut. WYATT crossed the Railway with three men and on his return journey encountered a party of four Germans - these were taken prisoners. Owing to these operations the party again lost direction and moved Northwards, eventually approaching our wire in front of the Hampshire Regt. about I.5.b.and d. They were naturally mistaken for a hostile patrol by the Hampshire Regt. who opened fire. One of the prisoners was killed. Another as wounded (he was searched for later but could not be found) The third escaped in the confusion of the moment and the fourth was successfully brought into our lines.

He belongs to the 362nd Regiment (Normal).

2. At 11.0 pm. gas was discharged from our trenches I.5.b.1.5. - C.29.c.6.4. Simultaneously our guns opened fire. Almost immediately red rockets bursting with golden rain were sent up from the German lines. but

(3).

but none of these were sent up from the Sector actually gassed.

At midnight two patrols were sent out to observe the effect of the gas. The first party went out from I.5.b.0.4. to a ruin at I.5.b.3.5. and to a hedge just East of this point, where they saw by the light of a fire in the German lines a party of the enemy moving from the MOUND. They were in single file. Seventeen were counted in all but there may have been more. The enemy patrol then divided into two, one party approaching our own patrol, who as they drew near attacked them with bombs and revolvers. The enemy patrol fled some being seen to drop. Our own patrol then withdrew.

Our patrol report that no machine gun fire or rifle fire came from the gassed sector, neither were there any rockets, etc. sent up from that part of the line. The Germans seen were wearing gas masks in an alert position.

NOTES ON RETALIATION ETC.

The enemy commenced to retaliate with 77 mm. shells and Minenwerfer at 11.10 pm. in reply to our bombardment. The latter caused considerable damage to the trenches on the left of our line though the loss in personnel was slight. It was not until 11.30 pm. that he retaliated with 5.9" and possibly larger shell. His main barrage lines appear to be in front of A 5 and along right front of ~~first~~ firing line - SUNKEN ROAD - DUCK WALK - S 23 and F 11. As soon as our fire died down the enemy's did likewise. The absence of enemy machine gun fire was most marked.

SIGNALS.

At 11.30 pm., i.e. when the guns lifted from the point of entry, the enemy sent up a flare which consisted of green and white stars rising together.

Otherwise the enemy did not appear to use any system in sending up flares.

Major-General,
Commanding 29th Division.

Appendix B(c).

SECRET.

REPORT ON RAID CARRIED OUT BY 2ND ROYAL FUSILIERS.

440

1. In accordance with your instructions a detachment of this Battalion carried out a raid on the German trenches at 2 a.m. on the 20th September.
I regret to report that the raid was not successful.

2. The original plan submitted on the 17th September was adhered to with the exception that from reconnaissance a gap through the two lines of the German wire was proved to exist, and two officers and a N.C.O. had actually passed through the gap on to the German parapet. In consequence of this it was determined to attempt a surprise by passing through the gap without attempting to widen it. As a precaution a bangalore torpedoe party went a short distance ahead to destroy hostile wire if necessary.

3. The raiding party left our trenches in accordance with the plan laid down. The bangalore party followed by about 12 of the raiding party actually passed through the gap in the first line of the German wire. Whilst going through the wire a hostile patrol (about 3 or 4 men) was reported to the North, but disappeared in the darkness. About the same time footsteps of a large number of men were heard in the German trench. These were believed to be, either a relief in progress, or else a working party. Up to this time the raid was apparently unperceived.

4. After passing through the gap in the first line of wire, the gap in the second line could not at once be located; it was either just missed, or probably been closed by two knife rests which were observed and which had certainly not been there when the previous reconnaissance was made. Without delay the officer in charge of the wire destroying party placed his torpedoe through the wire, and ignited the fuze, the whole party lying down. The fuze detonated all right, but the torpedoe failed to explode, just blowing the wooden stopper out and giving out a lot of smoke (the fuze had been firmly secured by wire). Almost immediately bombs were thrown from the hostile trench, and rifle shots fired.

5. Lieut. BIRD then got hold of the reserve bangalore torpedoe and placed it in position (this of course took a little time), meanwhile a strong German patrol came up from the South, between the two lines of wire entanglement, and at the same time another party of Germans, estimated at not less than thirty by an officer, came down from the North, between the second line of wire and the German parapet and opened fire. The man setting off the fuze of the second torpedoe was shot, and also wounded by splinters. Lieut. BIRD then tried to ignite the fuze, but before he could do so the torpedoe was drawn away by the enemy.
The raiding party then retired.
Casualties, one man killed, 5 wounded, and two injured (at duty).

I feel confident that Lieut. HURLE (a man of most
determined character) and the other officers with him
2/Lieut. MEREDITH and 2/Lieut. BIRD, did all in their power
for success, but that their efforts were defeated by :-

(1) The bangalore torpedoe failed to explode at a
    critical moment.

(2) The very good state of alertness maintained by
    the Germans and the large number of men, and the
    promptness with which they dealt with the situation.

The possibility of missing either, or both of the gaps
in the German wire had been forseen, but there was not
sufficient time to operate the second torpedoe after the
first one had failed.

                            (Signed) G. A. STEVENS,

                                  Lieut-Colonel,

20.9.16.   Commanding 2nd Royal Fusiliers.

Appendix 3(d).

Report on Raid made by 1st Border Regiment on night 30th Sept.1916.

The Covering Party consisting of a Sergeant and 6 riflemen to guard the left flank, a Sergeant and 7 men with Lewis Gun to guard the right flank, were posted at about 7.45 p.m. in the nearer line of trees opposite WIELTJE SALIENT. At 8.10 p.m. the raiding party began to leave our trench and were all in position in "NO MANS LAND" as arranged by 8.15 p.m.

During the first 15 minutes of the bombardment the party worked forward to the line of big trees without mishap, and crossed to the line of willows in front of enemy trench by 8.50 p.m. During this second stage of the advance one lance-corporal sustained a slight wound in the hand from a fragment of one of our shells.

At 8.50 p.m. the O.C. Raid left the head of the column by the willows and went forward to reconnoitre the wire. There were a great many enemy flare lights, but there was no firing from the enemy front line and it is probable that enemy were on the flanks or in the support trenches. The wire proved to have been very successfully knocked about by Trench Mortar fire but some inner belts of wire remained too high for easy passage. Accordingly wire-cutters were tried, but this method seemed slow, and at 8.55 p.m. the O.C. returned to party to begin advance through wire prepared to use bangalore torpedoes for any considerable obstructions near parapet. On a roll of concertina wire which remained little damaged in the line of advance, 3 bangalore torpedoes were tried. The fitting of the torpedoes in concertina wire turned out to be quite simple and was well done. Each of the torpedoes failed, however, to detonate owing to the dampness of fuzes. They had evidently been injured in the journey across "NO MANS LAND", as the very light cases used to protect them had come off.

The O.C. Raid then noticed an easy gap which had been blown in the wire to the right, and the party trampled down what was left of the wire, and made a rush for the parapet. All arrangements worked as they had been planned, the point

- 2 -

of entry being only a matter of yards away from that intended. The Right and Left Blocking Parties both experienced some bombing from enemy on flanks. The trench on right of point of entry had been rather badly blown in by our Artillery, and a group of men protected by the blockage sent up Very lights, and brought rifle fire and bombs to bear on right blocking party, from trench in rear of our right. Our bombers retaliated with evident effect, as the enemy party retreated and the sending up of Very lights ceased.

The right searching party found in the main communication trench for some 30 yards to right of the point of entry, 2 dugouts under the parapet. These were securely built, but small, and had merely wooden frames. They were carpeted with straw. In one of these a man was found who was made prisoner. The right communication trench was badly knocked about, and the large dugout shown in the aerial photo, was entirely demolished.

Several dead or unconscious bodies were found in the barbed wire in front of this sector, and several of the enemy who retreated down the communication trenches were fired on and chased, one at least was killed.

Left Blocking Party.

This party got into position opposite the left communication trench noticed in the aerial photo. The enemy threw a large number of bombs at them, but without effect. Our men replied vigorously throwing almost all the bombs they had and kept the enemy on the flank at bay, even if they did no further damage. Four dugouts were found in this section of trench and produced 6 prisoners. The dugouts were of the same pattern as those noted above and all under the parapet. Two of the enemy were killed, one shot and one bayonetted.

All prisoners (8) seemed unwilling to surrender themselves but were obviously frightened.

General.

The trenches were slightly deeper and wider than our

/ front

front line, they had no trench boards but a good wooden firestep. The revetting was for the most part, wooden trellis-work. The floor of the trench was covered with straw. A considerable quantity of bombs, equipment, clothing and papers were found. A large bell for Gas Alarm was found on the parapet at point of entry, and the trench seemed liberally supplied with long-handled bombs. About 25% of the men seen in the trench wore metal helmets. Uniforms and equipment were in a very good state of repair, and everything was noticeably clean and tidy.

The Sap search party.

A recent reconnaissance of the Boche front line by daylight had led us to suppose that this sap was now very little used, and would not produce anything of interest. This was confirmed in fact, and the junction of the sap and the trench had been so blown in by our shells as to be hardly recognizable. Accordingly the sap party which had been sent to search it returned to the main party for work in the front line trench.

Appendix 3(e).

445

REPORT ON RAID CARRIED OUT BY 1st LANCASHIRE FUSILIERS ON
THE NIGHT OF /30th SEPT. 1916.

The 1st Lancashire Fusiliers raiding party entered the enemy trenches to-night and spent some ten minutes there. A few identifications were obtained but no prisoners. No opposition was met with. The trenches entered were apparently held by a small bombing post who fled leaving their rifle behind them. No casualties excepting one man slightly wounded. The trenches were found to be considerably damaged by our Stokes Mortars.

A full report will be sent in to-morrow.

(Signed) W.L.WILLIAMS,
Brig. Genl.
30th September 1916.   86th Brigade.

"C" Form (Duplicate). Army Form C. 2123
MESSAGES AND SIGNALS.

Appendix 3(6).

Service Instructions.

Handed in at ...... 1/6c ...... Office 2375 m. Received ...... m.

TO 29" Div   447

Sender's Number: GA763 Day of Month: 30 In reply to Number: AAA

Corps Commander wishes his congratulations to be conveyed to both raiding parties on their successful and skillfully executed enterprises

FROM PLACE & TIME: 8th Corps 11 pm

"C" Form (Duplicate).
MESSAGES AND SIGNALS.

Army Form C. 2123.
(In books of 50's in duplicate.)

Appendix 3(f).

TO 29th Divn

446

Following received from 2nd Army timed 9.30 am aaa Begins aaa Army Commander wishes to congratulate 29th Divn on the successful results of last nights raids which reflect much credit on all concerned aaa The identifications gained are very valuable and the damage inflicted on the enemy is very satisfactory at this stage aaa The raids by this division have been carefully planned and well executed aaa Ends

Repeat to all units

FROM PLACE & TIME 8th Corps 10-30 am

SECRET.   Copy No......1......

29TH DIVISION ORDER NO. 62.

                                            20th Sept. 1916.

1. A total of 45 full and 155 empty gas cylinders will be removed from the left sector (A.5.a, A.6, A.7) front line on the night 20th/21st September.

2. The 87th Brigade will detail carrying parties in the following order :-

First party.   - 1 officer, 4 N.C.Os., 120 men.

Second party. - 1 officer, 4 N.C.Os., 120 men.

Third party.   - 1 officer, 4 N.C.Os., 90 men.

Fourth party. - 1 officer, 4 N.C.Os., 80 men.

Fifth party.   - 1 officer, 4 N.C.Os., 80 men.

3. These parties will report at the junction of POTIJZE ROAD and the FRONT LINE TRENCH (A.6), where each party will be met by a guide from "J" Coy. R.E. at the following times :-

   1st party - 8.30 p.m. (to carry 30 full cylinders).
   2nd   "   - 9.0 p.m.   (to carry 15 full and 30 empty
                                  cylinders).
   3rd   "   - 9.30 p.m. (to carry 45 empty cylinders).
   4th   "   - 10.0 p.m. ("   " 40   "   "   ).
   5th   "   - 10.30 p.m. ("   " 40   "   "   ).

   Four men will be detailed to each full cylinder, 2 carrying and 2 in relief, and 2 men will carry each empty cylinder.

4. Parties will leave trench by DUKE STREET and proceed along HAYMARKET and POTIJZE ROAD to the dump at I.4.c.2.9 (POTIJZE) where the cylinders will be loaded into lorries.
   Carrying parties will wear Box or P.H.G. Helmets in "Alert" position.
   DUKE STREET and HAYMARKET will be kept clear of all traffic between the hours of 8 p.m. and 1 a.m. or until such time as the last carrying party reaches POTIJZE ROAD. Wounded men even will not be moved, but will be attended to on the spot, and medical arrangements will be made accordingly.
   Sentries will be stationed at junction of DUKE STREET and A.5.a and at junction of HAYMARKET and POTIJZE ROAD to enforce this order.

5. "J" Company R.E. will get cylinders out of the boxes and attend to the poling of such as may require it: they will also assist in the loading of the lorries at I.4.c.2.9 (POTIJZE).

6. The full cylinders to be carried by the first two parties will be prepared and placed ready in A.5.a North of DUKE STREET by "J" Coy. R.E. during the day.

7. Parties should be sized and numbered before arrival at A.6 and each man supplied with a sandbag to act as a shoulder pad.

8. Smoking will on no account be permitted.

- 2 -

9.   It is important that silence be maintained during the operation.

10.   All reference to these arrangements on the telephone is prohibited.

11.   Acknowledge by wire.

for Lieut-Colonel, G.S.,
29th Division.

Copies 1 - 5 General Staff.
       6   86th Brigade.
       7   87th Brigade.
       8   88th Brigade.
       9   VIII Corps.
       10   A.D.M.S.
       11   A.A. & Q.M.G.
       12   "J" Coy. Spec. Bde. R.E.

SECRET.   Copy No......1.

29TH DIVISION ORDER NO. 63.

Appendix 4(6).
4/0

20th September, 1916.

1.   A total of 40 full and 120 empty gas cylinders will be removed from the right sector front line trenches (between H.14 and No.4 Crater) on the night 21st/22nd September.

2.   The 86th Brigade will detail the carrying parties in the following order :-

First party.   -   1 Officer, 4 N.C.Os., 80 men.

Second party.   -   1 Officer, 4 N.C.Os., 80 men.

Third party.   -   1 Officer, 4 N.C.Os., 80 men.

Fourth party.   -   1 Officer, 4 N.C.Os., 80 men.

Fifth party.   -   1 Officer, 4 N.C.Os., 80 men.

3.   Carrying parties will proceed by the following route :- WEST LANE - F.12 - F.11 - MUD LANE to the junction of MUD LANE and FRONT LINE TRENCH (H.15), where each party will be met by a guide from "J" Coy. R.E., at the following times :-

First party.   -   8.30 p.m.   (to carry 20 full cylinders).

Second party.   -   9.0 p.m.   (to carry 20 full cylinders).

Third party.   -   9.30 p.m.   (to carry 40 empty cylinders).

Fourth party.   -   10.0 p.m.   (to carry 40 empty cylinders).

Fifth party.   -   10.30 p.m. (to carry 40 empty cylinders).

        Four men will be detailed to carry each full cylinder; two carrying and two in relief, and two men will carry each empty cylinder

4.   Carrying parties will leave the trench by the DUCK WALK proceeding along F.12 to the point where it crosses the RAILWAY TRACK. They will then proceed along RAILWAY TRACK and MENIN ROAD to a point due south of the WHITE CHATEAU where cylinders will be placed on lorries.
        Carrying parties will wear BOX or P.H.G. helmets in the "ALERT" position.
        DUCK WALK and F.12 will be kept clear of all traffic between the hours of 8 p.m. and 1 a.m. or until such time as the last carrying party reaches the RAILWAY TRACK. Not even wounded men will be moved, but will be attended to on the spot, and medical arrangements will be made accordingly. Sentries will be stationed at junction of F.12 and RAILWAY TRACK to enforce this order.

5.   "J" Coy. R.E. will, during the day, prepare the cylinders for removal and attend to the poling of such as may require it; the full cylinders being placed in one spot ready to be carried out by the first two parties. They will also assist in loading the lorries at the MENIN DUMP on the MENIN ROAD, South of WHITE CHATEAU (I.10.c.1.4)

6.   Parties should be numbered and sized before arrival at junction of MUD LANE and H.15, and each man supplied with a sandbag to act as a shoulder pad.

7.   Smoking will on no account be permitted.

8.   It is important that silence be maintained during the operations..

                                                                /9.

- 2 -   451

9.   Any reference to these arrangements on the telephone is prohibited.

10.   Acknowledge by wire.

                                        D. M'Ey
                                        Major, G.S.,
                                    for Lieut-Colonel, G.S.,
                                          29th Division.

Issued at ....11.45 pm.

            Copies 1 -x5 General Staff.
                   6   86th Brigade.
                   7   87th Brigade.
                   8   88th Brigade.
                   9   A.D.M.S.
                   10   A.A. & Q.M.G.
                   11   "J" Coy. Special Brigade, R.E.
                   12   VIIIth Corps.

Appendix 5

HEADQUARTERS.
29TH DIVISION.
INTELLIGENCE

No. 452

29TH DIVISION DAILY SUMMARY.
From 10 a.m. 31.8.16. to 10 a.m. 1.9.16.

OPERATIONS.

GAS. A full report on the gas attack carried out from our Right Sector has already been forwarded.

ARTILLERY.

The enemy's artillery was active yesterday afternoon firing several heavy shells behind OUTPOST FARM and in YPRES. ST. JEAN and B.11 also received attention during the morning.
In retaliation for our bombardment at night, enemy fired some 15 c.m. on our front trenches A.5.a. to A.8. inclusive, causing six casualties, but very little damage to our trenches.
Between 1.35 a.m. and 3 a.m. he also bombarded B.9. He also fired some light shells on MUDDY LANE and DUCK WALK commencing about 8 minutes after our first emission of gas.
Some 60 shells were fired into LA BRIQUE during the day.

Machine Guns. During the night the enemy machine guns were active as usual against ROULERS RAILWAY, and they enfiladed the following trenches from the North - X.5, X.4 and B.11.
Our Right Brigade reports that six or seven hostile machine guns kept up a slow rate of fire along our front during the gas attack.
Our own machine guns were particularly active last night, those in the Left Sector alone firing some 8500 rounds on to the enemy's front line and selected points behind it.

Trench Mortars. The enemy bombarded B.9 at 9.30 a.m. but however very soon stopped on our artillery retaliating.
Our Stokes mortars fired a considerable number of rounds during the gas attack last night.

Patrols. Two patrols went out from our Right Sector after the gas attack and reported that the enemy were sending up Very lights about every second bay and though they could not get through the enemy's wire, they heard the enemy coughing a great deal, and they report that great excitement prevailed. An officer with one of these patrols reported that the enemy were running up and down the duckboards of the trench.

INTELLIGENCE.

Enemy Work. Work was heard close to KAISER BILL throughout the whole night in spite of our Lewis Gun fire.
By day sounds of bailing were heard.
Work still proceeds at OSKAR FARM, fresh earth having been thrown up in front of the parapet.

MISCELLANEOUS.

Flares. At 1.30 a.m. and again at 2.15 a.m. red flares were sent up by the enemy which broke into gold.

Smoke. Smoke was seen coming from the rear of OSKAR FARM at 7.30 a.m.

Aeroplanes. Considerable activity of anti-aircraft firing took place on both sides. At 10.30 a.m. a hostile aeroplane was driven back by two of our aeroplanes, and at 5.45 a.m. two more flew over the SALIENT but retired as soon as they were fired at.

Major, G.S.,
1.9.16.   29th Division.

29TH DIVISION DAILY SUMMARY.

From 10 a.m. 1.9.16. to 10 a.m. 2.9.16.

OPERATIONS.

Artillery. Enemy's artillery has been more active during this period. Between 9 a.m. and 10 a.m. HELLFIRE CORNER and HASLER HOUSE received attention. MONMOUTH TRENCH was shelled about midday. LA BRIQUE also was shelled with H.E. at about 6 p.m.

Machine Guns. Enemy's machine guns inactive.
Our machine guns fired a great deal on the usual targets.

Trench Mortars. Enemy's trench mortars were active between 4 p.m. and 5 p.m. Bombs fell mostly in front of our trenches H.19 and H.20 and behind No.6 Crater, doing little damage.
An enemy trench mortar was observed firing from I.6.c.3.3.

Patrols. A listening patrol out in front of A.7 from 9 p.m. till midnight returned reporting no enemy's patrols or working parties to be seen or heard.

INTELLIGENCE.

Enemy Movements. A/enemy sniper's post is suspected in a tree near I.5.b.6.0. Our trench mortar fired on this post, one direct hit was observed.
Another sniper's post has been located at I.12.a.1.8.
At 4 p.m. two motor lorries and a Red Cross wagon were observed moving south towards WESTHOEK in J.1.d. on main road.

Enemy Work. A small party of the enemy was observed at 3 p.m. near the enemy's front line I.18.b.7.6, and another party of about 20 men was observed at 2 p.m. working on road which runs north-east along J.1.b.
Enemy were heard knocking in stakes near point I.5.b.8.2 during the night.
Enemy was working on KAISER BILL throwing up earth on the parapet, between 7.30 a.m. and 9.50 a.m. on the 1st instant.

MISCELLANEOUS.

Aeroplanes. At 11 a.m. on the 1st instant, a hostile plane approached our lines. It was fired on and one of our machines appeared on the scene. The enemy plane retired.
At 6 a.m. this morning a hostile plane flew over the SALIENT.

2.9.16.

Major, G.S.,
29th Division.

HEADQUARTERS.
29th DIVISION.
D.S.137.
No. 454
Date.

29TH DIVISION DAILY SUMMARY.

From 10 a.m. 2.9.16. to 10 a.m. 3.9.16.

OPERATIONS.

Artillery. Enemy's artillery very quiet on our left in response to our bombardment of KAISER BILL in the afternoon. Our front trenches between C.29.c.8.2 and C.29.c.7.4 were shelled with H.E. at 11.30 p.m.
RAILWAY FARM and HELL FIRE CORNER also received attention. Some heavy shells were fired on DUCK WALK and MUDDY LANE at 11.20 p.m.
Our parapets and trenches near No.6 Crater were damaged in several places.

Machine Guns. Enemy's machine gun fire was about normal. It increased during our bombardment at 11.20 p.m.
Our machine guns were very active, the following being some of the targets fired at :- Enemy front line between ODER HOUSE and OSKAR FARM, their second line from east of WHITE COTTAGE (C.29.b.0.5) to C.29.d.9.2, the communication trench from JASPER FARM (C.23.d.55.00) to APPLE VILLA (C.24.b.15.00), and BILL COTTAGE (I.6.b).

INTELLIGENCE.

Enemy Work. Hostile working party of 20 men was again seen on road in J.1.b.
In J.1.b. 5 men were seen at 5 p.m. near WILDE COTTAGE running towards a dugout.
Near I.12.a.08.92 is a small bridge over enemy's trench possibly used at night by working parties.
Working parties were heard in the MOUND, and along the enemy's front trench between C.29.d.4.1 and C.29.d.4.4.

MISCELLANEOUS.

Aeroplanes. A hostile aeroplane was driven away from our lines N.E. by E. of YPRES by one of our aeroplanes at 9.30 a.m.

Signals. At 11 p.m. Strombos Horns were heard from our right. The enemy immediately put up a red rocket which broke into silver stars from C.29.d.0.0, followed shortly afterwards by two rockets from I.5.b.6.3 each rocket broke into one green and one white light remaining suspended in the air for a considerable time. No gas was emitted by the enemy.
It is reported from our Right Sector that two further gas alarms occurred during the night, one at 1.40 a.m. and another at 2.30 a.m., both coming from some distance to our right, and that on the gas alarm being given the enemy fired an orange flare which broke into five smaller ones, similar to one they had fired on the night when we discharged gas.
During the our bombardment the enemy sent up an exceptionally large number of flares.

3.9.16.

Major, G.S.,
29th Division.

HEADQUARTERS.
29th DIVISION.
D.S.138.
No. 455
Date.

29TH DIVISION DAILY SUMMARY.
From 10 a.m. 3.9.16. to 10 a.m. 4.9.16.

OPERATIONS.

Artillery. Enemy shelled working party in B.11 and B.12, also X.8 with high velocity gun knocking in part of the trench and obtaining a direct hit on House at C.27.d.78.45. At 1 p.m. 4 shells dropped near a machine gun emplacement in ST. JEAN. The emplacement was destroyed without however any injury to the gun.

Machine Guns. The enemy traversed at intervals between 8 p.m. and midnight the front of the right half sector between C.29.c.9.1 and I.5.b.05.50.
Our machine guns fired amongst other targets at the Cross Roads C.20.c.9.6, JASPER and UHLAN FARMS, and the trench trams in C.30.a.

Trench Mortars. At 2.30 a.m. the enemy opened fire with his trench mortars in retaliation to bursts from ours. The greater part of his bombs fell in No.2 Crater, and did little damage to our front line. The action of these mortars appears similar to our Stokes guns, except that at night his bombs can be seen.

INTELLIGENCE.

Enemy Movements. At 5.15 p.m. a German officer was seen looking over the parapet near I.12.a.08.92, dressed in light blue uniform with peak cap. Again at 6.30 p.m. two officers were seen at the same point one of them using Field glasses. A Lewis gun was fired at them and one was seen to fall. They were dressed similarly to the first officer observed.
An enemy machine gun was observed to fire from either the first or the second line at a true bearing $76\frac{1}{2}°$ from I.5.b.08.33.

Enemy Work. Throughout the night the enemy worked on the MOUND.
A small working party at C.29.d.4.2 was fired at by our snipers.
Another enemy working party was dispersed by our Lewis gun opposite No.2 Crater at 1 a.m. this morning.
New sandbags have been placed along enemy front line for several yards at C.5.d.10.8.

MISCELLANEOUS.

Signals. At 2.30 a.m. the enemy sent up a white flare which broke into green stars.

4th September, 1916.

Captain, G.S.,
29th Division.

D.S.139.

29TH DIVISION DAILY SUMMARY.
From 10 a.m. 4.9.16. to 10 a.m. 5.9.16.

OPERATIONS.

Artillery. The enemy's artillery has been exceptionally quiet during this period. A few shells were fired near RAILWAY WOOD during the afternoon, at least half of these failed to explode.

Machine Guns. Normal activity on the part of our own and the enemy's machine guns. Our guns fired at the usual targets.

Trench Mortars. Our trench mortars in the right sector were very active during the afternoon firing at the enemy's trenches opposite Nos.3 and 4 craters. The enemy retaliated with his trench mortars but we replied on every occasion by firing twice the number he fired at us. We fired 60 rounds altogether.
Rifle grenades were also fired by both sides.

Patrols. A patrol went out from DUKE STREET to inspect the enemy's wire at I.5.b.8.0. The wire is reported to be comparatively thin at one point.

INTELLIGENCE.

Enemy Work. The enemy was heard working on his front trenches in C.29.d. and KAISER BILL.
At 3 p.m. a party of about 6 men were observed carrying something heavy along trench at I.6.a.0.1 near OSKAR FARM. Another party was seen at 2.30 p.m. moving along a trench at the same place.

MISCELLANEOUS.

More movement than usual was observed in the Salient opposite H.20, 3 periscopes being seen there during the day, usually none are to be observed.

An attempt was made to locate the position of an enemy sniper who had been very active about I.6.c.1.2, by shewing a dummy head over the parapet. The sniper shot at it four times but unfortunately missed it each time.

Major, G.S.,
5th September, 1916.
29th Division.

29TH DIVISION DAILY SUMMARY.
From 10 a.m. 5.9.16. to 10 a.m. 6.9.16.

OPERATIONS.

Artillery. Enemy artillery was practically inactive throughout the day.

Machine Guns. Enemy machine guns were very active between 11 p.m. and 2 a.m. We retaliated on the usual targets.

Trench Mortars. Enemy trench mortars fired between 50 and 60 rounds between 3 p.m. and 3.45 p.m. Our parapet was damaged behind No.2 crater. Very slight damage was also done to the SUNKEN ROAD and No.6 crater. Our Stokes guns retaliated effectively.

Snipers. At 10 a.m. a sniper was observed at C.29.d.18.88. He had on a large ringed shrapnel helmet which covered his ears. A Lewis gun opened fire on him and the sniping hole has not since been used.

INTELLIGENCE.

Enemy Movements. Enemy transport was heard on road I.6.a.2.2.5 towards WILDE COTTAGE.
Trench tramways were also busy right up to daybreak.
A man was seen at C.29.d.18.88 wearing a round forage cap with a thin yellow band and a round yellow badge about the band.

Enemy Work. The enemy was working between 9 p.m. and 12.30 a.m. in his trenches at about I.5.b.central. Lewis guns were brought to bear on the spot but the enemy did not discontinue his work, which was probably low down in the trench.
    New wire (knife rests) has been put up in front of OSKAR FARM and the trench at approximately I.12.a.1.9 has been repaired.
    At 8.15 a.m. a party of 30 men was seen to the right of LAKE WOOD approximately J.7.c.4.8.

Shell. In WARWICK LANE just near WARWICK FARM there is an unexploded 5.9" enemy shell. It is painted green with black rings and a black nosecap marked "Kg". It also has the words "Lab Sch" on it. If further information is desired it can be obtained.

L. Carden Roe Captain, G.S.,

6th September, 1916.   29th Division.

HEADQUARTERS.
29th DIVISION.
INTELLIGENCE.
D.S. 141.
No.
Date.........

458

29th DIVISION

Daily Intelligence Summary

from 10.0 am. 6/9/1916 to 10.0 am. 7/9/1916.

OPERATIONS.   ARTILLERY.   The enemy artillery was generally inactive.
About 15 18-pdr. shells were fired at Battalion Headquarters
POTIJZE at about 11.45 am.   LA BRIQUE was shelled
between 6.0 pm. and 6.30 pm. with high velocity gun.

TRENCH MORTARS.   At 11.0 am. enemy trench mortars fired
about 50 rounds into front line at I.11.b.6.4. and
SUNKEN ROAD. The parapet was badly damaged in one or two
places. Our artillery and Stokes Mortars replied
effectively.

MACHINE GUNS.   Enemy machine guns were active at night,
firing on Railway and wiring party in front of S 21.

PATROLS.   A patrol went out from C.28.b.7.8. at 1.45 am.
and reconnoitred "No Man's Land". No hostile patrols were
encountered but enemy was heard working on his front line
from C.23.c.25.00 to C.29.a.50.65.   Lewis gun fire was
brought to bear on this area but failed to stop the enemy's
work.
Another patrol went out from A.4. at 10.0 pm., remaining
out until 1.0 am. They report that the enemy was busy
repairing wire and trenches.

AEROPLANES.   About 12.45 pm. a hostile aeroplane was
engaged by two of our aeroplanes. It was observed to
retire and is believed to have been driven down.
Between 10.15 and 10.45 pm. sounds were heard as though
one of our aeroplanes was proceeding towards the enemy's
trenches. Searchlights were turned on by the enemy
apparently endeavouring to locate it.

SNIPING.   One of our snipers claims to have hit one of the
enemy who was pumping water from a trench at approximately
C.23.c.3.4.

INTELLIGENCE.   ENEMY WORK.   The enemy work opposite Crater 2A has been
renewed.

ENEMY MOVEMENTS.   Motor lorries were heard at 5.0 am.
moving South on the WESTHOEK - CLAPHAM JUNCTION Road.

L. Carden Roe   Captain. G.S.

7th September 1916.   29th Division.

D.S. 142.

29TH DIVISION DAILY SUMMARY.
From 10 a.m. 7.9.16. to 10 a.m. 8.9.16.

OPERATIONS.

Artillery. At 12 Noon our front line and MUDDY LANE were bombarded with 77 mm. and trench mortars. One shell which burst in MUDDY LANE did considerable damage. ~~During our retaliation for the bombardment men were seen running back to the rear from enemy saps.~~
At the same hour a salvo of 4 shrapnel shells burst over the POTIJZE WOOD, followed a few minutes later by two more rounds.

Trench Mortars. At 8.15 p.m. the enemy sent up a red and green flare and shortly afterwards a heavy bombardment was opened on our lines with trench mortars. His fire was chiefly directed on our right and on GULLY and No.6 Crater. Our mortars and artillery retaliated. Men were seen running back to the rear from enemy saps.

Machine Guns. Enemy machine guns were more active than usual all along our front.
Our machine guns continued to search the enemy's communications in rear of the front line, apparently with effect as sounds of galloping transport and shouting could be heard, while firing was in progress.

Patrols. One of our patrols which went out from A.4 at 9 p.m. report that the enemy were wiring and working hard in their trenches. As they were returning through our wire an enemy patrol threw two bombs after them. Our patrol got into the trench safely and Lewis gun fire was at once opened. At 11.30 p.m. another patrol was sent out but no trace of the enemy patrol was found. This patrol brought in a board from "NO MANS LAND" on which the word "Tommy" was written.
Another patrol which went out from the GULLY at 11 p.m. report that enemy transport could be heard quite close to the line. It appeared that on a signal of two whistles, two carts could approach the line at a time.

INTELLIGENCE.

Enemy Work. During the day work was in progress in enemy front line in C.23.c. At night parties were working in front line south of C.29.d.4.0, but work was stopped by a bombardment from our artillery at 9.45 p.m.

Enemy Movements. An Officer on duty in B.9 reports that at 2.5 a.m. tramping of feet was heard within the enemy trenches. At the time no work could be heard and no flares were sent up, nor was there any rifle fire. This possible denotes that a relief was taking place.
At 2 a.m. a steam engine or pump was heard in enemy trenches in XXIX I.12.a. near front line trench.
Handling of iron and timber could be distinctly heard in the same direction.

MISCELLANEOUS.

Signals. Preceeding the bombardment at 8.15 p.m. a red and green rocket followed shortly afterwards by a white one breaking into five white lights, were seen to go up near RAILWAY WOOD.

Shell. An unexploded enemy shell was found marked :-
  H 2 0 5 G Y
   S P 15 N
     M p.

Captain, G.S.,

8.9.16.   29th Division.

D.S.143.

29TH DIVISION DAILY SUMMARY.

From 10 a.m. 8.9.16. to 10 a.m. 9.9.16.

460

OPERATIONS.

Artillery. The enemy did very little shelling throughout the day. Between 8 p.m. and 10 p.m. the enemy fired a few shells on YPRES, and between 10.30 p.m. and 11 p.m. along the MENIN ROAD.

Aeroplanes. At 7 p.m. five of our aeroplanes passed over the enemy lines on to which they appeared to drop bombs. At 10.15 p.m. this performance is reported to have been repeated.

Patrols. Our patrols were active during the night and all report enemy very busy working on his trenches. One patrol reconnoitred the enemy wire North of the MOUND and report that a considerable number of fresh coils have been put out there.

Enterprise. At 4 p.m. we successfully exploded a camouflet in front of No.2.A. Crater. Smoke and dust were seen to come from the part of the trench where enemy entrance to mine was supposed to be. Our own artillery and trench mortars immediately opened fire on enemy trench and received but little retaliation.

INTELLIGENCE.

Enemy Work. Enemy was working along the whole of his line in large parties last night.
Trucks were heard along the Railway opposite our ~~left~~ right sector from 11.30 p.m. to 5.15 a.m.

Trench Mortar. Enemy trench mortar fired from I.6.c.1.8.

Machine Gun. A machine gun is located at I.5.b.7.4.

MISCELLANEOUS.

At 3.40 p.m. a rocket landed behind our trench near BARWICK FARM. On reaching the ground it emitted a thick white vapour. Herewith fragments of the rocket.

At 7.10 a.m. this morning a slight underground shock was felt in the front line and also at YPRES.

There is a decoy "head and shoulders" with steel helmet at point I.11.b.96.70.

Herewith documents in German which were picked up in our lines and were evidently intended to be dropped in those of the enemy.

W. Carden Re Captain, G.S.,

9.9.16.   29th Division.

29TH DIVISION DAILY SUMMARY.
From 10 a.m. 9.9.16. to 10 a.m. 10.9.16.

OPERATIONS.

Artillery. Enemy artillery and trench mortars extraordinarily inactive. At 1 a.m. a few field gun shells were fired into A.5 but no damage was done.

Machine Guns. Enemy's machine guns were active during the night opposite our Left Sector.
Our Lewis guns fired on enemy working parties between 11 p.m. and 12 midnight.

INTELLIGENCE.

Enemy Work. The enemy was again working all along his line throughout the night.
A patrol examined the enemy's wire at I.11.b.9.7 and found that at point of small salient the wire is very thick and strong, but on the left face of the salient is much less so and appears to consist of scraps of wire pulled together. There was no new wire.

Enemy Movements. Transport was heard between 12.50 a.m. and 1.20 a.m. behind enemy's line opposite WIELTJE.
Men were seen carrying timber at :-
       (1) BELLEWAARDE FARM.
       (2) GREY RUIN (C.30.a.9.1).

MISCELLANEOUS.

A man has been seen several times to-day looking through the broken roof of OSKAR FARM as if observing with glasses.

10th Sept. 1916.

Captain, G.S.,
29th Division.

D.S.145.

HEADQUARTERS.
29th DIVISION.
INTELLIGENCE.

No. ....
Date 462

29TH DIVISION DAILY SUMMARY.
From 10 a.m. 10.9.16. to 10 a.m. 11.9.16.

OPERATIONS.

Artillery. Enemy's artillery almost inactive. B.12 was slightly shelled at about 5 p.m., it is believed by a high velocity gun. Our guns retaliated.

Machine Guns. Enemy's machine guns were active during the night. Our guns fired on the usual targets.

Trench Mortars. The enemy's trench mortars were more active than usual. About 40 bombs were fired at the right sector, 10 of which were of large calibre. SUNKEN ROAD and S.21 were slightly damaged. About 20 more bombs were fired at A.8 and B.9.

Snipers. Enemy's snipers were active.

Patrols. One N.C.O. and one man left I.5.a.96.95 at 10.30 p.m. and went towards the MOUND in front of which place they heard a large enemy working party.
Other small patrols reported the enemy working on and in front of their front line in C.23.c.

INTELLIGENCE.

Enemy Work. New wire has been placed along the southern face and point of small salient south of ROULERS RAILWAY (I.11.b.9.7). The old wire has been supplemented and a new line put out about 15 yards in front of it. Enemy continually exposes himself here. 3 or 4 different men were observed looking over the parapet during the day.
Our snipers observed a party of about 6 of the enemy working on their front line at C.23.c.3.4 at about 2.30 p.m. They fired on this party and it disappeared.
Enemy was heard working, shouting and hammering in his front line trench from about I.5.b.4.9 to I.5.b.5.5 from 6.30 a.m. to 7.30 a.m.
The wire in the re-entrant of the enemy's line at C.29.d. appears to be weaker than usual.

Enemy Movements. At 6.30 p.m. a wagon was seen on the road leading to UHLAN FARM. The usual train activity was heard during the night.
Enemy's transport heard coming down the ST. JULIEN ROAD about midnight close up to front line. This transport left again at 1.30 a.m.
About 20 of the enemy were seen crossing the road behind FREZENBOURG (D.25.c.8.8).

MISCELLANEOUS.

Signals. At 8.15 p.m. enemy put up coloured rockets from about a mile behind their front line. They were sent up in the following order :- 1 white, 2 green, 2 red, 2 white, 1 green.
At 8.35 p.m. several flares went up opposite A.6 and A.7 from behind the enemy's front line trench. They broke into colours - red, white and green - nothing followed.

Smoke. Smoke was seen from behind the ridge behind KAISER BILL true bearing from C.29.c.6.8 was 39°66'.

Balloon. An observation balloon could be seen over enemy's lines between 6.30 a.m. and 8 a.m.

Band. A band was heard playing behind the German lines during "Stand to" in the evening.

11/9/16.

Captain, G.S.,
29th Division.

29TH DIVISION DAILY SUMMARY.

From 10 a.m. 11.9.16. to 10 a.m. 12.9.16.

OPERATIONS.

Artillery. Enemy artillery slightly more active than usual.
(1) Between 11 a.m. and 11.30 a.m. enemy fired 6 heavy H.E. in vicinity of WEST LANE in I.10.d.
(2) Between 4 p.m. and 6 p.m. he shelled ST. JEAN with 77 mm. and 4.2" Howitzer shells.
(3) About 14 light shrapnel shells were fired over dump at junction of RAILWAY and CAMBRIDGE ROAD at midnight.
(4) At 9.50 a.m. this morning 12 heavy shrapnel burst over CORK Cots.

Trench Mortars. At 6 p.m. enemy fired 7 trench mortar shells about the GULLY. We immediately retaliated with excellent results, 6 direct hits into enemy's trench being recorded, much material being blown in the air.

Machine Guns. Enemy machine guns were very active during the night opposite our left sector. Our field guns opened fire on them and they were gradually silenced.

Snipers. Enemy's snipers were reported to be more active opposite both sectors.

Patrols. An enemy patrol of about 14 men were seen about 11 p.m. coming through enemy wire in front of A.5.a. They were dispersed by Lewis gun fire.
Another enemy patrol was encountered by one of our patrols in front of A.6. On seeing our patrol they withdrew to their lines and did not return.

INTELLIGENCE.

Enemy Work. No sounds of work at all were heard in the German lines opposite our left sector.
On our right sector new earth has been thrown up and new sandbags have been placed at both sides of Railway at I.6.c.2.0.
There were small working parties at BILL COTTAGE (I.6.b.2.8) all day.

Enemy Movements. Several men have been seen at different times of the day moving in the vicinity of MOUSE TRAP FARM. They do not appear to be carrying anything.
At 5 p.m. two large lorries loaded with bales were seen passing along road towards VERLORENHOEK.

Enemy Defences. Enemy wire from C.29.d.4.0 to C.29.d.4.3 consists of low entanglements. The grass outside is much trodden, suggesting frequent patrolling.

Sniper's Post. There appears to be a sniper's post at I.5.d.9.8.

MISCELLANEOUS.

Pigeons. 3 pigeons flew from east to west over A.7 at 4.10 p.m. 2 from west to east at 5.30 p.m.

12.9.16.

Captain, G.S.,
29th Division.

HEADQUARTERS.
29th DIVISION.
INTELLIGENCE.
No. 464

29TH DIVISION DAILY SUMMARY.
From 10 a.m. 12.9.16. to 10 a.m. 13.9.16.

OPERATIONS.

Artillery. At 12 midday when our 2" trench mortars sent 6 shells into enemy front line, the enemy retaliated with H.E. and shrapnel on the GULLY and continued this shelling intermittently all day.
During the afternoon our 6" howitzers registered various points, and enemy retaliated on S.25 and DOVER STREET, and at 5.35 p.m. shelled No.6 Crater and GULLY, doing a little damage.
At 5.15 p.m. enemy fired 10 rounds of shrapnel and H.E. about A.6 and A.7 and 20 rounds into POTIJZE WOOD. Several of those shells failed to explode. Our guns retaliated.

Machine Guns. Enemy machine guns were on the whole quiet, but snipers were active both by day and night.

Patrols. A patrol of one officer and 4 men reconnoitred "Stable Mud" at I.5.b.65.00. They could see no signs of enemy work there and everything appeared to be very quiet. They reported the depression to be about 25 yards in diameter.
Two small enemy patrols one near TUR HOUSE and the other near C.29.d.1.5 were dispersed by our Lewis gun fire.

INTELLIGENCE.

Enemy Work. A little more wire is noticeable round small salient South of ROULERS Railway at I.11.b.95.80, and a good deal more immediately North of the Railway.
There appears to be new work which has been carefully camouflaged running from point I.12.a.20.75 in a direction East by South.
Enemy is also reported to be working on the MOUND and on his front line wire at C.29.d.

Trench Mortars. A trench mortar battery is located about I.12.d.16.12, and a trench mortar fired from I.5.d.9.8. (Small piece of covering from German trench mortar bomb is enclosed.)

Snipers Post. A sniper has been seen moving behind his loophole at point I.11.b.10.4. He was in a shell hole in front of his line. He has been fired at and has not been seen since.

Observer. An observer was seen at point I.11.b.95.80.

Enemy Bomb. One of our patrols last night found and brought in a German bomb. It consists of a piece of board roughly hairbrush shape with 14 packets of gun cotton fastened to it by a network of string, with about 2 feet of fuse ending in a brass cylinder (the size of a cartridge case) fitted with a safety pin. The board is some 2 feet long and 10 inches wide. It is believed to be meant to damage wire.

Pigeons. At 4.30 p.m. two pigeons flew from behind our line over A.7 and alighted in rear of the enemy's line.
At 5.30 p.m. a pigeon flew from the enemy's line towards YPRES.
At 7.45 a.m. one pigeon flew from YPRES towards the enemy lines and seemed to return a few minutes later.
The spot in the enemy's lines where these pigeons alight is being looked for.

13.9.16.

Captain, G.S.,
29th Division

29TH DIVISION DAILY SUMMARY.

From 10 a.m. 13.9.16. to 10 a.m. 14.9.16.

D.S.148.

OPERATIONS.

Artillery. Enemy artillery was again active opposite our right sector. From 11.45 a.m. to 12.15 p.m. the DUCK WALK and parts of F.5 and F.11 were heavily shelled. From 2.45 p.m. to 4 p.m. I.16.a. & b was also heavily shelled. Our Heavy Artillery began to retaliate at 4.45 p.m. At 7.30 a.m. the enemy fired 6 light shrapnel shells over junction of F.13 and ROULERS Railway.

Machine Guns. Enemy's machine guns were not active.

Patrols.
(1) Our patrols were active during the night.
One patrol went out to the MOUND about midnight and placed a bomb in the enemy's wire. To this they attached a string and returned. They then put up a flare and pulled the string and on the explosion taking place, swept the enemy's parapet with Lewis guns.
(2) Another patrol left A.6 at 1 a.m. and returned at 2 a.m. They encountered a small enemy patrol which hurriedly withdrew to their own line.
(3) A small patrol went out from our left battalion to identify a dead German in our own wire. He appeared to have been there about a month. The only distinguishing marks were buttons with a figure "5" on them.
(4) A patrol which went out at 11 p.m. reported a large German working party working some distance in front of their line in C.22.d., probably working on the saps between C.22.d.8.4 and C.22.d.9.9. This was reported to the Artillery who opened fire on the working party.
(5) A small sniper patrol found the body of another German (locality not stated). They brought back 3 bombs of the usual stick type and buttons with the figure "5" on them.

INTELLIGENCE.

Enemy Work. A good deal of work is going on just south of OSKAR FARM. At 10.15 a.m. two parties of 20 men each were seen revetting and building up the parapet.
A small working party was seen carrying trench boards along trench at I.12.d.0.0.
Sounds of stakes being driven were heard opposite A.8 during the night.

Enemy Movements. Men still continually moving in 2's and 3's in the vicinity of BILL COTTAGE and GREY RUIN. At 2.30 p.m. an officer dressed in field grey with red tabs on collar and large peaked cap with red band was seen observing from enemy O.P. at I.11.b.95.80.
At 1.20 p.m. a train was seen getting up steam and moving away TYNE COTTAGE approximately D.17.c.2.8½.

Trench Mortars. Enemy trench mortars are still firing from I.5.d.9.8.

Snipers. An enemy sniper was particularly troublesome firing from NO MANS LAND behind ARGYLL FARM.

Pigeons. At midday two pigeons flew over A.6 towards YPRES. At 4.30 p.m. two flew over from our rear towards the enemy. At 11 a.m. a man carrying something white was seen going in the direction of BOSSAERT FARM and between 11 a.m. and 12.30 p.m. six men left this farm one by one coming in the direction of MOUSE TRAP FARM.

L. Carden Roe
Captain, G.S.,
14.9.16.
29th Division.

29TH DIVISION DAILY SUMMARY.

From 10 a.m. 14.9.16. to 10 a.m. 15.9.16.

OPERATIONS.

Artillery. Our own artillery was active throughout the period but drew little retaliation from the enemy. GARDEN STREET was shelled with 4.2" and 5.9" shells, ten of these failed to explode.

Machine Guns. There has been a noticeable decrease in the enemy's use of machine guns. They were only active during morning "Stand to".
Our own machine guns fired on enemy's communications, and Railway crossing at J.1.a.85.55.

Rifle Grenades. Between 6 a.m. and 6.20 a.m. seven large rifle grenades were fired at A.8.

General. The day was most marked for the general quiet attitude of the enemy. His trench mortars did not fire at all, and his snipers were considerably quieter.

INTELLIGENCE.

Enemy Work. Much digging is going on in enemy front line system by OSKAR FARM. 6 loads of what appeared to be doors and boxes were seen to be brought up to the Farm in handcarts along the communication trench.
Working parties were seen at I.12.b.0.2, J.1.a.5.5 and BOESAERT FARM.

Enemy Movements. At 8 p.m. work was heard in FATHER BILL and at 2.30 a.m. in front line north of the MOUND. Both of these parties were dealt with by our Lewis guns.
Transport was heard between 6.30 p.m. and 8.15 p.m. on road C.29.d.10.2 – C.23.c.85.55.
At 8.14 a.m. two horse transport wagons were seen on road leading to FREZENBERG from the south.

Trains. At 1.14 p.m. a train arrived at D.17.b.3.6, it shunted one wagon containing field sacks and departed again at 1.17 p.m. (reported from Divisional O.P.).

Emplacements. A machine gun is suspected about C.23.c.6.2½. A gun position is suspected on bearing of 122° from point I.12.c.8.7½, this is being communicated to the gunners.

MISCELLANEOUS.

Signals. At 2.20 a.m. a white light was seen in rear of enemy's lines, it frequently changed colour to golden and went out at 2.35 a.m. No action followed. There was a remarkable lack of Very lights from enemy's lines last night.

Pigeons. At 8.20 a.m. 4 pigeons passed over the right of trench A.8 from the direction of POTIJZE and settled behind German front line.

Captain, G.S.,
29th Division.

15.9.16.

29TH DIVISION DAILY SUMMARY.

From 10 a.m. 15.9.16. to 10 a.m. 16.9.16.

OPERATIONS.

Enterprise (1). At 11 p.m. gas was discharged from A.5.a to A.7. Our guns simultaneously opened fire. Almost immediately the gas was discharged a red rocket was sent up from the German lines breaking into golden rain, followed by a considerable number of others.
At midnight two patrols went out to observe if possible, the results of the gas. The first patrol observed a hostile patrol moving from the MOUND in single file, 17 in all were counted and there were probably more. This patrol divided into two parties, one party going towards our trenches, the other moving North. When they arrived abreast of our patrol, our patrol attacked them with bombs and revolvers. Some of the Germans fled, others dropped down. One man fired 4 or 5 shots wounding one of our patrol. Our patrol then withdrew to our own trenches bringing in the wounded man. It was noticed that on the discharge of gas no flares were sent up immediately opposite the gas sector. Also no machine gun or rifle fire came from the German trenches while the patrol was out. The Germans seen were wearing gas masks in an "Alert" position.

Enterprise (2). Between 11.30 p.m. and 12.15 a.m. we raided the enemy's trenches just south of the ROULERS Railway. All returned having entered enemy's trenches, bombed a dugout, and succeeded in bringing in one prisoner of 362nd Regiment, killing another of the same Regiment, and another who has not yet been found. Pay books of prisoner and dead man herewith.

ARTILLERY.

From 11.15 a.m. to 3 p.m. the enemy fired 77 mm. H.E. on DUCK WALK, GULLY, RAILWAY TRENCH and S.23. Little damage was done.
When our artillery opened fire at 11 p.m. the enemy commenced retaliating about 11.10 p.m. His retaliation was not very effective until 11.30 p.m. His main barrage lines appeared to be - in front of A.5 - along right front of firing line - SUNKEN ROAD - DUCK WALK - S.23 and F.11. When our fire died down, the enemys did likewise.
Our artillery bombardment appeared to be most effective. A fire was started in the enemy's lines which blazed until 3.30 a.m. Judging by the small explosions, puffs of smoke, and occasional extreme brightness of the fire, it appeared that a very light store has been set on fire. Men were seen trying to put it out but were dealt with by our Lewis guns. Location of fire I.6.c.2.4.
Machine Guns. The absence of machine gun fire along the whole line was most marked last night.

INTELLIGENCE.
At 11.30 p.m. when our guns lifted from the enemy's line, the enemy sent up a flare which consisted of a green and white star rising together. 20 minutes later he sent up two more such flares. Other than this the enemy did not appear to use any system in use of flares.
At 10 a.m. this morning a man in a green cap was seen working at C.22.b.5.6. There is a good deal of new earth at this point.
A large steel structure about 80 feet high is at C.17.b.3.9. A hut appears to have been recently erected at its foot.
At 3 p.m. 3 wagons were seen going along road behind VERLORENHOEK. The same thing was seen at 5 p.m.
At 4.30 p.m. 5 pigeons went over Right Sector to enemy's lines from direction of POTIJZE.

16.9.16.

Captain, G.S.,
29th Division.

29TH DIVISION DAILY SUMMARY.
From 10 a.m. 16.9.16. to 10 a.m. 17.9.16.

OPERATIONS.

Artillery. The enemy was not very active during the period. Between 9 a.m. and 12 Noon enemy heavy gun either 4.2" or 5.9" enfiladed the right of H.19 doing damage to trench. At 10 a.m. enemy fired 20 H.E. and shrapnel along ST. JEAN ROAD. Our guns retaliated.

Machine Guns. Enemy machine guns were active during the evening "Stand to". One gun was particularly active firing from C.29.d.4.3.
Our Lewis guns fired throughout the night at gaps made by our artillery in the enemy's wire.

Snipers. Enemy snipers were quiet except opposite the right of our Left Brigade.
One of our snipers shot a man looking over the parapet at I.12.a.1.5. He was wearing a bluish forage cap with thin red band.

Patrols. One of our patrols went out towards KAISER BILL last night. They reported a working party without a covering party on the North side. Enemy wire here has many gaps caused by our shell fire. Our patrol returned and informed our Lewis gunners who opened fire. One of the enemy working party was heard to scream.

Another of our patrols went out along the VERLORENHOEK ROAD and found the enemy repairing his wire on both sides of the Road. We dispersed them in similar manner with Lewis gun fire.

INTELLIGENCE.

Enemy Work. The enemy has not yet repaired the damage done to his wire on the night of the 15th instant, but he has been busy repairing his trenches both by day and night. Parties were seen working during the day in the -
   MOUND
   I.6.a.5.2
   J.1.a.3½.5.

Enemy Movements. About 75 yards south of the sap at C.29.d.4.1 and 100 yards in front of the German lines there is a small semi-circular trench about 50 yards long neither wired nor traversed. Sniping from here is suspected and it is being kept under observation by our patrols.

At 2.15 a.m. sounds of moving a gun or wagon were heard at approximately I.6.a.2.1. As small shells have been coming from that direction it seems possible that a damaged gun was being removed from an emplacement.

About 2.30 a.m. the noise of a train was heard in the distance along the ROULERS Railway. About 30 minutes afterwards a heavy gun fired 30 shells in the direction of YPRES. The noise of the discharge had a peculiarly metallic sound and it is thought the shells may have been fired from a naval gun mounted on a railway truck.

Usual horse transport was heard last night.

MISCELLANEOUS.

Dump. A dump is suspected about point I.6.c.2.8. Trolleys come up to this point and are unloaded there.

Captain, G.S.,
29th Division.

17.9.16.

29TH DIVISION DAILY SUMMARY.

From 10 a.m. 17.9.16. to 10 a.m. 18.9.16.

OPERATIONS.

<u>Artillery.</u> At 7.45 a.m. the enemy bombarded our line from AIR STREET to the extreme right of the line. The bombardment was very heavy and did considerable damage along MUDDY LANE, SUNKEN ROAD, S.21, JUNCTION TRENCH, and F.11. The front line trench has been broken in in several places and the wire is considerably damaged from H.16 to H.21. Many large trench mortars were fired at No.6 Crater at the same time, but damage to the line North of the Railway was not so great as on the south side. This bombardment was continued until about 9.30 a.m.

<u>Machine Guns.</u> Enemy machine guns were again quiet. One at G.29.d.4.3 was attacked by us with rifle grenades from A.6. There was some retaliation with rifle grenades but the gun has not fired since.

<u>Patrols.</u> One of our patrols went out at 8 p.m. to search the house in NO MANS LAND at I.5.b.3.5. The house was empty but appears to have been used by both sides. Two German bombs, a quantity of old .303 ammunition, some German telephone wire and a disused gun pit were found. The patrol visited the enemy wire at the MOUND and reported fairly thick and in good condition. The enemy were very quiet, no flares or machine gun were used while the patrol was out. The patrol waited at the house a hour and a half and then returned.

Another patrol went out to ARGYLL FARM to see if this is occupied at night but no signs of the enemy could be seen.

INTELLIGENCE.

A large trench mortar was firing this morning from I.6.c.1.5 and several smaller ones were firing about the same spot.

A large party of about 20 men was observed near BILL COTTAGE during the bombardment.

<u>Aeroplanes.</u> Enemy aeroplane tried to cross our line at B.9. It was driven back by our Anti-aircraft guns.

Capt. G.S.,
29th Division.

18.9.16.

D.S.153.

29TH DIVISION DAILY SUMMARY.

From 10 a.m. 18.9.16. to 10 a.m. 19.9.16.

HEADQUARTERS
29th DIVISION,
INTELLIGENCE

No.
Date 470

OPERATIONS.

Artillery. Enemy's artillery was quiet but machine guns were more than usually active.
At 5.45 a.m. a mine was exploded by the enemy in front of 2.A Crater. The earth was not thrown up but men in the trenches felt the earth shake and clouds of smoke issued just in front of our wire.
On the left sector enemy's artillery was quiet.
At 3 p.m. they dropped 10 shells about 25 yards behind X.4 and at the same time about 6 on the junction of B.11 and JOHN STREET.

Machine Guns. Enemy's machine guns active during the night on the right sub-sector, otherwise quiet.
Our own artillery was active on I.5.b. and silenced every machine gun on left sub-sector between 8 p.m. and 11.15 p.m. Rifle Grenades were used on the left sector, again attacking the machine guns mentioned yesterday and a suspected machine gun position in the MOUND, and sending several into KAISER BILL. No retaliation followed. Machine guns did not fire after the rifle grenades were used.

Our rifle battery at junction of DURHAM TRENCH and B.10.a. fired on the Cross Roads at C.22.b.9.1 and C.23.c.15.70 during the night - results unknown.

Patrols. Right Sector. A patrol of 10 men under 2/Lt.GIBBS and 2/Lt. TRIBER went out at 1 a.m. from I.5.b.1.3. The patrol report they could not get close enough to enemy's wire to find out the strength of the enemy.

In the **Left Sector** a patrol of 1 N.C.O. and 5 men went out at 9 p.m. to the MOUND and again examined the house at I.5.b.3.5, it was unoccupied. They reported a wiring party 15 strong on the MOUND. The patrol got close to them but saw no covering party. The wiring party retired to their trenches after half an hours hurried work. Transport from a southerly direction was heard coming close to the MOUND. No enemy patrols were seen. The patrol returned at 11.30 p.m.

Another patrol of 1 N.C.O. and 5 men went out at 9 p.m. to observe sap at KAISER BILL. At 10.45 p.m. they observed a wiring party come out to repair gap at the foot of KAISER BILL. They were only out about five minutes. A bomb was picked up just outside the sap. Wire at the sides is not very strong consisting of barbed wire on low stakes.

A patrol under 2/Lt. PRAYNE went out at 11.30 p.m. 15 yards south of WIELTJE ROAD. About 50 yards from our wire, sounds of a hostile patrol were heard. Our patrol tried to cut them off, but they retired too quickly towards their own lines. The patrol returned and got Lewis gun trained on the line the hostile patrol retired on and on the German parapet. The direction they took was towards KAISER BILL.

INTELLIGENCE.

On the right sector enemy was quiet during the night, but hammering was heard between 7 a.m. and 9 a.m. this morning opposite 2.A Crater.

At 9.30 p.m. a green flare was sent up by the enemy followed by a red one on our extreme right. Nothing followed.

- 2 -   471

On the left sector opposite the right sub-sector the
Germans were seen in front line wearing rounds caps, some
with white, some with red bands.   Also one was observed
wearing steel helmet with white diamond shaped badge
similar in shape to ours.

Another German looked over the parapet at point C.22.b.3.2.
He was fired on by our snipers and disappeared at once.
There is apparently a periscope at this point taken down
about every 5 minutes and put up again; also there is
a good deal of fresh work there.

Another periscope was seen at C.22.d.8.10.   Our snipers
claim a direct hit on it.

O.P. at WEST LANE reports :-

At 12.5 p.m. small party at point D.27.c.5.1.   Horse transport
was observed at the road from BROODSEINDE to PAASSCHENDAELE.
4 men proceeded along the same road at 5 p.m.
At 8.10 p.m. a searchlight was seen apparently coming from
a peculiarly shaped tripod.
There was a very heavy mist.

                                                Captain, G.S.,

19th Sept. 1916.   29th Division.

D.S.154.

29TH DIVISION DAILY SUMMARY.

From 10 a.m. 19.9.16. to 10 a.m. 20.9.16.

OPERATIONS.

Artillery. On the right sector enemy artillery very quiet both by day and night. The enemy reply to our bombardment on the left sector at 2 a.m. was feeble.

Machine Guns. Right sub-sector enemy machine guns active from 9 p.m. to 9.30 p.m. and about midnight. They were also active on the left sub-sector about 1 a.m. The left sector machine guns traversed front line; fire ceased at 2 a.m., it is presumed it was due to raiding party coming in contact with strong enemy patrol.

Trench Mortars. On the left sector a few rounds landed near A.7 soon after the commencement of our bombardment. In WIELTJE Salient enemy trench mortars were inactive, although some 40 of our 2" trench mortar bombs were fired into the enemy trench lines between C.23.c.3.0 and C.29.a.8.7.

Snipers. Snipers on the right sector were quiet.

Patrols. A patrol reports an enemy machine gun on the right sector at I.5.b.5.4.
An enemy patrol of about 4 men approached our wire at H.15 at 11 p.m. They were fired on and withdrew.
A patrol under 2/Lieut. GIBBS and 2/Lieut. TULFER went out from A.5 at 11.30 p.m. Enemy heard working at point 54 south of HITEL FRITZ FARM. They also report machine gun mentioned above at I.5.b.5.4. They returned safely at 12.45 a.m.

Raid. At 11 p.m. the 2nd Royal Fusiliers attempted a raid on the German front line between KAISER HILL and the MOUND. A full report has been sent in separately.

INTELLIGENCE.

Enemy Work. Enemy was heard working between 2.30 a.m. and 5 a.m. on the front and support lines on the left sector, probably repairing damage caused by our bombardment.
It is reported that a working party was seen at about 3 p.m. on the high ground in front of MOUSETRAP FARM on what appears to be a redoubt.

Enemy Movements. Transport could be heard after 5 a.m. in the direction of the ST. JULIEN ROAD.
A machine gun is suspected at C.29.a.5.6 firing from a sap head near WHITE COTTAGE.
Snipers posts are also suspected at C.28.b.5.9 and C.22.b.7.8.
On the right sector trains were heard at 6 a.m. and 11.30 p.m. on ROULERS RAILWAY. Transport movements were previously heard, possible due to the Company relief referred to in the examination of prisoner mentioned in the Summary of 18th September. This is born out by the fact there was little firing during the night.
Our snipers saw two of the enemy carrying a load opposite A.5, which they dropped when fired upon and scrambled into their trench.

MISCELLANEOUS.

Aeroplanes. Our aeroplanes were very active between the hours of 10 a.m. and 12 Noon and 5 p.m. and 7 p.m. They were heavily fired on by the enemy but without result.

Flares. On the left sector very few flares were sent up during the night, but on the right sector several flares were sent up without result.

20.9.16.

Capt. G.S.
29th Division.

D.S.155.

29TH DIVISION DAILY SUMMARY.

From 10 a.m. 20.9.16. to 10 a.m. 21.9.16.

HEADQUARTERS.
29th DIVISION.
INTELLIGENCE.

No. 473
Date.

OPERATIONS.

Artillery. Enemy artillery showed slightly increased activity. The principle targets were POTIJZE WOOD, ST. JEAN, GARDEN STREET, POTIJZE ROAD, POTIJZE DEFENCES, X Line between CAMBRIDGE ROAD and F.13. Our artillery retaliated vigorously on all occasions.

Machine Guns. Enemy machine guns quieter than usual along the whole front. On the left sector our machine guns systematically traversed the enemy's communication routes throughout the night.

Snipers. Between 5 a.m. and 7 a.m. enemy snipers were active in the WIELTJE sub-sector but could not be located. At I.12.a.3.4 an enemy sniper was engaged but quickly stopped firing.

Patrols. On the right of the right sector patrol from H.16 reported enemy working in his front line. On the left of the right sector a patrol under 2/Lt. GIBBS and 2/Lt. TELFER reported the enemy working about I.8.b.5.4. An enemy patrol was seen in front of A.6. Our patrol returned safely at 1.15 a.m.

On the right of the left sector a patrol consisting of one officer and seven other ranks left A.7 at 8.50 p.m. It proceeded S.E. towards the MOUND. When within 80 yards of the MOUND, observed an enemy party of at least 16 cross its line of advance in a south-westerly direction. Enemy party was in extended order and was seen to lie down in NO MANS LAND at a distance of about 100 yards from our wire. Patrol returned at 9.30 p.m. and reported the above with a view to having fire opened on the enemy patrol.

At 12.30 a.m. another patrol under 2/Lt. WEBB left B.9 at C.29.a.1.4. They proceeded to a row of trees between C.29.a.2.6 and C.29.a.2.7 and remained there one hour. They then advanced through a small hedge on the road between WHITE COTTAGE and the POTIJZE ROAD. As they were moving a rifle exploded about 2 yards from them which it is thought was attached to a trip wire but could not be found and being searched for. The patrol continued its advance towards enemy wire at C.29.a.4.5 just to the left of enemy sap and there turning sharply to the left struck the sap head on the road above mentioned at the point C.29.a.19.78. An enemy working party of about 20 strong were digging or draining at the sap head but not wiring. The enemy working party immediately dashed into the sap and opened rapid fire on the patrol which continued its advance and dropped into a disused trench at about C.29.a.09.78 where it remained for about half an hour during which time a hostile machine gun fired at them from the sap head. The protection of the old parapet was sufficient of the disused trench was sufficient to protect the patrol and as soon as things quietened it continued its advance along the line of the road to the point at C.29.a.0.49 after which they returned to our lines at the point of egress without any casualties.

474

INTELLIGENCE.

At 10 p.m. and 5.30 a.m. enemy transport was heard opposite H.19 apparently close to the front line and proceeding in a north-westerly direction.
At 10 a.m. two horse transports were seen on the road N.E. of BROODSEINDE.
On the WIELTJE sub-sector transport was heard during the night and up to 6 a.m.
At 5 a.m. a heavy motor was heard moving along the ST. JULIEN ROAD. It appeared to be hauling wagons.
Horse transport was observed at 5 p.m. about I.1.d.6.8.

Work was going on along the whole front all night, the enemy making a considerable amount of noise, hammering nails, sawing, pumping, scooping of mud and water, was heard. The enemy was also scooping mud during the day at I.12.c.8.5. He took no pains to conceal the fact that the work was going on and could be heard shouting and whistling all night, and opposite the left sub-sector was speaking English.
His small trench railway was heard east of KAISER BILL just before 8 a.m.
Clay was thrown up at 5 p.m. at I.7.b.5.3.

At 1.45 a.m. opposite H.14 a bell was heard and at 3 a.m. a gong was beaten for about a minute, but no result followed.

An Observation Balloon was up in the direction of ST. JULIEN before 10 a.m.

No signs of enemy aerial activity on our side this morning.

At 11.45 a.m. a man was seen walking across the field and getting in the second line trench at 1575. I.5.6.7.5.

At 1.40 p.m. a party was working at C.24.c.6.4 and at 2.40 p.m. a man with a wheelbarrow was observed at C.30.b.5.4.

Between 6.2 and 6.12 p.m. 29 men crossed field at D.22.a.5.3 in threes and fours proceeding in a south-easterly direction.

At 7.40 a.m. a party of about 6 men were seen at D.20.c.8.8.

At 7.50 a.m. a party was seen working at D.23.c.2.8 apparently erecting a screen.

A party was also working at D.17.c.5.1 at 9.35 a.m. on the same road.

Captain, G.S.,
21st Sept. 1916.   20th Division.

D.S.156.

29TH DIVISION DAILY SUMMARY.

From 10 a.m. 21.9.16. to 10 a.m. 22.9.16.

OPERATIONS.

Artillery. POPERINGHE was shelled with heavy guns between 9.15 a.m. and 9.45 a.m.; little damage was done. On the left sector enemy showed but little activity and did not reply to our afternoon bombardment. He was also quiet on the right sector but a little damage was done to H.19, H.20 and A.5. In replying some of our own shells dropped behind our lines; both H.E. and shrapnel.

Machine Guns. Enemy machine guns quiet. Enemy gun located at I.12.a.3½.3.

Trench Mortars. No trench mortar activity.

Patrols. On the left front patrol of one officer and 6 other ranks reconnoitred wire round KAISER BILL. It returned at 10.50 p.m. and reported small party of the enemy sandbagging the trenches in the Salient. Enemy wire is in good condition and consists of loose plain wire on wooden stakes.

A patrol under 2/Lt. WILTON, one other officer and 8 other ranks left B.10 at 12.30 a.m. and proceeded along the ST. JULIEN ROAD and halted for half an hour at C.22.d.6.3. The patrol then proceeded along the road and encountered a snipers post in a hollow tree at C.22.d.70.35. Telephone wires connecting the post about 50 yards apart were discovered and cut. Enemy was observed walking down the sap from the second "T" in WELL COTTAGE towards the road. There was wire in front of the S.W. of the sap but it does not extend as far as the road. It is thought an enemy machine gun was firing from L.R.B. COTTAGE. Patrol returned safely at 4.30 a.m.

On the right front a patrol under 2/Lt. GIBBS and 2/Lt. TELFER left A.5 at 11.30 p.m. and reported enemy party moving heavy objects, possibly gas cylinders, at I.5.b.5.4. They were working very quietly and were using a hand trolley in the trench. Patrol returned safely at 2.30 a.m.

Aeroplanes. On the left front there was some aerial activity during the afternoon and reconnaissances were made in the face of heavy shelling, aeroplanes replied with Lewis gun.

Enemy observation balloons were up during the afternoon. One is reported on the authority of a Sergeant and a Corporal of the 2nd South Wales Borderers stationed at X.8, to have been brought down in a cloud of smoke.

Another balloon reported at 5.30 a.m. this morning. This appeared to be nearer our lines than balloons usually are.

Enemy aeroplane was observed at 9 a.m. this morning West of YPRES. It appeared to return safely to its own lines.

Squadron of our aeroplanes flew N.N.E. over enemy's lines this morning.

The right sector also reports considerable aeroplane activity. At 12.30 p.m. one of them brought down an observation balloon by rocket fire. (This apparently is the same balloon as reported by left sector.)

- 2 -

476

INTELLIGENCE.

On the left front transport was heard during the night on the ST. JULIEN ROAD but ceased for a time when fired on by machine guns.

Trains were heard at 10 p.m. and 12.15 a.m. on the right front.

A number of red flares were sent up at intervals between 9 p.m. and 1 a.m. along the whole front. Nothing was observed to result from them.

Between 8.30 p.m. and 11.30 p.m. periodic flashes were seen from I.10.d.5¾.5 (magnetic bearing 5½°) at intervals of 3 seconds, from distant gun fire.

Throughout the day several men were at work with wagons at D.20.d.8.8 apparently manuring the ground.

At 1 p.m. a train was seen at D.17.b.3.6.

At 6.21 p.m. and 8.3 a.m. horse transport was seen on the road to BROODESEINDE going S. and N.E.

Smoke was seen rising at JASPER FARM at 3.30 p.m. and 3 men were seen moving about.

Sentries report metallic clinking sounds from the enemy lines between I.5.b.5.4 and the MOUND.

[signature]

Captain, G.S.,

22nd Sept. 1916.   29th Division.

29TH DIVISION DAILY SUMMARY.
From 10 a.m. 22.9.16. to 10 a.m. 23.9.16.

HEADQUARTERS.
29TH DIVISION
INTELLIGENCE.
No. 477
Date.

OPERATIONS.

<u>Artillery.</u> Enemy artillery quiet on the left front and made no response to our afternoon bombardment.
On the right more active than usual, reserve and support lines were shelled.
On the morning of the 22nd, five 7.7 cm. shells burst near an observation post at B.9. No damage was done.
At 6.30 p.m. 8 rounds fell in the neighbourhood of HAYMARKET.
There are still complaints of our own shells falling short.
Enemy aircraft was shelled over POPERINGHE at 8.30 a.m.

<u>Machine Guns.</u> More than usually active during the night along the whole front.

<u>Trench Mortars.</u> No trench mortar activity.

<u>Snipers.</u> Were quiet along the whole front.

<u>Rifle Grenades.</u> We retaliated with trench mortars and artillery on the right sector, in reply to enemy rifle grenades fired into our front line between 6 and 7 p.m. and 5 and 6 a.m.

<u>Aircraft.</u> At 10 p.m. aircraft noises were heard very plainly which led officers of the 1st K.O.S.Bs. to suspect that they were produced by a Zeppelin. Machine guns were active during that period and no enemy flares were put up.
Our aeroplanes were active during the night and one was observed at 5 a.m. above the left Brigade Headquarters flying eastwards, shortly after which explosions due to bombs were heard.

<u>Patrols.</u> On the right front two strong patrols under 2/Lieuts. GIBBS and TELFER report enemy wiring parties working south-west of KITEL FRITZ FARM, and also work being done in enemy's front line at I.6.c.
Careful reconnaissance was made of the left front by a patrol of the 2nd South Wales Borderers, but after strenuous endeavours, they did not succeed in obtaining enemy identifications. Patrol reports, in its opinion, that apart from machine guns the front line is lightly held.
On the right of the left sector a patrol left A.6 at 9 p.m. and returned at 10 p.m. They reported work going on in the MOUND, and it appeared that corrugated iron was being handled.
Another patrol consisting of 1 officer, 2 N.C.Os. and 10 men left trench at 1 a.m. and returned at 3.45 a.m. They went North of the VERLORENHOEK Road, but heard and saw no movements of any kind.

INTELLIGENCE. Enemy transport heard opposite H.16 at 9 p.m. and at D.17.b.3.6 a train was observed to move off at 1.25 p.m. Men were seen during the morning moving about the neighbourhood of BOSSAERT FARM (C.23.b.) Artillery were informed.
Transport during the night and the early morning was heard moving round the ST. JULIEN Road.

Captain, G.S.,
29th Division.

23rd Sept. 1916.

D.S.158.

29TH DIVISION DAILY SUMMARY.
From 10 a.m. 23.9.16. to 10 a.m. 24.9.16.

OPERATIONS.

Artillery. Enemy artillery inactive. What shells were fired did no damage to our line, neither did he retaliate to our bombardment during the night. He took no steps to fire at six of our aeroplanes which flew over his lines at 6 p.m.

Machine Guns. Generally quiet along the whole front.

Trench Mortars. No trench mortar activity.

Snipers. Several loopholes have been spotted and are being watched on the right front.
On the left one of our snipers firing at B.9 claims a victim at C.29.a.6.6. The spot in question is close to a concrete cupola which is thought to be the top of a machine gun emplacement and can be plainly seen with the aid of a telescope. There is also a large periscope there.

Patrols. A patrol under 2/Lt. MAXWELL and 12 other ranks left A.7 at 10 p.m. and returned at midnight. They advanced towards ODER HOUSE and within 50 yards of the enemy lines and they extended northwards and laid down. They report work going on, but no workers could be seen. No hostile patrols or covering parties were encountered.

Another patrol under 2/Lt. WILTON, 2nd South Wales Borderers, and 6 other ranks, left B.10 at 10.30 p.m. and proceeded along the ST. JULIEN ROAD to the barbed wire entanglements in front of the sap head at C.22.d.85.42. Here the patrol was challenged by a sentry. Patrol halted and laid down, the challenge was repeated. After the third challenge our patrol threw bombs into the sap, to which the enemy replied by throwing one bomb and by rifle fire, without effect. Patrol could not obtain an entry into the sap because of a thick apron of barbed wire, but they are of opinion that the sap is not occupied by more than 4 men. Patrol returned safely after remaining over half an hour at the above point.

INTELLIGENCE. At 7 p.m. enemy was heard working in front of No.2.A Crater, right front. He was dispersed by Lewis gun fire.

At 9.45 p.m. two green lights were observed to the North from the left of the right sector, but no action appeared to follow their appearance.

On the left front enemy were seen working during the day in the trenches E. of ARGYLL FARM.

Transport was heard on the ST. JULIEN ROAD as usual.

No enemy observation balloons were up, neither were any hostile aeroplanes seen during the day. One was observed this morning flying high South of YPRES, not far from a second machine, the nationality of which could not be distinguished.

MISCELLANEOUS.

Signals. A light, possibly a signal, was seen from X.8 about the point C.27.d.50.82 about 11.30 p.m. on the night of the 21st instant, in the direction of DEAD END, but its exact location could not be determined. It appeared to be moved at regular intervals from place to place, but has not been seen since.

479

<u>Pigeons.</u>   A pigeon was observed to fly from the German lines over our parapet between A.7 and A.8 at a low elevation.   It rose gradually in a bee line for POTIJZE WOOD over which it passed out of sight flying strongly along the line of the BELLEWAARDEBEEK.   Enquiries made show that the same thing occurred about the same time on the two previous evenings.   On these occasions two birds and not one were flying.

[signature]

Captain, G.S.,

24th Sept. 1916.   29th Division.

29th DIVISION DAILY SUMMARY.
From 10 a.m. 24.9.16 to 10 a.m. 25.9.16.

OPERATIONS.

Artillery. Enemy artillery showed but slight activity. At 5 p.m. five 105 mm. shells fell between HUSSAR FARM and POTIJZE, and during the night five 77 mm. shells burst over a working party in B.10.a., without doing any damage. At the request of the infantry our own artillery fired on and dispersed an enemy party which was working in the front trench of the sector in C.22.d., at 12.15 p.m.

Machine Guns. Enemy machine guns were active during both the morning and evening "Stand to".

Trench Mortars. During the evening "Stand to" enemy fired five trench mortar bombs into H.16. At the same time a dozen rifle grenades were fired into H.14 and H.16. No damage was done.

Aeroplanes. At 10.30 a.m. two hostile aeroplanes attempted to cross our line, but were driven back by our anti-aircraft fire.

Patrols. We sent out several patrols during the night, all of which brought back useful information concerning the enemy's defences (see Intelligence Summary).

One patrol visited the enemy sap opposite No.3 Crater and found a wiring party on each side of the sap, protected by a small covering party. Fire was opened on the wiring party. The enemy retaliated with bursts of machine gun fire, after which he sent up a red rocket immediately followed by white rockets fired crosswise. This formed a bright stream of light down the middle of NO MANS LAND, behind which their parties retired.

INTELLIGENCE.

Enemy Work. Working parties were located at the following points :-
(1) At 2.11 p.m. at C.30.d.9.8.
(2) At 2.30 p.m. at J.1.d.7.9.
(3) During the night in the sap opposite No.1 Crater.
(4) During the night at No.3 Crater. Here the enemy were wiring on either side of the sap.
(5) The enemy worked noisily all night between C.29.d.3.8 and C.29.a.8.3.

Enemy Defences. The sap at C.29.a.15.80 is not occupied by the enemy. From the ST. JULIEN ROAD to the above sap the wire is about 70 yards distant from the front trench, and is in good condition. It consists of an outer row of stiff concertina wire 5 feet high. Inside this and close to the borrow trench there is a second system of wire which consists mainly of loose tangles. In front of the sap head there is a single row of concertina wire with large gaps in it

Enemy Movements. At 3.50 p.m. two transport wagons were seen on road to BROODSEINDE from the south.

25th Sept. 1916.

Captain, G.S.,
29th Division.

D.S.160.

HEADQUARTERS,
29th DIVISION.
INTELLIGENCE.

No. ....
Date ...481

29TH DIVISION DAILY SUMMARY.

From 10 a.m. 25.9.16. to 10 a.m. 26.9.16.

OPERATIONS.

Artillery. Enemy's artillery quiet.
Some shelling with small guns along the POTIJZE ROAD during the afternoon, and 2 or 3 large shells in the direction of MUD LANE towards the evening.
This morning there was ranging on CAMBRIDGE ROAD.

Trench Mortars. A number of trench mortar shells fell in the right sector about 7 p.m. Enemy was silenced by our artillery.

Machine Guns. Enemy machine guns fairly quiet both by day and night.
Our machine guns searched the ST. JULIEN ROAD and ZONNEBEKE ROAD, also the connecting trenches.

Snipers. A sniper was observed to fire from point C.22.b.55.05. He stopped on being fired at.

Patrols. A patrol under 2/Lt. HENNING observed a strong party wiring in front of the MOUND.

An officers patrol proceeded from the left sector towards KAISER BILL. They saw a party wiring south of the Salient at C.29.c.5.9. They were fired on by a machine gun which appeared to be in a shell hole in NO MANS LAND.

Patrols on the right front report work going on in the enemy's front line.

Standing patrol in Crater No.6 reports metallic noises in the enemy's line, possibly due to gas cylinders being moved about.

Aeroplanes. Our aeroplanes were active during the day and were heavily shelled by enemy guns.

An aerial encounter was observed at 8.15 a.m. from the Left Brigade Headquarters, in the direction of the LILLE GATE. The enemy plane appeared to receive injury, as it dived and made off for the west as if about to land.

An enemy aeroplane flying low passed over the right sector near the RAILWAY, and was fired at by one of our Lewis Guns. She dropped star lights which were followed by Shrapnel and H.E. on RAILWAY FARM.

INTELLIGENCE.

Several men were seen walking round VON HUGEL FARM (C.23.d.) between 4 and 4.30 p.m. This place is being kept under observation.

Enemy parapet and wire appears to have been strengthened at I.5.d.10.9. Some of our artillery shells fell here at 3.50 p.m.

Captain, G.S.,
29th Division.

26th Sept. 1916.

D.S.161

HEADQUARTERS.
DIVISION.
INTELLIGENCE.
No.
Date. 6.8.2

29TH DIVISION DAILY SUMMARY.
From 10 a.m. 26.9.16. to 10 a.m. 27.9.16.

OPERATIONS.

Artillery. Hostile activity below normal.
At 5.5 p.m. the enemy fired 4 high velocity shells into S.10.a. between C.29.b.0.2 and OXFORD ROAD.

Machine Guns. Normal.

Trench Mortars. Enemy trench mortars were quiet throughout the day.
About 9 p.m. enemy fired 3 rifle grenades which fell very short in front of Trench A.4. We fired a dozen from H.16 which provoked no retaliation.

Patrols. One of our patrols examined the enemy wire at C.29.d.19.78 and brought back useful information (see Intelligence). To assist in the inspection of the wire Very lights were put up from the row of trees which run from N.W. to S.E. immediately south of ARGYLL FARM. This caused a considerable amount of excitement in the German lines, which appear to be strongly held here, for tramping of feet on the trench boards and a lot of talking could be distinctly heard. Enemy also put up a number of flares in the direction from which our flares had come.

INTELLIGENCE.

Enemy Work. An enemy working party was heard in the MOUND driving in stakes during the night and early morning. Our bombers fired rifle grenades into the MOUND, whereupon work ceased.
From daybreak to 8.15 a.m. earth was being thrown up at C.29.d.40.45 and piles of new earth are visible at this point.
During the same period planks were being carried along the front line trench between C.29.d.4.5 and C.29.d.25.78. Enemy was also seen working at WILDE COTTAGE and at D.27.d.1.5.

Enemy Defences. Enemy wire was examined between the sap at C.29.d.19.78 and C.23.c.30.05. The distance between the outside of the wire and the enemy parapet is nearer 50 than 70 yards. The latter was reported by a patrol which went out on the 25th instant. At one point a gap was seen in the wire which seemed to go on through the wire in zig-zags. Several new coils have been added to those previously noticed. They show up quite plainly by daylight.
The outer wire is of the concertina pattern standing about 3ft. 6in. high (not 5ft. as previously reported). Behind this there are two or three rows of ordinary wire at intervals of about 10 yards. Then there is a quantity of low wire: still further inside there is a good deal of old wire. Three machine guns were observed to fire, one from the angle at C.23.c.29.05, C.29.a.3.95 and also at L.R.B. COTTAGE.or From between L.R.B. COTTAGE. and the enemy lines. (Patrol report).

Enemy Movements.   At 5.10 p.m. 6 men crossed field at D.22.a.5.3 going S.E.

Between 6.10 and 6.25 p.m. 17 men crossed the same field.

4 horse transports left field at D.20.d.8.8 at different times during the day.

At 3.45 p.m. a cart was seen on the UHLAN FARM - VERLORENHOEK ROAD.

It is believed that PASCHENDAELE FARM [Tower] is used as an O.P. Movements have been seen in it at different times.

           p.p. L Cordier Rose
                    Captain, G.S.,
27th Sept. 1916.   29th Division.

29th DIVISION DAILY SUMMARY.   D.S.162.
From 10 a.m. 27.9.16. to 10 a.m. 28.9.16.

**HEADQUARTERS.
29th DIVISION.
INTELLIGENCE.
No............
Date 484**

OPERATIONS.

Artillery.   Enemy's artillery quiet.
4 shrapnel shells were fired on the X line between 4 p.m. and 5 p.m.
At 6.50 p.m. and at 6.57 p.m. H.E. shells were fired by the enemy at a spot about 300 yards West of the CROSS ROADS FARM. These gave out heavy white gas which rolled low along the ground for about 15 minutes.

Machine Guns.   Enemy machine guns were normal, except that heavy fire was directed on WIELTJE Estaminet about midnight.

Enemy trench mortars and snipers were inactive.

Rifle Grenades.   We again engaged enemy's saps in front line at various points with rifle grenades.   His reply was feeble.

Aeroplanes.   Enemy aircraft was considerably more active than usual.
At 10.30 a.m. and again at 11.45 a.m. machines flew over POTIJZE WOOD.
Two more machines attempted to cross our lines, one at 12 Noon, and the other at 5.30 p.m.   They were fired on by our Machine Guns and anti-aircraft guns, and driven back.

Patrols.   Our patrols were active throughout the night.
One patrol located an enemy wiring party about I.12.a.3.4. The patrol took cover in shell holes and directed Lewis gun fire on to the wiring party, who hurriedly retired.   At 10.45 p.m. the enemy party attempted to renew their work. Again our Lewis guns opened fire, this time apparently with better effect, as cries were heard.   Our patrol immediately followed up their success by bombing the enemy's covering party, who had taken shelter in shell holes.
A hostile patrol reached C.29.a.6.1 about midnight, but were dispersed by Lewis gun fire.

INTELLIGENCE.

Enemy Work.   The enemy was working hard at his defences at OSKAR FARM, and at several points between that place and the MOUND.
Working parties were observed at D.26.c.8.5 and D.29.a.3.7.

Enemy Movements.   At 11.55 a.m. horse transport was seen on road to BROODSEINDE from the south.
At 10.5 a.m. 4 men were seen in field at D.20.d.8.5, and later two horse transports wagons were seen in the same field.
At 1.10 p.m. a train arrived at D.17.b.3.6 and left again at 1.16 p.m.
At 4.55 p.m. another train was seen arriving at the same point, departing at 5.55 p.m.

MISCELLANEOUS.

Lights.   At 8.30 p.m. the enemy fired red flares from C.29.d.30.93, and at 1.30 a.m. a single green flare from the MOUND.

28th Sept. 1916.

Captain, G.S.,
29th Division.

29TH DIVISION DAILY SUMMARY.

From 10 a.m. 28.9.16. to 10 a.m. 29.9.16.

OPERATIONS.

Artillery. Although our guns did a considerable amount of firing, the only retaliation reported on the part of the enemy was the firing of a few 77 mm. shells over FLEET STREET at 11.45 a.m., and about 30 similar shells at 5 p.m. at the WIELTJE Salient, S.10.a. and the junction of GARDEN STREET and B.11.

Machine Guns. A machine gun firing from C.29.d.43.38 was silenced by our artillery at midnight. At 5 a.m. it fired again in short bursts.
Otherwise enemy machine guns were unusually quiet.

Rifle Grenades. About 9 p.m. the enemy fired three rifle grenades which fell short of No.6 Crater.

Snipers. There was a lot of sniping during the night opposite the right sub-sector of the right brigade. A German working party about I.6.c.1.5 was dispersed by our own snipers.

INTELLIGENCE.

The enemy was working during the night and early morning between the MOUND and the VERLORENHOEK ROAD.

At 7 a.m. planks were again seen being carried northwards down front line trench at C.29.d.30.75.

Working parties were also seen at I.12.c.8.4 and D.26.c.8.8.

A wiring party was heard at I.12.a.0.4 at 5.15 a.m.
Small parties of men were seen at different times crossing field at D.22.d.2.8 going S.E.

At 3.10 p.m. two horse transport wagons were seen in field at D.20.d.8.5.

A train is reported to have been heard between 5 a.m. and 6 a.m. North-east of the right sector of the left brigade.

L. Carden Roe
Captain, G.S.,
29th Sept. 1916. 29th Division.

D.S.164.

HEADQUARTERS, 29th DIVISION. INTELLIGENCE.

No. 486

29TH DIVISION DAILY SUMMARY.

From 10 a.m. 29.9.16. to 10 a.m. 30.9.16.

OPERATIONS.

Artillery. Our own artillery was active between midnight and 12.35 a.m. on our left, and between 8.30 a.m. and 8.45 a.m. on our right.
Enemy activity normal. A few 77 mm. shells burst over B.9, and six 105 mm. shells burst in ST. JEAN, between 9.30 a.m. and 10 a.m.
A few rounds of 105 mm. calibre were also observed to fall near battery positions around POTIJZE.
A few shells fell in YPRES at different times.

Machine Guns. Normal, but it was noticed that when our artillery were firing at night, the volume of hostile machine gun fire diminished considerably.

Trench Mortars. About 3 p.m. the enemy bombarded our trenches in C.29.a., and did some damage to about 30 yards of the parapet. It is reported that they were firing from C.29.b.2.4, but there is nothing in the air photographs to indicate that there is a trench mortar emplacement at this point. It is more likely to have been UHLAN FARM, where there appears to be a trench mortar emplacement.

Patrols. A small hostile patrol 3 strong was observed from our bombing post near the ROULERS Railway at 8.45 p.m., but they retired almost as soon as they were observed.

INTELLIGENCE.

Enemy Work. Enemy working parties were busy the whole night.
A tramway was in use opposite the left sector of the Right Brigade, and no attempt seemed to be made to conceal the noise.
The enemy was again working in strength on the MOUND. He also worked on the parapet about C.29.a.3.9, but ceased on rifle fire being opened.

Enemy Movements. There was considerable enemy movement at OSKAR FARM and BILL COTTAGE.

MISCELLANEOUS.

Flares. The enemy fired several flares which landed behind our lines between the MOUND and the VERLORENHOEK ROAD. They were evidently fired from NO MANS LAND.

Shells. It is reported that the enemy is using a new heavy type of H.E. shell for anti-aircraft purposes.

L. Carder

Captain, G.S.,

30th Sept. 1916.   29th Division.

Appendix 6

29TH DIVISION WEEKLY OPERATION REPORT.

From 10 a.m. 21.9.16. to 10 a.m. 28.9.16.

ARTILLERY.
Enemy artillery quiet during the whole week.
On the evening of the 27th some H.E. shells were fired near CROSS ROADS FARM. They gave out a heavy white gas which rolled along the ground for about 15 minutes.
The enemy did not retaliate to our daily bombardments.

MACHINE GUNS.
Enemy machine guns quiet on the whole during the week, excepting on the night of the 27th/28th, when considerable fire was directed on WIELTJE Estaminet, about midnight.
An enemy gun has been located at I.12.a.3½.3.

TRENCH MORTARS.
There was some trench mortar and rifle grenade activity on the evening of the 24th and 25th. No damage was done. Enemy stopped firing when our artillery came into action.

AEROPLANES.
Enemy aeroplanes have been more active than usual, during the week, but showed little inclination to cross our lines, and have usually been driven back by our aeroplanes and gun fire.
On the afternoon of the 21st instant enemy balloon was brought down by one of our machines.
Our aeroplanes have made several reconnaissances over the enemy's positions, during the week.

PATROLS.
A considerable amount of patrolling in NO MANS LAND has been done during the week, by the various battalions in the front line.
On the night of the 21st, a snipers post was observed in a hollow tree at C.22.d.70.35.
Wire reported good around KAISER BILL.
From ST. JULIEN ROAD to C.29.a.15.80, wire is reported to be in good condition. There is a second system of wire between these points, consisting mainly of loose tangles.
Wire has been put up in the enemy sap opposite No.3 Crater.
On the night of the 21st, a patrol reported noises in the trench at I.5.d.5.4, and it is suggested that they were possibly due to movement of gas cylinders.
A wiring party seen on the night of the 27th at I.12.a.3.4, was dispersed by our Lewis gun fire, and the covering party who were taking shelter in shell holes, were bombed out.

CASUALTIES.
A list of casualties for the week is subjoined :-

KILLED.		WOUNDED.		MISSING.	
OFF.	O.R.	OFF.	O.R.	OFF.	O.R.
-	7	1	25	-	-

Captain, G.S.,
28th Sept. 1916. 29th Division.

Casualties from 12 noon 21st to 12 noon 28th September 1916.   488

Unit	Killed Off.	Killed O.R.	Wounded Off.	Wounded O.R.	Missing Off.	Missing O.R.
2/ Royal Fusrs.	–	1	–	–	–	–
1/ Lancashire Fus.	–	1	–	5	–	–
1/ R. Dublin Fus.	–	–	1	4	–	–
16/ Middlesex Regt.	–	1	–	2	–	–
2/ South Wales Borders.	–	–	–	1	–	–
1/ K.O.S.B.	–	2	–	5	–	–
1/ R. Innis. Fus.	–	1	–	–	–	–
1/ Border Regt.	–	1	–	5	–	–
87th M.G. Coy.	–	–	–	1	–	–
1/1 West Riding Fd.Co.	–	–	–	1	–	–
147th Bde. R.F.A.	–	–	–	1	–	–
Total	–	7	1	25	–	–

28/9/16.

M.R.24.

29TH DIVISION WEEKLY OPERATION REPORT.

From 10 a.m. 14.9.16. to 10 a.m. 21.9.16.

HEADQUARTERS.
29th DIVISION.
INTELLIGENCE.
No. 489
Date.........

ARTILLERY. 1. The enemy's artillery has been normally active during the period except on the morning of the 18.9.16. when he bombarded our line from AIR STREET to the extreme right of the line. The bombardment which begun at 7.45 a.m. was very heavy and did considerable damage along MUDDY LANE, SUNKEN ROAD, S.21, JUNCTION TRENCH and P.11. The front line trench was broken in in several places and the wire was considerably damaged from H.16 to H.21. Many large trench mortars were fired at No.6 Crater at the same time. This bombardment was continued until about 9.30 a.m. The other places which received most attention were the POTIJZE DEFENCES, ST. JEAN, GARDEN STREET, DUCK WALK and RAILWAY TRENCH.

MACHINE GUNS. 2. Enemy machine guns have been much quieter than usual, but one gun at C.29.d.4.3 was very active and was attacked by us with rifle grenades, and has not fired since. Our machine guns systematically traversed the enemy's communications nearly every night.

TRENCH MORTARS. 3. A few rounds fired near A.7 on 19.9.16. but on the whole enemy's trench mortars have been inactive during the week except on 18.9.16. when they assisted in bombardment of RAILWAY WOOD.

SNIPERS. 4. There has not been so much sniping as usual but one of our snipers shot a man said to be wearing a bluish forage cap with a thin red band.

PATROLS. 5. Our patrols have been active during the period and have directed Lewis gun fire on to several working parties. They have also visited ARGYLL FARM and the house in NO MANS LAND at I.5.b.3.5 to see if they were occupied by the enemy, but this was not the case. One of our patrols located a Machine Gun at I.5.b.5.4.
One hostile patrol of 4 men approached our wire at H.15, but drew off on being fired at.
On 20.9.16. one of our patrols observed a hostile patrol of sixteen men going in a S.W. direction from the MOUND, and fire was opened by Lewis guns from our trench, but the result is not known.

ENTERPRISE. 6. At 11 p.m. on 16.9.16. gas was discharged by us from trenches A.5.a to A.7. The enemy immediately discharged a red rocket which broke into a golden rain which was followed by a lot of others. Two patrols went out to observe if possible the results of the gas. One of these ran into a hostile patrol of 17 men or more and attacked it with bombs and revolvers. The enemy drew off and were observed to be wearing gas masks in "Alert" position.
A party raided the enemy's trenches between 11.30 p.m. and 12.15 a.m. just south of the ROULERS Railway, and brought back one prisoner of the 362nd Regiment, having killed one and possibly another, who has not been found.

CASUALTIES. 7. A list of casualties for the week is subjoined.

KILLED.		WOUNDED.		MISSING.	
OFF.	O.R.	OFF.	O.R.	OFF.	O.R.
2	28	2	64	-	1

21st Sept. 1916.

Major, G.S.,
29th Division.

Weekly Strength, weekending 23rd Septr, 1916.

490

Unit	Strength		Details detached		Fighting Strength	
	Off.	O.R.	Off.	O.R.	Off.	O.R.
86th Bde. Hdqtrs	5	43	-	-	5	43
2/Royal Fusrs.	39	722	14	146	25	576
1/Lancashire Fus.	34	714	7	138	27	576
1/R. Dublin Fusrs.	36	821	10	213	26	608
16/Middlesex Regt.	38	623	9	154	29	469
86th M.G. Coy.	12	150	1	3	11	147
87th Bde. Hdqtrs.	3	30	-	-	3	30
2/South Wales Bordrs.	40	642	12	185	28	457
1/K.O.S.B.	36	700	13	142	23	558
1/R. Inniskilling Fus.	29	509	11	110	18	399
1/Border Regt.	33	644	10	147	23	497
87th M.G. Coy.	9	139	-	6	9	133
88th Bde. Hdqtrs.	5	48	1	7	4	41
4/Worcester Regt.	37	735	12	169	25	566
2/Hants. Regt.	39	898	16	229	23	669
1/Essex Regt.	38	891	13	196	25	695
1/Newfoundland Regt.	30	646	5	141	25	505
88th M.G. Coy.	10	151	-	15	10	136
1/2 Monmouth Regt.	37	976	10	113	27	863
Total - Infantry	510	10082	144	2114	366	7968
D.H.Q.	20	111	-	-	20	111
R.E. Hdqtrs.	3	13	-	1	3	12
1/1 West Riding Fld. Coy.	8	210	1	17	7	193
1/2 London Field Coy.	8	202	-	3	8	199
1/3 Kent Field Coy.	9	212	-	-	9	212
29th Divl. Train	25	453	3	23	22	430
18th Mobile Veterinary Sect.	1	24	-	2	1	22
87th Field Ambulance	9	225	3	9	6	216
88th " "	8	231	-	21	8	210
89th " "	10	246	4	22	6	224
16th Sanitary Section	1	40	-	-	1	40
29th Divl. Signal Coy.	6	148	2	8	4	140
Total	618	12197	157	2220	461	9977

24/9/16.

R. Morgan Capt.
D.A.A. & Q.M.G.

Casualties from 12 noon 14th to 12 noon 21st Septr.

Unit	Killed		Wounded		Missing	
	Off	O.R.	Off	O.R.	Off	O.R.
2/Royal Fusiliers	-	3	-	7	-	-
1/Lancashire Fusrs.	-	2	-	8	-	-
1/R. Dublin Fus.	-	-	-	1	-	-
16/Middlesex Regt.	-	1	-	4	-	-
86/T.M. Battery	2	-	-	-	-	-
2/South Wales Borders	-	1	-	2	-	-
1/K.O.S.B.	-	-	-	1	-	-
4/Worcester Regt.	-	11	1	18	-	1
2/Hants. Regt.	-	1	-	1	-	-
1/Essex Regt.	-	4	-	10	-	-
1/Newfoundland Regt.	-	2	-	3	-	-
88th M.G. Company	-	-	-	1	-	-
1/2 London Field Coy.	-	-	-	1	-	-
1/3 Kent Field Coy.	-	-	1	-	-	-
Total	2	25	2	57	-	1
4th Divl. Artillery						
24 T.M. Battery	-	2	-	4	-	-
14th Brigade R.F.A.	-	1	-	3	-	-
Total	-	3	-	7	-	-

21/9/16.

H.C. Ryan, Capt.
D.a.a.q.m.g.

29TH DIVISION WEEKLY OPERATION REPORT.

From 6 p.m. 7.9.16. to 6 p.m. 14.9.16.

ARTILLERY.

1. Generally speaking the enemy's artillery has shown little activity during the past week; on some days hardly a shell has been fired. The places that received most attention are - POTIJZE WOOD, MUDDY LANE, DUCK WALK, F.5, F.11, GULLY.
Our artillery effectively retaliated on every occasion.

TRENCH MORTARS.

2. The enemy's trench mortars have been rather more active against our right sector, particularly about the GULLY, SUNKEN ROAD and H.21.
Our retaliation has been very thorough.

MACHINE GUNS.

3. The enemy's machine guns have been rather more active than usual at night, especially against our left sector.
Our machine guns have fired nightly at the usual targets.

SNIPERS.

4. The enemy has done rather more sniping than usual.

PATROLS.

5. Our patrols have been active and have succeeded in bringing Lewis gun and Artillery fire on to several hostile working parties during the week. Five hostile patrols have been met with. The enemy is still reported to be working on his wire and front trenches.

MISCELLANEOUS.

6. We successfully exploded a camouflet in front of 2A Crater on the 8th instant. Smoke and dust were seen to come from part of the trench where it is thought the enemy's mine shaft commenced. Our Artillery and Trench Mortars opened an immediate fire on this spot. There was little hostile retaliation.

CASUALTIES.

7. A list of casualties for the week is subjoined :-

KILLED.		WOUNDED.		MISSING.	
Off.	O.R.	Off.	O.R.	Off.	O.R.
-	7	2	47	-	-

14th Sept. 1916.

Major, G.S.,
29th Division.

493

Strength Return W.E. Saturday 16th Sept, 1916.

Units	Total Strength		Men away from Unit		Effective Strength	
	Off.	O.R.	Off.	O.R.	Off.	O.R.
86th Bde. Hdqtrs.	5	43	-	-	5	43
2/Royal Fus.	40	731	15	124	25	607
1/Lancashire Fus.	31	687	5	122	26	565
1/R. Dublin Fus.	39	817	13	202	26	615
16/Middlesex Regt.	38	627	6	106	32	521
86th M.G. Coy.	11	151	1	3	10	148
87th Bde. Hdqtrs.	3	30	-	-	3	30
2/South Wales Bordrs.	40	638	11	192	29	446
1/K.O.S.B.	37	708	13	158	24	550
1/R. Innis. Fus.	29	518	9	127	20	391
1/Border Regt.	34	653	8	137	26	516
87th M.G. Coy.	9	139	-	4	9	135
88th Bde. Hdqtrs.	5	48	-	9	5	39
4/Worcester Regt	33	761	8	156	25	605
2/Hants. Regt.	38	894	11	188	27	706
1/Essex Regt.	33	903	13	152	20	751
1/Newfoundland Regt.	30	640	4	96	26	544
88th M.G. Coy.	10	151	-	8	10	143
Infantry Totals	465	9139	117	1784	348	7355
1/2 Monmouth Regt.	38	916	8	90	30	826
D.H.Q.	20	110	-	-	20	110
R.E. Hdqtrs.	3	13	-	-	3	13
1/2 London Fld. Coy.	8	201	-	2	8	199
1/1 West Riding Fld. Coy.	8	208	1	21	7	187
1/3 Kent Field Coy.	9	208	-	-	9	208
29th Divl. Signal Coy.	6	150	2	4	4	146
87th Field Ambulance	9	225	4	12	5	213
88th " "	9	231	-	20	9	211
89th " "	11	244	4	22	7	222
16th Sanitary Sect.	1	39	-	-	1	39
29th Divl. Train	27	468	5	23	22	445
18th Mobile Vet. Sect.	1	25	-	2	1	23
Totals	615	12177	141	1980	474	10197

W.R.21.

29TH DIVISION WEEKLY OPERATION REPORT.

From 6 p.m. 31.8.16. to 6 p.m. 7.9.16.

ARTILLERY. 1. The enemy's artillery has been generally inactive during the past week. The following points have received most attention :- HELLFIRE CORNER, LA BRIQUE, RAILWAY WOOD, but few shells have fallen any where.

MACHINE GUNS. 2. Enemy's machine guns have been normally active; our guns have fired a considerable number of rounds on the usual targets.

TRENCH MORTARS. 3. The enemy has been very active with his trench mortars lately, particularly against RAILWAY WOOD and all the craters, he did very little damage however; our trench mortars retaliated vigorously and effectively on every occasion.

SNIPERS. 4. There has been practically no hostile sniping. One of our snipers claims to have hit a hostile sniper, and we turned a Lewis Gun on to another at C.29.d.18.88 effectively checking his ardour, that particular sniping hole has not since been used.

PATROLS. 5. Our patrols again report that they have met with no hostile patrols, the enemy appears to be working on his front line and trenches.

CASUALTIES. 6. A List of Casualties during the week is subjoined :-

KILLED.		WOUNDED.		MISSING.	
Off.	O.R.	Off.	O.R.	Off.	O.R.
-	8	4	56	-	-

7th September, 1916.

Major, G.S.,
29th Division.

Casualties from 12 noon 30th Aug.
to 12 noon 4th Sept.   495 LK

	KILLED	WOUNDED	
	O.		O.R.
1st Lancs. Fus^{rs}			3
2^d S.W.Bⁿ			11
1st K.O.S.Bⁿ	1		4
1st Roy Irish Fus^{rs}			1
1st Border Reg^t			15
87th M.G. Coy			2
4th Worcester Reg^t	1		6
2^d Hants "			9
1st Essex "			1
1st Newfoundland "			4
88th T.M. B^{tty}			2
1/2^d Monmouth Reg^t	1		4
93^d Bde R.F.A.			1
V.20 T.M. B^{tty}			1
1/3^d Kent Field Coy. R.E.	1		
	4		64

SUMMARY

KILLED		WOUNDED		MISSING	
O.	O.R.	O.	O.R.	O.	O.R.
-	8	4	56	-	-

Index_____ _____

SUBJECT.

WAR DIARY

No.	Contents.	Date.

GENERAL STAFF
29th DIVISION

October
1916

CONFIDENTIAL

WAR DIARY

GENERAL STAFF

29TH. DIVISION.

FOR THE PERIOD

1ST. - 31ST. OCTOBER, 1916.

VOLUME XX.

-o-o-o-o-o-o-o-o-o-o-o-o-o-o-o-

SECRET

Headquarters,

    29th Division.
_____

        The Brigade was attached to the 12th Division and took up trenches about Gueudecourt on the night of 10th October, relieving the 37th Brigade.

        The Newfoundland occupied the firing line with the Essex Regt. in support.

        Heavy shelling all day on the 11th with fairly severe casualties to the Newfoundland Regt.

        On the night of the 11th, the Essex Regt. took over the left of the firing line preparatory to a joint attack on the following day with the Newfoundland Regt. The objective of the attack was HILT trench and the ground to the North of it. The 35th and 36th Brigades were attacking on our left and right respectively. Zero hour was fixed for 2-5 p.m. At this hour the two Battalions had left their trenches, and following up our barrage as closely as possible, had no difficulty in getting into HILT trench. There was very stiff fighting in the trench and heavy casualties in killed and prisoners were inflicted on the Germans. The attack on our left failed completely. That on the right was partially successful.

        The two Battalions on gaining HILT trench at once sent parties forward under a barrage to establish posts further on, but this, it was found impossible to do owing to the Brigades on the right and left not having got on. The men of the Essex Regt. went well beyond GREASE trench, but had to retire. A hot fight developed on their left flank, and they were bombed out of the portion of HILT trench they were holding, and eventually retired to their original line.

        The Newfoundland Regt. with difficulty established touch with the Brigade on their right. On finding that the Essex Regt. had retired, the officer in command proceeded to bomb

bomb/
along the trench and recovered most of what the Essex had given up and established a block. Meanwhile the enemy made a determined counter-attack on him from in front, which was repulsed with heavy loss to the enemy, largely by Lewis Gun fire and by the fire of Machine Guns which had most gallantly gone forward with the advance.

The Newfoundland Regt. held their own till nightfall, when they were reinforced by the Hampshire Regt., and the position won was properly consolidated, a communication trench being dug during the night to connect up with the original firing line.

The total number of prisoners taken was about 150. Three machine guns were captured and brought back, and others were buried and broken in the trench.

The Brigade remained in position in the line under constant and heavy shelling which caused numerous casualties.

A fresh attack was ordered for the night of 18/19th October. The Worcestershire and Hampshire Regts. were ordered to carry this out, the Hampshire on the right, and Worcestershire on the left. The objective was GREASE trench. The attack was to be made in conjunction with the Brigades on the right and left.

The day of the 18th was very wet, and the rain continued all night. Zero hour was fixed at 3-40 a.m. and there was no preliminary bombardment. At Zero hour the Battalions were lined up in front of their trenches ready to advance. Immediately our barrage began they advanced close behind it, and reached the hostile trench with very little loss and almost as a surprise to the enemy. On the left there was stout opposition, and many Germans were found in dug-outs in a Sunken Road. Severe casualties were inflicted on them by bombing, and a considerable number were captured. On the right the trench was found to be unfinished. A German working party with an officer were surprised and captured. The Hampshire Regt. found that the Brigade on on/their right had not got on, so extended their right for nearly 300 yards, beat off a strong hostile bombing attack, and thus helped the Battalion on their right to establish themselves in MILD trench. The Hampshire Regt. held, and consolidated this extra 300 yards of trench. They were in close touch with the Worcestershire Regt. who sent patrols up the Sunken Road to their front and bombed many dug-outs.

The objective of the left Company of the Worcestershire Regt. was that portion of HILT trench still in hostile possession running back towards our original line. The attack on this failed the first time owing largely to wire, but the officer Commanding the Company at once reorganised his Company and attacked again with complete success. Thus, the whole of our objectives were attained. As the Brigade on the left had failed, the whole left flank was in the air, but a strong block was established in BAYONET trench, and successfully held against bombing attacks.

The enemy attempted to gather for counter-attacks, but was beaten off every time by artillery fire, and by the covering fire of our machine guns from Gueudecourt. In this attack too, some machine guns advanced with the attacking troops and proved themselves invaluable in assisting to hold the position.

After nightfall parties of engineers came out and the trench was properly consolidated. At the same time a new trench connecting HILT trench and GREASE trench was dug to protect the left flank.

The total number of prisoners captured in this attack was over 80.

The Brigade continued to hold the line till the night of the 21st October, when they were relieved by the 87th Brigade.

Brigadier General,
9-11-16.   Commanding 88th Infy. Brigade.

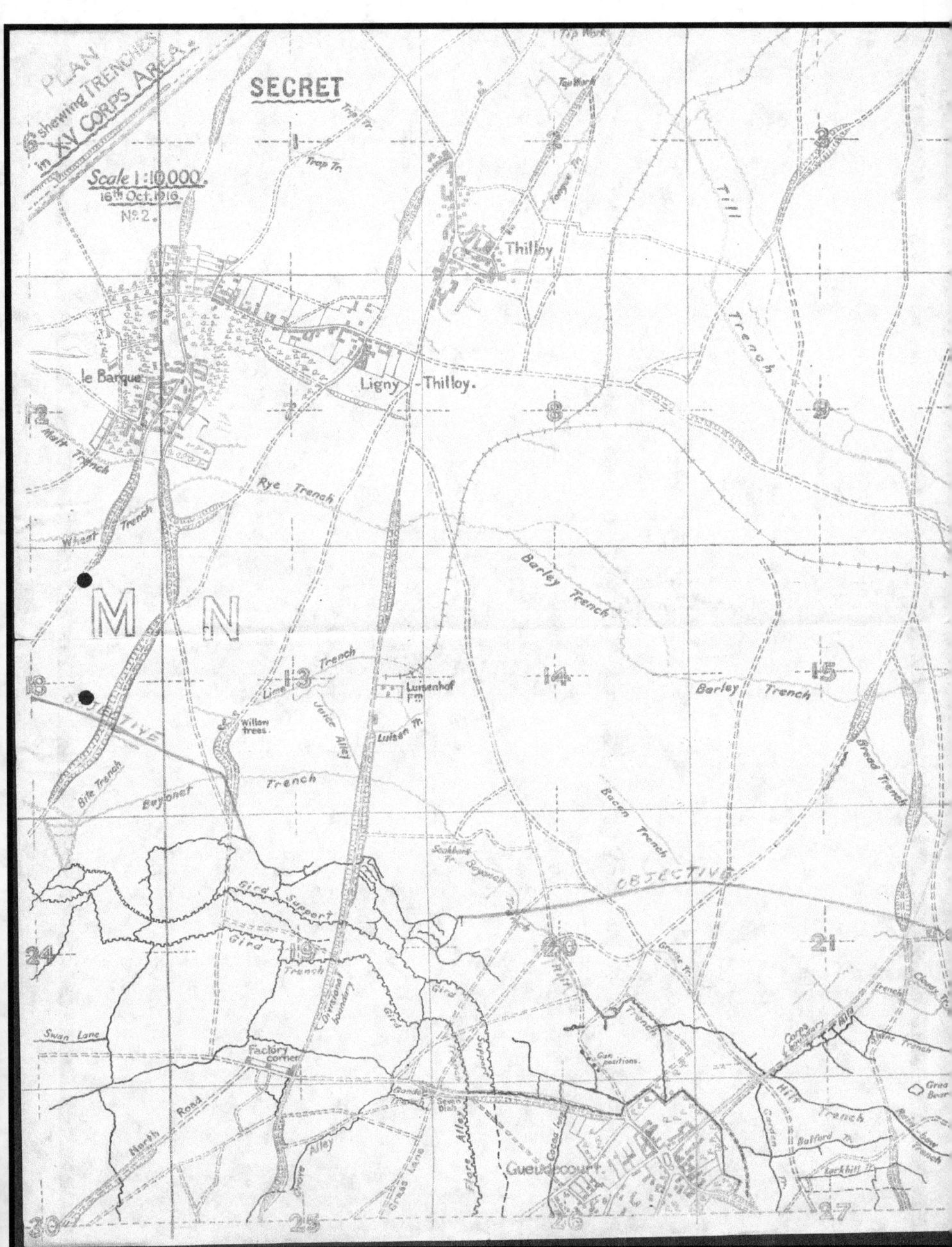

606

Another sap was cut from this post running North to a bank about 20 yards distant. This work was completed on the night of the 28th/29th, during which time another prisoner was captured belonging to the 101st Regiment.

Two German Machine Guns of the 1916 pattern, were captured in the SUNKEN Road about N.20.b.80.15, on the night of the 27th/28th, and brought in.

On the night of the 29th/30th the 29th Division were relieved by the 1st Australian Division.

(Sd) H de B de Lisle

Major-General,
9th November, 1916.   Commanding 29th Division.

Appendix 1(a).

514

SECRET.   Copy No. 4

29th DIVISION ORDER NO. 65.

Referencd. Trench Map 10.000,   1st October 1916.
Sheets 27 & 28 1/40,000.

1. The 29th Division (less Divisional Artillery) will be relieved by the 55th Division, commencing on October 3rd. The relief will be completed by the night 5th/6th October.
   The 29th Divisional Artillery will remain in the line in support of the 55th Division and will be attached to the 55th Division. It will probably be relieved and proceed on the 10th October.

2. 164th Inf. Bde. will relieve 86th Inf. Bde. in Div. Reserve.
   166th   "   "   "   87th   "   "   Left Sector.
   165th   "   "   "   88th   "   "   Right Sector.
   Details of reliefs will be arranged between G.Os.C. Infantry Brigades concerned.

3. Movements will be carried out in accordance with the attached Table. Instructions regarding Train Service during the relief will be issued by the A.A.&Q.M.G., 29th Division. The Division will entrain, commencing probably on the evening of the 6th October.

4. Machine Gun Companies and Trench Mortar Batteries of the 87th and 88th Brigades will be relieved on the night previous to that on which the Infantry relief in the trenches is carried out.

5. Details of relief of Field Companies R.E. and Field Ambulances will be arranged respectively between the C.R.Es. and A.Ds.M.S. of Divisions in accordance with the attached Table.

6. Advanced parties of 13 Officers and 17 N.C.Os. from each of the 166th and 165th Brigades will be attached to the 87th and 88th Brigades on the afternoon of October 2nd, and will remain attached till their units arrive in the trenches.
   These advanced parties will be conveyed direct from the detraining station to the Asylum, YPRES, where the Brigades concerned will make arrangements to meet and guide them. They will be rationed by the 29th Division from the 3rd October inclusive.

7. The 87th Brigade and if possible the 88th Brigade will leave a proportion of Officers and N.C.Os. attached to the units of 166th and 165th Brigades respectively for 24 hours after completion of relief.

8. Units will hand over 29th Division Defence Schemes, secret trench maps and secret instructions to the incoming units relieving them.

9. All trench stores must be handed over and receipts obtained.

(2).

10. (a). From 10.0 am. October 3rd the 3 Battalions of 164th Infantry Brigade in B, C, O Camps will come under the command of the G.O.C. 29th Division as Divisional Reserve. The Battalion in ELVERDINGHE and L Works will be under the control of VIIIth Corps.

(b). The G.Os.C. 87th and 88th Brigades will hand over command of their Sectors of the line to the G.Os.C. 166th and 165th Brigades on completion of relief on the nights 4th/5th and 5th/6th October respectively.

11. Completion of all reliefs will be reported to Divisional Headquarters.

12. All units will send Interpreters and advanced parties ahead to take over Camps and Billets. The 86th Brigade advance party will move by bus, starting from BRANDHOEK Cross Roads at 2.0 pm. on 2nd inst.

13. Railhead for 29th Division will remain at EDE AARTHOEK throughout. The 86th Brigade at WORMHOUDT will be supplied by Supply Column lorries; re-filling point on the WORMHOUDT - CASSEL Road.

14. The Divisional School of Instruction will close at midday on October 5th, and all students will rejoin their units. The Divisional Anti-Gas and Grenade Schools will close on October 3rd, when all under instruction will rejoin their units.

The Staffs of the above Schools will entrain with Divisional Headquarters.

15. The G.O.C. 29th Division will hand over command of the line to G.O.C. 55th Division at 7.0 am. on October 6th, at which hour Division Headquarters will close at A. 25. d. and will open at POPERINGHE.

Divisional Headquarters, including Divisional Band and Divisional Reserve Co. will be billeted in POPERINGHE, under arrangements to be made by Camp Commandant and Liaison Officer. Staff Officers will change over as the corresponding Staffs of the 55th Division arrive.

16. Acknowledge by wire.

Issued at 11 p.m.

A.G. Fuller.
Lieut. Colonel, G.S.
29th Division.

```
          Copies 1 - 5    General Staff.
                    6     86th Brigade
                    7     87th Brigade.
                    8     88th Brigade.
          9    C.R.A.              13-17.  A.A.&.Q.M.G.
         10    C.R.E.               18     VIIIth Corps.
         11    Off. i/c Sigs.       19     38th Division.
         12    1/2nd Monmouths      20     2nd Australian D
                          21     55th Division.
```

MOVEMENTS OF 29TH DIVISION (continued).

Positions on nights of

Unit.	2nd/3rd October	3rd/4th October	4th/5th October	5th/6th October
No.1 Coy. Div. Train	F.29.c.2.0	F.29.c.2.0	F.29.c.2.0	F.29.c.2.0
No.2 Coy. Div. Train	F.28.b.5.2	WORMHOUDT	WORMHOUDT	WORMHOUDT
No.3 Coy. Div. Train	F.29.c.3.5	F.29.c.3.5	F.29.c.3.5	F.29.c.3.5
No.4 Coy. Div. Train	F.28.b.8.0	F.28.b.8.0	F.28.b.8.0	F.28.b.8.0
Divisional Headquarters	A.25.d.3.5	A.25.d.3.5	POPERINGHE & A.25.d.3.5	POPERINGHE & A.25.d.3.5
Pioneer Battalion	1 Coy. H.7.c.5.8 3 Coys. YPRES	A. Camp	A. Camp	A. Camp
16th Sanitary Section	LAITERIE PROVEN ROAD F.30.a.central	LAITERIE PROVEN ROAD F.30.a.	LAITERIE PROVEN ROAD F.30.a.	LAITERIE PROVEN ROAD F.30.a.
Mobile Vet. Section				

516

MOVEMENTS OF 29TH DIVISION.
Positions on nights of

Unit.	2nd/3rd October	3rd/4th October	4th/5th October	5th/6th October
86th Reserve Infantry Brigade.				
Headquarters	C. Camp	WORMHOUDT	WORMHOUDT	WORMHOUDT
Battalion	B. Camp			
Battalion	C. Camp	WORMHOUDT	WORMHOUDT	WORMHOUDT
Battalion	O. Camp			
Battalion	ELVERDINGHE Defences	and	and	and
	BRANDHOEK vicinity	HERZEELE	HERZEELE	HERZEELE
M.G. Coy.	Bde. H.Q.			
T.M. Bty.				
87th Infantry Brigade.			*PROVEN*	*PROVEN.*
Headquarters	YPRES	YPRES	POPERINGHE	POPERINGHE
Battalion	Trenches	Trenches	M. Camp	M. Camp
Battalion	Trenches	Trenches	J. Camp	J. Camp
Battalion	YPRES	K. Camp	K. Camp	K. Camp
Battalion	Canal Bank	L. Camp	L. Camp	L. Camp
M.G. Coy. & T.M. Bty.	Trenches	J. Camp	J. Camp	J. Camp
88th Infantry Brigade.				
Headquarters	YPRES	YPRES	YPRES	YPRES
Battalion	Trenches	Trenches	Trenches	G. Camp
Battalion	Trenches	Trenches	Trenches	BRANDHOEK
Battalion	YPRES	YPRES	POPERINGHE	POPERINGHE
Battalion	YPRES	YPRES	POPERINGHE	POPERINGHE
M.G. Coy. & T.M. Bty.	Trenches	Trenches	POPERINGHE	POPERINGHE
1st West Riding Field Coy.	H.1.d.8.8	HOUTKERQUE	HOUTKERQUE	HOUTKERQUE
1/3rd Kent Field Coy.	H.7.a.5.9	H.7.a.5.9	HOUTKERQUE	HOUTKERQUE
1/2nd London Field Coy.	A.28.d.8.2	A.28.d.8.2	A.28.d.8.2	HOUTKERQUE
89th Field Ambulance	POPERINGHE	PROVEN	PROVEN	PROVEN
87th Field Ambulance	L.21.a.central	L.21.a.central	WATOU	WATOU
88th Field Ambulance	G.5.d.9.2	G.5.d.9.2	G.5.d.9.2	WATOU
		WATOU	WATOU	

MOVEMENTS OF 55TH DIVISION.

Unit.	2nd/3rd October	3rd/4th October	4th/5th October	5th/6th October
164th Infantry Brigade.				
Headquarters 164th Brigade	POPERINGHE	C. Camp	C. Camp	C. Camp
1 Battalion	POPERINGHE	B. Camp	B. Camp	B. Camp
1 Battalion	BRANDHOEK	C. Camp	C. Camp	C. Camp
1 Battalion	G. Camp	O. Camp	O. Camp	O. Camp
1 Battalion	POPERINGHE	ELVERDINGHE & L Works	ELVERDINGHE & L Works	ELVERDINGHE & L Works
L.G. Coy.	POPERINGHE	BRANDHOEK vicinity	BRANDHOEK vicinity	BRANDHOEK vicinity
T.M. Bty.	POPERINGHE	G. Camp	C. Camp	C. Camp
166th Infantry Brigade.				
Headquarters 166th Brigade	POPERINGHE	POPERINGHE	YPRES (left sector)	YPRES (left sector)
1 Battalion	K. Camp	YPRES	Trenches	Trenches
1 Battalion	L. Camp	YPRES(Canal Bank)	Trenches	Trenches
1 Battalion	M. Camp	H. Camp	YPRES	YPRES
1 Battalion	J. Camp	J. Camp	YPRES(Canal Bank)	YPRES(Canal Bank)
L.G. Coy.	J. Camp	Trenches	Trenches	Trenches
T.M. Bty.	J. Camp	Trenches	Trenches	Trenches
165th Infantry Brigade.				
Headquarters 165th Brigade	ESQUELBECQ	POPERINGHE	POPERINGHE	YPRES (right sector)
1 Battalion	WORMHOUDT	POPERINGHE	YPRES (right sector)	Trenches
1 Battalion	and	POPERINGHE	YPRES (right sector)	Trenches
1 Battalion		BRANDHOEK	BRANDHOEK	YPRES (right sector)
1 Battalion	HERZEELE	G. Camp	G. Camp	YPRES (right sector)
L.G. Coy.	HOUTKERQUE	POPERINGHE	Trenches	Trenches
T.M. Bty.	HOUTKERQUE	POPERINGHE	Trenches	Trenches
Field Coy.	HOUTKERQUE	H.1.d.8.8	H.1.d.8.8	H.1.d.8.8
Field Coy.	HOUTKERQUE	HOUTKERQUE	H.7.a.5.9	H.7.a.5.9
Field Coy.	WORMHOUDT	A.28.d.8.2	A.28.d.8.2	A.28.d.8.2

MOVEMENTS OF 55TH DIVISION (continued).

Unit.	2nd/3rd October	3rd/4th October	4th/5th October	5th/6th October
Field Ambulance	VATOU	POPERINGHE	POPERINGHE	POPERINGHE
Field Ambulance	PROVEN	PROVEN	HILLHOEK	HILLHOEK
Field Ambulance	WORMHOUDT	G.5.d.9.2	G.5.d.9.2	G.5.d.9.2 RED FARM
H.Q. Coy. Div. Train	ESQUELBECQ	PROVEN	PROVEN	PROVEN
Coy. Train	PROVEN	F.28.b.5.2	F.28.b.5.2	F.28.b.5.2
Coy. Train	PROVEN	PROVEN	PROVEN	PROVEN
Coy. Train	WORMHOUDT	PROVEN	PROVEN	PROVEN
Divisional Headquarters	ESQUELBECQ	ESQUELBECQ	(A.25.d.3.5 ESQUELBECQ	(A.25.d.3.5 ESQUELBECQ
Pioneer Battalion	POPERINGHE	3 Coys. YPRES 1 Coy. BRANDHOEK	3 Coys. YPRES 1 Coy. BRANDHOEK	3 Coys. YPRES 1 Coy. BRANDHOEK
Sanitary Section	LAITERIE PROVEN ROAD	LAITERIE PROVEN ROAD	LAITERIE PROVEN ROAD	LAITERIE PROVEN ROAD
Mobile Vet. Section	F.30.a.central	F.30.a.central	F.30.a.central	F.30.a.central

SECRET.

86th Brigade.	O.C. 1/2nd Monmouth Regiment.
87th Brigade.	A.A. & Q.M.G.
88th Brigade.	VIIIth Corps.
C.R.A.	38th Division.
C.R.E.	2nd Australian Division.
Officer i/c Signals.	55th Division.

Amendment to 29th Division Order No. 65 dated 1st October, 1916.

1. Reference table of movements the following movements will now take place on the 4th October, instead of on the 3rd October.

   (a) The move of the 86th Brigade from B. C. and O. Camps and ELVERDINGHE Defences, to the WORMHOUDT and HERZEELE Area.

   (b) The move of the 164th Brigade from POPERINGHE to B. C. O. Camps and ELVERDINGHE.

   (c) The move of the 165th Brigade from WORMHOUDT and HERZEELE Area, to POPERINGHE, BRANDHOEK and G. Camp.

2. The 3 battalions of the 164th Infantry Brigade will come under the orders of the G.O.C. 29th Division at 10 a.m. on October 4th, and not as stated in para. 10 (a).

3. All other movements remain unchanged.

4. Acknowledge.

C.J. Fuller.
Lieut-Colonel, G.S.,
29th Division.

3rd October, 1916.

No. C.G.S.71.

SECRET.

86th Brigade.
87th Brigade.
88th Brigade.
C.R.A.
C.R.E.
Officer i/c Signals.
O.C., 1/2nd Monmouth Regiment.
A.A. & Q.M.G.
VIIIth Corps.
38th Division.
2nd Australian Division.
55th Division.

====================

Amendment to 29th Division Order No.65,

dated 1st October, 1916.

================================

In "Movements of 29th Division" Table, column 5, opposite 88th Infantry Brigade Headquarters, for "YPRES" read "POPERINGHE".

(Signed) C.G.FULLER, Lieut-Colonel, G.S

3rd October, 1916.   29th Division.

SECRET.

86th Brigade.
87th Brigade.
88th Brigade.
C.R.A.
C.R.E.
Officer i/c Signals.
O.C., 1/2nd Monmouth Regiment.
A.A. & Q.M.G.
VIIIth Corps.
38th Division.
2nd Australian Division.
55th Division.

Amendment to 29th Division Order No.65 dated 1st Oct. 1916.

      In table of "Movements of 29th Division" columns 4 and 5, opposite 87th Infantry Brigade Headquarters, for "POPERINGHE" read "PROVEN".

                (Signed) C.G.FULLER, Lieut-Colonel, G.S.,
4th October, 1916.   29th Division.

"C" Form (Duplicate).
MESSAGES AND SIGNALS.

Handed in at... M5 ... Office 11.0 a.m. Received 11.08 m.

TO Z5

Sender's Number	Day of Month	In reply to Number	A A A
a 571	2		

Please detail six lorries to
report at 12 noon tomorrow
as follows aaa Two Z5
Hq "C" Camp aaa One
"B" Camp aaa One batt'n
by "C" Camp aaa one batt'n
hq "B" Camp aaa One
batt'n by ELVERDINGHE CHATEAU aaa
These lorries will be required
to proceed to WORMHOUDT aaa
return journey not required aaa
addressed amb park repeated Z5

FROM PLACE & TIME M5

"O" Form (Duplicate).
MESSAGES AND SIGNALS.

Service Instructions. M6

Handed in at .... Office 0905 m. Received 0901 m.

TO Z5

Sender's Number	Day of Month	In reply to Number	A A A
Q 578	3		

Second Army wires begins aaa Handcarts for stokes mortars will be left behind ~~xxx~~ ends please hand carts over to incoming units

FROM PLACE & TIME M5

Form (Duplicate).
MESSAGES AND SIGNALS.

Army Form C. 2123.

| Service Instructions. | M5 | | Charges to Pay. | Office Stamp. |

Handed in at .... Office 0940 m. Received 0945 m.

TO: Z5

Sender's Number: GR170 Day of Month: 5/10 In reply to Number: AAA

Reference my CGS71 aaa STAND aaa acknowledge

FROM: M5
PLACE & TIME: 9.40 am

SECRET.

HEADQUARTERS,
29th DIVISION,
GENERAL STAFF.

No. C.G.S. 71
Date 3/10/16.

H.Q.
86th Brigade.
~~29th Divisional Train.~~
~~29th Divisional Supply Column.~~

   Reference the time table attached to 29th Division Order No.65, it is extremely probable that the move of the 86th Brigade from B. C. & O. Camps and the ELVERDINGHE Defences to the WORMHOUDT and HERZEELE Area on relief by the 164th Infantry Brigade, will be postponed for 24 hours, i.e. the move will take place on October 4th instead of October 3rd.

   Definite instructions cannot yet be issued as the railway service affected, is in the hands of the French Authorities, who have not yet replied to the request that all the arrangements may be postponed 24 hours.

   As soon as a reply is received, all concerned will be notified by wire, the following code will be used :-
"MOVE" signifies that previous arrangements, hold good.
"STAND" signifies stand fast for 24 hours.

   In the event of the 86th Brigade's move being postponed 24 hours as above, they will be considered as Corps Reserve until relief.

   Acknowledge.

[signature]

Lieut-Colonel, G.S.,
29th Division.

3rd October, 1916.

A/858

O.C., 2nd Royal Fusiliers.
     1st Lancashire Fusiliers.
     16th Middlesex Regiment.
     1st Royal Dublin Fusiliers.

With reference to move, the following transport will be available for Units in addition to Reg: Transport Limber Wagons:-

2nd Royal Fusiliers.   1 Lorry   for Blankets.
                         2 G.S.Wagons   Baggage.
                         1 " Wagon   Battle stores, etc.

1st Lancashire Fusiliers.
                         1 Lorry   for Blankets.
                         2 G.S. Wagons Baggage
                         1 Lorry   Battle Stores, etc.

16th Middlesex Regiment.
                         1 Lorry for Blankets.
                         2 G.S.Wagons   Baggage.
                         1 Lorry   Battle stores, etc. (part of this Lorry for use of 86th T.M.Battery.)

1st Royal Dublin Fusiliers.
                         1 Lorry   for Blankets.
                         2 G.S. Wagons Baggage.
                         1 Lorry   Battle stores, etc.

86th Machine Gun Company.
                         1 G.S. Supply Wagon- (part for use for baggage also).
                         1 G.S.Wagon in place of broken G.S.Limber, and for extra stores.

86th Trench Mortar Battery.
                 Part of 16th Middlesex Regt. lorry, as stated above.

All the above will report to Units at 10-30 a.m. to-morrow, 3rd instant. The G.S.Wagons will move with the 1st Line Transport. Lorries will move independently; a small unloading party being sent with them from each unit.

                                                   Captain,
October 2nd, 1916.   Staff Captain, 86th Infantry Brigade.

Appendix 1 (6).
529

Copy No... 5   S E C R E T.

29TH DIVISION ORDER NO. 66.

9th October, 1916.

1. The 29th Division (less Artillery and 88th Infantry Brigade group) will move from the XIVth Corps to the XVth Corps Area on October 10th as follows :-

(Mobile Vet. Section)
(a) Divisional Headquarters, Divisional Signal Coy., Divisional Reserve Coy., and Hd.Qrs. Divisional Train, from CORBIE to RIBEMONT via BONNAY, under arrangements to be made by the Camp Commandant.

(b) The 86th Brigade Group (consisting of 86th Brigade, 1st West Riding Field Coy., 89th Field Ambulance and No.2 Coy. Divisional Train) will march from DAOURS to DERNACOURT at 9 a.m. Route:- LA NEUVILLE - BONNAY - HEILLY - BUIRE.

(c) The 87th Brigade Group (consisting of 87th Brigade, 3rd Kent Field Coy., 87th Field Ambulance and No.3 Coy. Divisional Train) will march from ALLONVILLE to BUIRE at 1 p.m. Route via QUERRIEUH - LA HOUSSOYE - Cross Roads D.16.b.9.2. The head of the column must not pass bridge head at QUERRIEU before 1.30 p.m.

2. Intervals of 200 yards will be maintained between Companies and between Company and Battalion Transport. Intervals of 400 yards will be maintained between Battalions. All other details will be arranged by Brigades concerned.

3. Two Battalions of the 88th Brigade, the 88th Machine Gun Coy. and Trench Mortar Battery will proceed by bus to Camp S.26.c, to-night under orders, which have already been issued. The remainder of the 88th Brigade, the 2nd London Field Coy., and No.4 Coy. Divisional Train, will march at 8 a.m. to-morrow 10th instant to Camp S.26.c.; Route - BONNAY - HEILLY - BERNANCOURT - MEAULTE - FRICOURT - POMMIERS. If weather permits, the horse track North of HEILLY - BERNANCOURT - MEAULTE - FRICOURT Road will be used in order to avoid congestion of traffic. 100 yards interval between Companies and 500 yards between Battalions and regimental transport will be kept.

On arrival, the above troops will come under the command of the G.O.C. 12th Division.

The 88th Field Ambulance will remain at CORBIE.

4. Divisional Headquarters will close at CORBIE and reopen at RIBEMONT at 12 noon on the 10th instant.

5. Acknowledge.

C.G. Fuller.
Lieut-Colonel, G.S.,
29th Division.

Issued at ... 10.30 p.m.

Copies 1 - 5   General Staff.   19   12th Division.
       6   86th Brigade.   20   30th Division.
       7   87th Brigade.   21   Camp Commandant.
       8   88th Brigade.
       9   C.R.A.
     10   C.R.E.
     11   Officer i/c Signals.
     12   1/2nd Monmouth Regt.
   13-17   A.A. & Q.M.G.
     18   XVth Corps.

"A" Form. Army Form C. 2

MESSAGES AND SIGNALS.

No. of Message

Prefix	Code	in	Words	Charge	This message is on a/c of:	Recd. at m.
Office of Origin and Service Instructions			Sent		Service.	Date
SECRET			At m.			From
			To			
			By		(Signature of "Franking Officer.")	By

TO 86. Bde & Q.

| Sender's Number. | Day of Month | In reply to Number | |
| G. 1207 | 9th | | A A A |

Warning Order. The 86. Bde Group will be prepared to march to-morrow morning to DERNANCOURT AAA Detailed Orders will be issued later AAA 86. Bde Staff will arrange to warn all units of the Bde Group and to detail order of march AAA Co. of Divl train with Group should march first. Addressed 86. Bde and Q.

From 29. Divn HdQrs
Place
Time 4.50 p.m.

C. J. Fuller

(Z)

March Table of Infantry Moves to accompany 29th Division Order No. 67.

Unit.	From.	To.	Replacing.	Who proceed to	Route.	Remarks.
29TH DIVISION.						
86th Inf. Bde. Group including 1/3rd Kent Field Coy. R.E. No. 2 Coy. Div. Train. 89th Field Ambulance.	DERNANCOURT	Trench Shelters S.20.a.0.5	123rd Inf. Bde. 41st Div.	DERNANCOURT	DERNANCOURT-MEAULTE-FRICOURT Road. If weather permits Horse Track just North of Road will be used.	Starting point - Forked Roads L.21.a.8.9 Time - 8 a.m.
87th Inf. Bde. Group including 1/1st W. Riding Field Coy. R.E. No. 3 Coy. Div. Train. 87th Field Ambulance.	BUIRE	FRICOURT CAMP (F.8.c.)	124th Inf. Bde. 41st Div.	BUIRE	-do-	Starting point - Road junction D.30.a.7.4 Time - 1 p.m.
41ST DIVISION.						
123rd Inf. Bde.	Trench Shelters S.20.a.0.5	DERNANCOURT	86th Inf. Bde.	Trench Shelters S.20.a.0.5	-do-	March at 8 a.m.
124th Inf. Bde.	FRICOURT CAMP (F.8.c.)	BUIRE	87th Inf. Bde.	FRICOURT CAMP (F.8.c.)	-do-	March at 1 p.m.

Appendix 1(c).
524

SECRET.   Copy No. 5

29TH DIVISION ORDER NO. 67.

                                12th. October, 1916.

1. Moves will take place to-morrow, 13th October, in accordance with the attached March Table.

2. Intervals of 200 yards will be kept between each Company and Regimental transport, and 400 yards between Battalions.

3. Arrangements for handing over billets and camps will be made between the Brigades concerned.

4. Please acknowledge receipt.

                                        C.G. Fuller.
                                    Lieut-Colonel, G.S.,
                                        29th Division.

Issued at 8 p.m.

Copies 1 - 5 General Staff.   12.   1/2nd Monmouth Regt.
        6   86th Brigade.   13-17 A.A. & Q.M.G.
        7   87th Brigade.   18   12th Division.
        8   88th Brigade.   19   30th Division.
        9   C.R.A.   20   41st Division.
        10 C.R.E.   21   XV Corps.
        11 Officer i/c Signals.

Appendix 1 (d).
596

SECRET.   Copy No....5......

29TH DIVISION ORDER NO. 68.

                                                    17th October, 1916.
Reference Maps :-
(a) Sheet 57 C S.W. 1/20,000.
(b) Trench Map attached.

1. The III, XIV and XV Corps will attack on 18th October, in conjunction with the 6th French Army at an early hour before daylight. The exact Zero hour will be notified later.

2. The attack of the XV Corps will be carried out by the 12th Division (with the 88th Infantry Brigade attached) on the RIGHT - final objective the green line in N.20 and 21; and by the 30th Division on the left - final objective the green line in N.19 and 13 and M.18.(See attached map, which also marks boundaries between Corps and Divisions.)

3. The 6th Division XIV Corps will attack on the right of the 12th Division, and the 9th Division III Corps on the left of the 30th Division.

4. The 29th Division (less 88th Infantry Brigade) will be in reserve, and the 86th and 87th Infantry Brigades will hold themselves in readiness to move at 2 hours notice after Zero.

5. Watches will be synchronised at 6 p.m. 17th October by telephone from Div. Headquarters.

6. Acknowledge by wire.

                                        Lieut-Colonel, G.S.,
                                             29th Division.

        Issued at 12 noon.

        Copies 1 - 5   General Staff.
               6   86th Brigade.
               7   87th Brigade.
               8   War Diary.
               9   C.R.A.
              10   C.R.E.
              11   Officer i/c Signals.
              12   O.C. 1/2nd Monmouth Regiment.
              13 - 17 A.A. & Q.M.G.
              18   12th Division.
              19   30th Division.
              20   41st Division.
              21   XV Corps.

Appendix 1(e).
527

SECRET.   Copy No. 5.

29TH DIVISION ORDER NO. 69.

Refce. 1/20,000 Sheet 57.C.S.W.   18th October, 1916.

1. The 29th Division will relieve the 12th Division on the ~~night of~~ 19th/~~20th~~ October in the sector from N.21.d.0.7 to N.19.b.4.7.

2. The boundaries of the Divisional Area are as follows :-
On the East.   N.21.d.0.7 - N.27.a.8.3 - N.32.c.5.5 - T.1.d.9.8 - T.1.d.3.3 - S.18.b.6.0 - S.22.d.8.2.

On the West.   LIGNY - THILLOY - FACTORY CORNER - FLERS Road (inclusive to 29th Division) - M.36.b.5.0 - M.36.d.3.3 - S.11.b.5.5 - S.11.c.8.5 - S.11.c.2.0 - S.16.d.0.6 - S.22.a.5.6.

3. The relief will be carried out in accordance with the attached march table.
   Troops moving by road will maintain the following distances :-
       200 yards between Companies, and between Companies and Battalion Transport.
       400 yards between Battalions.
   North of LONGUEVAL, troops will move in small detachments.

4.(a) The 86th Brigade (with Headquarters at S.12.b.8.8) will take over from the 35th Brigade the Left Sector extending from N.20.c.8.1 to N.19.b.4.7 on the 19th instant.
  (b) The 87th Brigade will replace the 36th Brigade in BERNAFAY Camp (S.22.d.9.4) on the 19th instant, and will relieve the 88th Brigade in the Right Sector, extending from N.21.d.0.7 to N.20.c.8.1 on the 20th instant, moving their Headquarters to S.12.b.8.3.
  (c) The 88th Brigade on relief will be in Divisional Reserve with Headquarters at S.22.d.9.4.
  (d) Details of reliefs will be arranged between Brigadiers concerned.
  (e) The Boundary between the Right and Left Sectors will be as follows :- N.20.c.8.1 - T.1.b.3.1 - S.12.b.7.8.

5. Artillery support will be provided by the Divisional Artillery Group, under the command of Brigadier-General S. LUSHINGTON, C.B., C.M.G., R.A., with Headquarters at POMMIERS Camp.

6. The reliefs of the Field Companies R.E. and Field Ambulances will be arranged direct between the Cs.R.E. and A.Ds.M.S. of the Divisions respectively.

7. The 1/2nd Monmouth Regiment (Pioneers) will remain at their present Camp at S.27.c.7.6 and come under the command of the G.O.C. 29th Division.

8. The line on the right is held by the 71st Brigade (6th Division) with Headquarters at T.8.a.
   The line on the left is held by the 21st Brigade (30th Division) with Headquarters at S.6.a.6.8.

- 2 -

9. All grenades, S.A.A. and Trench Stores will be taken over in the line and receipts given.

10. Completion of reliefs will be notified to these Headquarters.

11. The G.O.C. 29th Division will take over command of the line at 5 p.m. on the 19th instant, at which hour Advanced Divisional Headquarters will open at POMMIERS Redoubt (with Rear Divisional Headquarters at E.11.central) and close at RIBEMONT.

12. Acknowledge by wire.

C.F. Fuller.
Lieut-Colonel, G.S.,
29th Division.

Issued at 11.30 p.m.

```
Copies 1 - 5   General Staff.
       6       86th Brigade.
       7       87th Brigade.
       8       88th Brigade.
       9       C.R.A.
      10       C.R.E.
      11       Officer i/c Signals.
      12       O.C. 1/2nd Monmouth Regt.
      13 - 17  A.A. & Q.M.G.
      18       XV Corps.
      19       12th Division.
      20       30th Division.
      21       6th Division.
```

529

MARCH TABLE.

Unit.	From.	To.	Time.
86th Bde. H.Q.	MARETZ WOOD CAMP S.20.a.	S.12.b.8.8.	Any convenient time.
1 Bn. 86th Bde. x	-"-	Trenches(support) S. of FLERS.	Leading platoon to be at Grand Place, LONGUEVAL at 11 a.m.
1 Bn. 86th Bde. x	-"-	Trenches(support) SMOKE TRENCH.	-"- 12 Noon.
86th M.G. Company.) x 86th T.M. Battery.) -"-		Trenches.	To be at -"- 1 p.m.
1 Bn. 86th Bde.	-"-	Trenches (N.E. of DELVILLE WOOD).	Leading platoon -"- 2 p.m.
1 Bn. 86th Bde. x	-"-	Front line trenches .20.c.8.1 - N.19.b.4.7.	-"- 4.30 p.m.
87th Bde. H.Q.	FRICOURT CAMP F.8.c.	QUARRY S.22.d.9.4.	Any convenient time.
1 Bn. 87th Bde.	-"-	BERNAFAY WOOD CAMP S.23.c.1.4.	Leading Coy. to leave Camp at 10 a.m.
1 Bn. 87th Bde.	-"-	-"-	-"- 10.30 a.m.
1 Bn. 87th Bde.	-"-	-"-	-"- 11 a.m.
1 Bn. 87th Bde.	-"-	-"-	-"- 11.30 a.m.
87th M.G. Coy.) 87th T.M. Battery)	-"-	-"-	To leave Camp at 12 Noon.

Note I. Guides from 12th Division will meet units marked x at the Grand Place, LONGUEVAL, at the times shown above.

Note II. The 86th Brigade will march by the most convenient route. The transport of the 87th Brigade will march via F.4.c.5.2 - F.4.c.5.4 - MARETZ - POMMIERS - MONTAUBAN - S.28.d.2.1 - S.23.c.1.4. The Infantry will march by cross country route as much as possible.

Appendix I (f).

520
Copy No. 3

S E C R E T.

29TH DIVISION ORDER NO. 70.

Refce. Sheet 57 C S.W. 1/20,000)
      Map marked "G" attached.)   23rd October, 1916.

1.   The XV and III Corps in conjunction with the Reserve Army will attack on the 26th October, at an hour zero to be notified later. The XV Corps is attacking on the whole of its front. The 8th Division (XIV Corps) on our right are attacking to-day the objectives shewn in Brown on Map "G". They will make no attack on the 26th October. The 5th Australian Division (XV Corps) will attack on our left. Boundaries are shewn on Map "G". The 1st Australian Division (XV Corps) will be in reserve.

        The troops believed to be opposite us are the 19th Reserve Division (92nd Regiment) and the 6th (Brandenberg) Division (396th and 24th Regiments).

2.   The main object of the operation is to advance our present line to a favourable position from which to attack BARLEY, RYE and WHEAT trenches.

        The immediate objectives of the 29th Division are :-
(a) to establish the right of the Division firmly on the spur, which runs from N.21.b. to N.15.d., and thus secure good observation of the valley through which TILL trench runs;
(b) to establish the centre of the Division about N.15.c.4.0 with the same object in view;
(c) to join up on the left with the right of the 5th Australian Division, so as to afford protection to their right flank.

3.   The attack of the 29th Division will be carried out in two stages. The first objective is marked BLUE, and the second objective GREEN on the attached Map "G".

        The 87th Brigade will carry out the attack on the right and the 86th Brigade on the left. The boundary between Brigades is shewn on the attached Map "G". The 88th Brigade will be in Divisional Reserve. To enable the 86th Brigade to carry out a converging attack on the hostile trenches at N.20.d.4.5, the 87th Brigade will place the following trenches at the disposal of the 86th Brigade; Saphead at Western end of GREASE TRENCH, Western communication trench from GREASE to HILT Trench, and HILT Trench from N.20.d.7.4 to N.20.d.6.6.

4.   The first objective will be consolidated forthwith by special parties of Infantry told off for the purpose, by a series of strong points, approximate positions of which are shewn on the attached Map "G". Two sections of a Field Coy. R.E. are allotted to each Brigade to assist in this operation.

        The second objective will be consolidated as far as possible during daylight by the infantry, and after dark special working parties will be pushed forward to complete the work. The O.C. 1/2nd Monmouths will detail two Companies to each of the 86th and 87th Brigades for the purpose of digging communication trenches by night for the use of each Brigade, as shewn on Map "G" attached.

5.   The attack will be preceded by a Heavy Artillery bombardment which has already commenced. There will be no intense fire before Zero.

/ The

The assault will be carried out under cover of a creeping artillery barrage, which will lift as follows :-

(a) At Zero, the artillery barrage will commence on the first objective and on a line 150 yards short of the enemy's front trench, and the infantry will immediately leave their trenches and get as close to it as possible.

(b) At 0.3 the barrage will creep forward at the rate of 50 yards per minute until at 0.9 it has reached a line 150 yards beyond the first objective, where it will halt till 0.13.

At 0.6 the barrage passes over the first objective and the infantry will enter the trench.

(c) At 0.10 the infantry, less clearing up parties previously detailed, will leave the first objective, and get close under the barrage, which will commence to creep at 0.13, at the rate of 50 yards per minute until it reaches a line 150 yards beyond the second objective, where it will halt, whilst the second objective is being consolidated.

The details of the Artillery Barrage are given in Appendix "A", a copy of which will be in the possession of every Company Commander of the assaulting Battalions.

During the attack the Divisional Artillery Howitzers and Heavy Artillery will engage the further objectives, and lift off them, when the assault is launched.

6. The attack will be carried out by each Brigade, with two Battalions in the front line, one in support and one in Reserve.

Special "mopping-up" parties will be detailed to clear up the trenches captured by the assaulting troops.

The Brigades will cover their assault as far as possible by (a) pushing forward Lewis Guns into shell-holes or wherever covering fire can be obtained;

(b) Mobile Machine Guns pushed forward to engage any hostile Machine Guns encountered.

7. The 88th Machine Gun Coy. will arrange to bring indirect fire to bear on the enemy's rear trenches and approaches thereto, under instructions which have been issued separately.

8. The 86th Brigade will detail a special left flank Company with 2 Vickers Machine Guns to cover the right of the 5th Australian Division, and to hold the gun-pits at N.14.c.4.4. and N.14.c.4.6., and the bank at N.14.c.6.6. The 86th Brigade will also arrange to place machine guns in the N.W. end of BACON TRENCH to keep down the hostile fire from BARLEY TRENCH in the direction of LUISENHOF FARM.

9. The two leading Brigades will arrange to garrison their own trench system during the attack, and to leave a proportion of Machine Guns with the garrison.

10. The two leading Brigades will be assembled in the trenches in their Brigade Areas North and clear of SWITCH TRENCH by 12 midnight on the 25th/28th October. The Reserve Brigade will be responsible for the defence of SWITCH TRENCH and will occupy it after midnight with one Battalion, a second Battalion being located just South of the DELVILLE WOOD. The Remainder of the Reserve Brigade and the 1/2nd Monmouths (Pioneers) will remain in Camp at BERNAFAY WOOD ready to move at $\frac{1}{2}$ hours notice.

/ 11.

- 4 -

Existing arrangements for evacuation will be augmented by reinforcements from Field Ambulances under orders of the A.D.M.S. 29th Division.
In case of necessity the A.D.M.S. will call on the Reserve Brigade for up to 200 men to reinforce stretcher bearers.

19. Divisional Battle Stops will be established by the A.P.M. at road junction S.17.b.3.4 and at S.18.a.2.0.
Brigades will establish Battle Stops at Battalion Headquarters and on the line of BULLS ROAD.

20. As deep dug-outs are likely to be encountered, troops should carry two grenades per man.

21. Situation reports will be rendered by the 41st Divisional Artillery and the two leading Brigades to Divisional Headquarters at 0.30, and at every subsequent half hour after Zero, independently of special reports, which will be forwarded immediately. When runners and pigeons are the only methods of communication, the reports will be forwarded as often as circumstances permit.

22. Watches will be synchronised at 8 a.m. and 6 p.m. by telephone from Divisional Headquarters, on the 25th October.

23. 29th Divisional Headquarters will remain in their present position at the POMMIERS REDOUBT. The Brigade Headquarters of the 86th, 87th and 88th Infantry Brigades will remain in their present positions.

24. Acknowledge by wire.

C.F. Fuller
Lieut-Colonel, G.S.,
29th Division.

Issued at 10.30 p.m.

```
Copies  1 - 5  General Staff.
            6  86th Brigade.
            7  87th Brigade.
            8  88th Brigade.
            9  C.R.A.
           10  C.R.E.
           11  Officer i/c Signals.
           12  O.C. 1/2nd Monmouth Regt.
       13 - 17 A.A. & Q.M.G.
           18  XV Corps.
           19  5th Australian Division.
           20  1st Australian Division.
           21  8th Division.
```

- 3 -

11. Major B. C. S. CLARK, Worcestershire Regiment, and Captain C. W. MAFFETT, Royal Dublin Fusiliers, will act as Divisional Liaison Officers with the 5th Australian and 8th Divisions respectively during the operations.

Major D. OVEY (G.S.O.2) will be with the Headquarters of the 87th Brigade.

The 88th Brigade will detail a liaison officer to each of the Headquarters of the 86th and 87th Brigades. The 86th Brigade will have a liaison officer with the 87th Brigade, and vice versa.

An artillery officer will be attached to each Brigade Headquarters and each Battalion Headquarters during the operations. All liaison officers will report at their respective Headquarters at least one hour before Zero.

12. The C.R.E. will detail two sections of a Field Company to each of the 86th and 87th Brigades to assist in the consolidation of strong points. The remainder of the R.E. will be kept in Divisional Reserve under C.R.E. in their Camps. An officer from each Field Company R.E. will be at the Reserve Brigade Headquarters to receive instructions.

13. O.C. Divisional Signals will arrange to establish a system of runner posts between Divisional and Brigade Headquarters.

A Wireless Station will be established at S.6.d.4.1 (DELVILLE VALLEY) to supplement the telephone.

Eight additional pigeons per Brigade will be provided to supplement the existing allotment.

14. Two contact aeroplanes will be in the air from 0.3 for two hours, after which one contact aeroplane will be in the air until dark. Troops will indicate their positions to them by means of RED flares.

Flares will be lit,
    (a) on reaching the BLUE line;
    (b) on reaching the GREEN line;
    (c) at certain stated times to be ordered later, with the notification of the Zero hour.

Each man should carry one red flare, and groups of six flares should be lit at a time.

15. A Divisional Observation Station will be established in SWITCH TRENCH, and will be in telephonic communication with Divisional Headquarters.

16. Two men per Brigade will be employed under the Brigade Intelligence Officers in collecting information from dug-outs and enemy dead.

17. All unwounded prisoners will be sent under an escort to the Corps Cage at S.23.a.2.2 (S. of LONGUEVAL) where they will be handed over and the escorts will rejoin their units.

18. Bearer Relay Posts are established at N.25.b.6.1 and N.26.c.6.1, and Collecting Posts (with a Medical Officer at each) at N.31.b.4.0 (North FLERS) and N.32.c.0.8 (BULL LANE). A Main Collecting Post under a Medical Officer is established at S.6.b.8.0 (South FLERS) whence lying down cases will be evacuated by DECAUVILLE Railway to LONGUEVAL and thence by Horsed Ambulances to the Advanced Dressing Station on the LONGUEVAL - BERNAFAY road at S.23.c.2.8.

/ Existing

APPENDIX "A".

The arrangements for the creeping Artillery barrage are as follows :-

From Zero to 0.3, a heavy barrage will be placed on the first objective, and 150 yards short of the first objective, where this is possible.

This barrage will be placed on the Green line and the Areas shewn in shaded green on the attached map.

At Zero the troops leave our front line and get as close to the barrage as possible. The barrage creeps at the rate of 50 yards in one minute.

In the Right Brigade Area, at 0.3 the barrage creeps back to J.P. and J.E. to enable the troops on the right flank to enter the S.E. end of STORMY Trench.

At 0.6, it creeps back to E.L.P. to enable the troops in the centre to advance, and at 0.9 it creeps back beyond STORMY TRENCH to E.Z.N., where it remains till 0.13. At 0.9, the troops should enter the S.E. end of BACON TRENCH and establish a Lewis Gun post in it, but they should not advance up the trench, until the creeping barrage from the Left Brigade has passed over it at about 0.20.

In the Left Brigade Area, the barrage creeps back at 0.3 to B.B., which it passes at 0.6, and moves on to C.D., arriving there at 0.9, and remaining on C.D. till 0.13. At 0.6 the barrage on X.B., jumps to D.E. to enable the troops to attack the trenches at N.20.d.4.5 from the East.

At 0.13 the barrage in both Brigade Areas creeps to the line F.G., where it remains till 0.30. At 0.30 half the guns jump straight on to the BREAD and BARLEY trenches, and the remainder continue on F.G. until 1.0, or such time longer as may be required by the Infantry.

N.B. The times shewn against the barrage lines on the attached plan, are the times at which the barrage is timed to leave the line; thus at 0.9 the barrage leaves the Blue line. Where two figures are given thus 0. - 0.3, it means that the barrage remains on the Green line from Zero to 0.3, and starts creeping at 0.3.

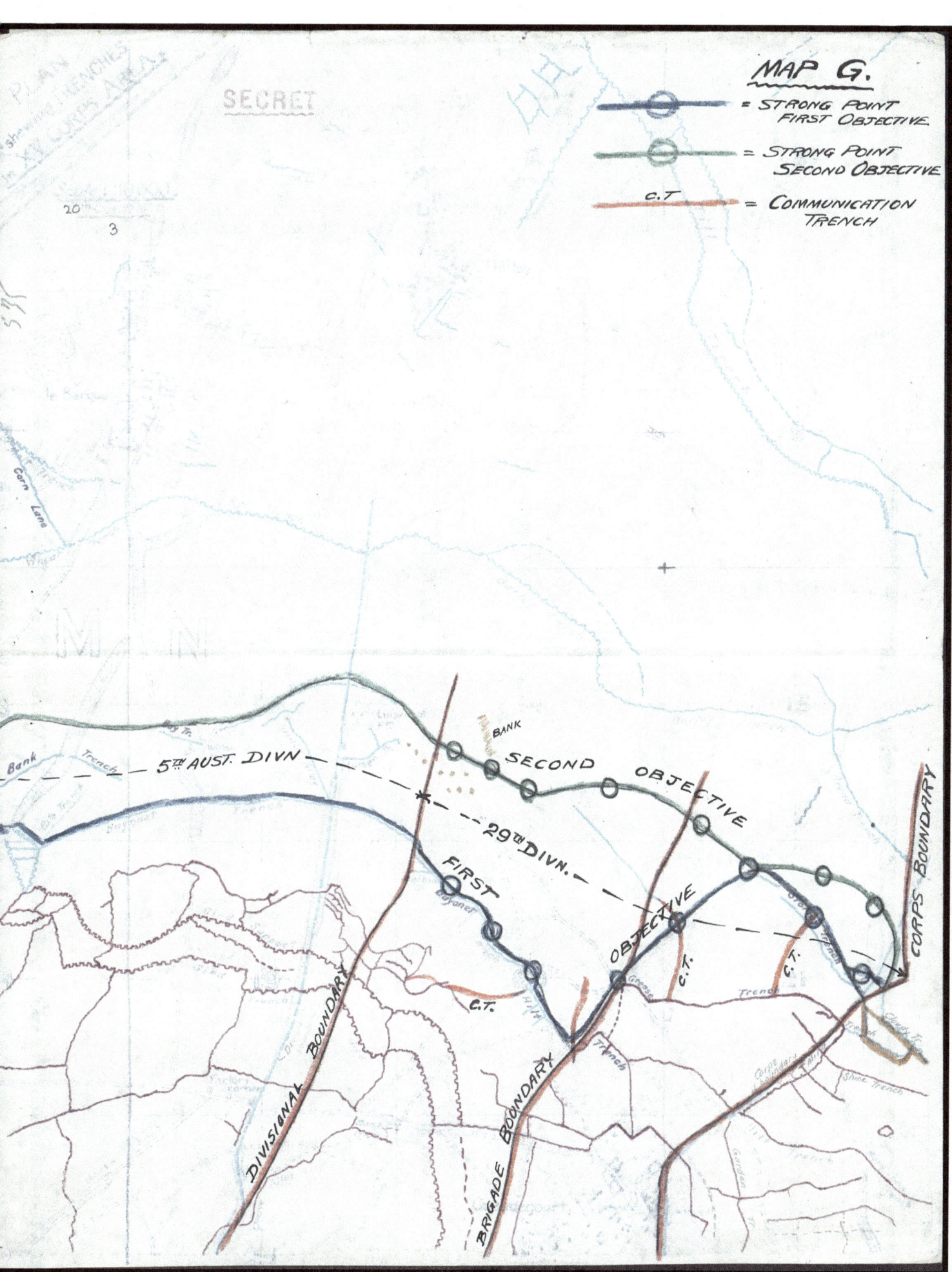

HEADQUARTERS,
29th DIVISION.
GENERAL STAFF.

No. G.S.125.
Date 24-10-16

Appendix 1(8).
536

S E C R E T.

86th Brigade.	O.C. 1/2nd Monmouth Regiment.
87th Brigade.	A.A. & Q.M.G.
88th Brigade.	XV Corps.
C.R.A.	5th Australian Division.
C.R.E.	1st Australian Division.
Officer i/c Signals.	8th Division.

1. The Operations ordered in 29th Division Order No. 70 will be postponed a further 48 hours.

They will now take place on October 28th.

2. 29th Division Order No. 70 will be amended as follows :-

   (a) Para. 1, line 2 and line 6, for "26th October"
                                            read "28th October".

   (b) Para. 10, line 3, for "25th/26th October"
                                            read "27th/28th October".

   (c) Para. 22, line 2, for "25th October"
                                            read "27th October".

   (d) Para. 10, line 3, delete from "The Reserve Brigade ...." to the end of the paragraph, and substitute the following :-

> "The 1/2nd Monmouths (Pioneers) will be responsible for the defence of SWITCH TRENCH, until required forward for digging, and will occupy it when vacated by the leading Brigades. One battalion of the Reserve Brigade will be located just South of DELVILLE WOOD on the night of the 27th/28th October. The remainder of the Reserve Brigade will remain in Camp at BERNAFAY WOOD, ready to move at ½ hours notice."

3. ACKNOWLEDGE BY WIRE.

C.P. Fuller
Lieut-Colonel, G.S.,
29th Division.

24th October, 1916.

Appendice 1(b).

537

SECRET.
B.G.S. 125

86th Brigade.	O.C. 1/2nd Monmouth Regiment.
87th Brigade.	A.A. & Q.M.G.
88th Brigade.	XV Corps.
C.R.A.	5th Australian Division.
C.R.E.	1st Australian Division.
Officer i/c Signals.	8th Division.

1. The Operations ordered in 29th Division Order No. 70 will be postponed a further 48 hours.

They will now take place on October 30th.

2. 29th Division Order No. 70 will be amended as follows :-

(a) Para. 1, line 2, for "28th October" read "30th October".

(b) Para. 10, line 3, for "27th/28th October" read "29th/30th October".

(c) Para. 22, line 2, for "27th October" read "29th October".

(d) Para. 1, line 4, delete from "The 8th Division - - - on the 28th October" and substitute the following :-

"Instructions will be issued later, giving information regarding the attack of XIV Corps, on our right."

3. Acknowledge.

C.G. Fuller.
Lieut-Colonel, G.S.,
29th Division.

26th October, 1916.

Appendix 1 (i).

538

SECRET.

C.G.S. 125.

86th Brigade.	O.C. 1/2nd Monmouth Regiment.
87th Brigade.	A.A. & Q.M.G.
88th Brigade.	XV Corps.
C.R.A.	5th Australian Division.
C.R.E.	1st Australian Division.
Officer i/c Signals.	8th Division.

1. The operations ordered in 29th Division Order No. 70 will be postponed a further 48 hours.

They will now take place on November 1st.

2. 29th Division Order No. 70 will be amended as follows :-

(a) Para. 1, line 2, for "30th October" read "1st November".

(b) Para. 10, line 3, for "29th/30th October" read "31st October/1st November".

(c) Para. 22, line 2, for "29th October" read "31st October".

(d) Para. 18, line 5, for "S.6.b.8.0 (SOUTH FLERS)" read "T.1.a.5.7 (S. of FLERS)".

(e) After para. 14, add fresh para. 14(a).

"14(a). The S.O.S. Signal during the operations will be two red Very lights followed by one White Very Light, fired in quick succession. This signal will be repeated until acted upon by the Artillery."

(f) Para. 5, page 2, line 20, after "assaulting battalions", add "but will not be carried in the attack".

(g) After para. 20, add fresh para. 20(a).

"20(a). No maps, papers or notebooks (containing any information) are to be carried by officers or other ranks in the assault."

3. Acknowledge.

C.G. Fuller.
Lieut-Colonel, G.S.,
29th Division.

28th October, 1916.

Appendix 1 (J)

539

S E C R E T.   Copy No... 5......

29TH DIVISION ORDER NO. 71.

26th October, 1916.

1. The 88th Brigade will place two battalions at the disposal of each of the 86th and 87th Brigades on the 27th instant, to enable the battalions taking part in the forthcoming offensive to be withdrawn to BERNAFAY (Reserve Brigade) CAMP.

2. The four battalions relieved will on arrival at the Reserve Brigade Camp, come under the orders of the G.O.C., 88th Brigade, and will be in Divisional Reserve.

3. The four battalions of the 88th Brigade, lent to the two forward Brigades, will be available to hold the front line for 48 hours, and will be relieved on the night of the 29th/30th October.

4. Details of reliefs will be arranged direct between Brigades concerned.

5. The rations for the two Battalions of each of the 86th and 87th Brigades under command of the 88th Brigade will be delivered at BERNAFAY CAMP with effect from to-morrow 27th instant. Rations for the 88th Brigade Battalions will be delivered at the 88th Brigade 1st Line Transport Camp and taken up under orders of the 86th and 87th Brigade Staff Captains. Pack Saddlery will be taken and handed over under mutual arrangements to be made between Brigades concerned.

6. Acknowledge by wire.

C.J. Fuller.
Lieut-Colonel, G.S.,
29th Division.

Issued at 7.15 p.m

```
Copies  1 - 5   General Staff.
            6   86th Brigade.
            7   87th Brigade.
            8   88th Brigade.
            9   C.R.A.
           10   C.R.E.
           11   Officer i/c Signals.
           12   O.C. 1/2nd Monmouth Regiment.
       13 - 17   A.A. & Q.M.G.
           18   XV Corps.
           19   5th Australian Division.
           20   8th Division.
```

Appendix 1 (K).

SECRET.   Copy No......... 5.   540

29TH DIVISION ORDER NO. 72.

Refce. 1/40,000 Albert (Combined Sheet)   28th October, 1916.
       1/20,000 France Sheet 57 C S.W.

1. The 29th Division will be relieved in the line by the 1st Australian Division on the night of the 29th/30th October.

2. The 86th Bde. will be relieved by the 1st Aust. Inf. Bde. in the Left Sector.
The 87th Bde. will be relieved by the 2nd Aust. Inf. Bde. in the Right Sector.
The 88th Bde. will be relieved by the 3rd Aust. Inf. Bde. in Divl. Reserve.

Details of the reliefs will be arranged between G.Os.C. Infantry Brigades concerned.

3. Moves will be carried out in accordance with the attached Movement Tables.

4. The Machine Gun Companies and Trench Mortar Batteries of the 86th and 87th Brigades will be relieved during daylight on the 29th instant, the relieving units marching up to the line in small parties. Stokes Mortars whether in the line or in reserve will be handed over to the relieving units, and receipts obtained. The number of mortars handed over will not exceed the number received in exchange.

5. Details of relief of Field Companies R.E. and Field Ambulances will be arranged respectively between the Cs.R.E. and A.Ds.M.S. of Divisions.

6. Units on relief will hand over to the incoming units all secret trench maps and instructions, and the secret Operation Orders issued.

7. All Camps are to be left standing, and government property in the shape of tents, tarpaulins, tables, chairs, &c. is on no account to be removed from them. All Camps will be taken over by Advanced Parties, and handed over by Rear parties, especially detailed for this purpose. The allotment of accommodation in a Camp will be carried out by the Brigade, whose Headquarters are situated in that Camp.

8. All Medium Trench Mortars in the line will be handed over to the incoming units. Details of relief to be arranged between Cs.R.A. concerned.

9. The 86th and 87th Brigades will be responsible for handing over 50 pack saddles each to the relieving Brigades.

10. The S.A.A. Sections and 1st line Transport of the three Infantry Brigades will move on the 30th at hours to be arranged by the Brigades concerned.

11. The Divisional Train, Mobile Veterinary Section and Sanitary Section will remain in their present Camps.

/ 12.

12. Completion of all reliefs will be reported to these Headquarters.

13. The G.O.C., 29th Division, will hand over command of the line to the G.O.C., 1st Australian Division, at 9 a.m. on October 30th, at which hour Divisional Headquarters will close at POMMIERS CAMP and reopen at BELLEVUE FARM (E.5.c.).

14. Acknowledge by wire.

C.F. Fuller.

Lieut-Colonel, G.S.,

29th Division.

Issued at 8 p.m.

```
Copies 1 - 5   General Staff.
        6      86th Brigade.
        7      87th Brigade.
        8      88th Brigade.
        9      C.R.A. 29th Division.
       10      C.R.A. 41st Division.
       11      C.R.E.
       12      Officer i/c Signals.
       13      O.C. 1/2nd Monmouth Regiment.
       14 - 18 A.A. & Q.M.G.
       19      1st Australian Division.
       20      5th Australian Division.
       21      8th Division.
       22      XVth Corps.
```

MOVEMENTS OF 29TH DIVISION.

	Positions on 28th Oct.	March on 29th at	To.	Route.	March on 30th at	To.	Route.
86th Infantry Brigade.							
H.Q.	DELVILLE VALLEY	On relief	MAMETZ Camp	Cross Country			
One Battalion	BERNAFAY	8 a.m.	MAMETZ Camp	Cross Country			
One Battalion	BERNAFAY	8 a.m.	ALBERT	MONTAUBAN			
One Battalion Res. Trenches)	Left) Sector	on relief	MAMETZ Camp	via BAZENTIN			
One Battalion " "	" "	"	"	-"-			
M.G. Coy. & T.M. Batty.	Left Sector	on relief					
87th Infantry Brigade.							
Hd. Qrs.	DELVILLE VALLEY	on relief	POMMIERS Camp	MONTAUBAN	8 a.m.	FRICOURT Camp	
One Battalion	BERNAFAY	8 a.m.	MAMETZ Camp	Cross Country	"	-"-	
One Battalion	BERNAFAY	8 a.m.			"	-"-	
One Battalion Res. Trenches)	Right) Sector	on relief	POMMIERS Camp	MONTAUBAN	"	-"-	
One Battalion " "	" "	"	-"-	-"-	"	-"-	
M.G. Coy. & T.M. Batty.	Right Sector	on relief					
88th Infantry Brigade.							
Hd. Qrs.	BERNAFAY Camp				8 a.m.	POMMIERS Camp	MONTAUBAN
One Battalion	Front) trenches Right Sector	on relief	BERNAFAY Camp		8 a.m.	-"-	"
One Battalion	Front trenches)	on relief	BERNAFAY Camp		"	MAMETZ	Cross Country
One Battalion	Left Sector				"	MAMETZ	-"-
M.G. Coy. & T.M. Batty.	BERNAFAY Camp.				"	POMMIERS Camp	MONTAUBAN
Pioneer Bn.	BERNAFAY Camp				10 a.m.	POMMIERS Camp	MONTAUBAN
2/London Field Co. R.E.	S.28.b.3.2					MAMETZ	-"-
3/Kent Field Co. R.E.	S.23.a.4.7					FRICOURT	
1/West Riding Field Co.R.E.	S.23.a.4.5					BELLEVUE	
Divl. Headquarters	POMMIERS						FARM
Divl. Reserve Coy.	REDOUBT						

N.B. Troops on the march will maintain the following distances:-
200 yards between Companies, and between Companies and Battalion Transport.
400 yards between Battalions.
North of LONGUEVAL, troops will move in small detachments.

MOVEMENTS OF 1ST AUSTRALIAN DIVISION.

	Position on 28th Oct.	March on 29th Oct.	To	
1st Aust. Inf. Bde.				
Headquarters	MAMETZ Camp		DELVILLE VALLEY	
One Battalion	" "	8 a.m.	BERNAFAY Camp	⎫ These 2 Bns. halt at BERNAFAY for dinners,
One Battalion	" "	8 a.m.	BERNAFAY Camp	⎬ and march on xkm to the Trenches (Left Sector) in the afternoon, head of column
One Battalion	" "	4 p.m.	Res. Trenches	⎭ to arrive at LONGUEVAL at 5 p.m.
One Battalion	" "	4 p.m.	Left Sector	
L.G. & Coy. & T.M. Batty.	" "	7 a.m.	Left Sector Trenches	
2nd Aust. Inf. Bde.				
Headquarters	POMMIERS Camp		DELVILLE VALLEY	
One Battalion	" "	8 a.m.	BERNAFAY Camp	⎫ These 2 Bns. halt at BERNAFAY for dinners,
One Battalion	" "	8 a.m.	BERNAFAY Camp	⎬ and proceed to the trenches (Right Sector) in the afternoon, head of column to arrive
One Battalion	ALBERT	8 a.m.	BERNAFAY	⎭ at LONGUEVAL at 5 p.m.
One Battalion	MAMETZ Camp	4 p.m.	Res. Trenches, Right Sector.	(for Reserve Trenches, Right Sector).
L.G. Coy. & T.M.Batty.		7 a.m.	Right Sector Trenches.	
3rd Aust. Inf. Bde.				
Headquarters and 4 Battalions	FRICOURT Camp	March on 30th at 8 a.m.	BERNAFAY Camp.	
Divl. Headquarters	BELLEVUE FARM	To reach POMMIERS REDOUBT at 9 a.m.		
Pioneer Bn.	POMMIERS Camp	10 a.m.	BERNAFAY	
1st Field Coy. R.E.	MAMETZ Camp	⎫		
2nd Field Coy. R.E.	POMMIERS Camp	⎬ to be mutually arranged between Cs.R.E.		
3rd Field Coy. R.E.	FRICOURT	⎭		

MOVEMENTS OF 29TH DIVISION.

	Positions on Oct.29th March on 30th at		To.	Route.
			VILLE & MERICOURT	
86th Inf. Bde.	MAMETZ WOOD	9.30 a.m.		MAMETZ & MEAULTE FRICOURT CEMETERY
H.Q.	"	"	"	"
One Bn.	"	"	"	"
	ALBERT	— a.m.		& MEAULTE
M.G. Coy. & T.M. Batty.	MAMETZ WOOD	9.30 a.m.	VILLE & MERICOURT	MAMETZ FRICOURT CEMETERY
87th Inf. Bde.	POMMIERS	"	"	"
H.Q.	"	10 a.m.	FRICOURT	MAMETZ and FRICOURT CEMETERY
One Bn.	"	"	"	"
	MAMETZ Village	"	"	
	ALBERT			
M.G. Coy. & T.M. Batty.	POMMIERS	10 a.m.	FRICOURT	MAMETZ and FRICOURT CEMETERY
88th Inf. Bde.	BERNAFAY CAMP	"	POMMIERS	MONTAUBAN
H.Q.	"	"	"	"
One Bn.	"	"	"	"
	MAMETZ Village	"	"	"
M.G. Coy. & T.M. Batty.	BERNAFAY CAMP	10 a.m.	POMMIERS	MONTAUBAN
Pioneer Bn.	BERNAFAY CAMP		POMMIERS CAMP	"
2nd London Fd.Co.R.E.	S.28.b.3.2		MAMETZ Village	"
3rd Kent Fd.Co.R.E.	S.23.a.4.7		MAMETZ WOOD	"
1st W.Riding Fd.Co.R.E.	S.23.a.4.5		FRICOURT Camp	"
Div. Headquarters	POMMIERS		CORBIE MERICOURT	
Div. Reserve Coy.	BECORDEL		CORBIE and MEAULTE }	MEAULTE, VILLE SUR ANCRE,
16th Sanitary Section	E.10.b.central		CORBIE	MERICOURT
Div. Train	E.10.b.			
Mob. Vet. Sect.	E.10.b.			
S.A.A. Section	E.10.b.			
87th Field Amb.	Trenches		FRICOURT Camp	
88th " " }				
89th " ")	BECORDEL			

Appendix 1 (6).

544

SECRET.   Copy No. 5

29TH DIVISION ORDER NO. 73.

29th October, 1916.

1. The 29th Division (less Artillery) will be transferred from the XV to the XIV Corps on November 1st.

2. In consequence of this, the movements Table for the 29th Division on the 30th instant issued with Order No.72 is cancelled, and the attached movement Table will be substituted for it.

3. Troops moving by road will maintain the following distances :-
   200 yards between Companies, and between Companies and Battalion Transport.
   400 yards between Battalions.
   An officer (or senior N.C.O., if an officer is not available) will march at the head and tail of every column to ensure that proper march discipline is preserved, troops to be well closed up and to keep to the right of the road.

4. Advanced parties and interpreters will be sent ahead by all units to take over Camps and billets from the outgoing units.

5. Brigades will be responsible for detailing the order of march of the Field Companies R.E. affiliated to them.

6. Divisional Headquarters will close at POMMIERS CAMP at 9 a.m. on October 30th, and reopen at the same hour at CORBIE, instead of at BELLEVUE FARM, as stated in Order No. 72.

7. Acknowledge by wire.

C.F. Fuller.
Lieut-Colonel, G.S.,
29th Division.

Issued at 9.30.p.m.

```
Copies 1 - 5   General Staff.
       6       86th Brigade.
       7       87th Brigade.
       8       88th Brigade.
       9       C.R.A.
       10      C.R.E.
       11      Officer i/c Signals.
       12      O.C. 1/2nd Monmouth Regiment.
       13 - 17 A.A. & Q.M.G.
       18      1st Australian Division.
       19      5th Australian Division.
       20      XVth Corps.
       21      XIVth Corps.
       22      8th Division.
```

SECRET.   Copy No. 3
                                                        546
                    Appendix 1 (w)

           29TH DIVISION ORDER NO. 74.
                                        30th October, 1916.

1. The Division will move to billets on the 31st October, and
    1st November, in accordance with the attached movement
    tables.

2. The following distances will be maintained by units on the
    march:-
            200 yards between Companies and between Companies
                and Battalion Transport.
            400 yards between Battalions.

    An officer (or senior N.C.O. if an officer is not
    available) will march at the front and rear of every column
    to ensure that proper march discipline is preserved.

3. Advanced parties and Interpreters will be sent ahead by all
    units to take over billets.

4. Brigades will detail the order of march for the units of
    their Brigade Groups.

5. Divisional Headquarters will remain at CORBIE.

6. ACKNOWLEDGE BY WIRE.

                                            J. Fuller
                                         Lieut-Colonel, G.S.,
Issued at 5 p.m.   29th Division.

                Copies Nos. 1-5   General Staff.
                           6   86th Brigade.
                           7   87th Brigade.
                           8   88th Brigade.
                           9   C.R.A.
                          10   C.R.E.
                          11   Officer in charge SIGNALS.
                          12   O.C. 1/2nd Monmouth Regt.
                       13-17   A.A. & Q.M.G.
                          18   1st Australian Division.
                          19   5th Australian Division.
                          20   1st Anzac.
                          21   XIV Corps.
                          22   8th Division.
                          23   17th Division.

MOVEMENTS OF 29TH DIVISION.

	Positions on October 30th.	March on October 31st to.	Route.	March on November 1st to	Route.
86TH INFANTRY BDE.GROUP.					
H.Qrs., 86th Brigade.	VILLE & MERI COURT.			ALIONVILLE and	
One Battalion.	"			GARDINETTE.	GUEUX HK.
One Battalion.	"	CONTE.			
One Battalion.	ALBERT				
M.G.Coy & T.M.Battery.	VILLE & MERI COURT.		AMIENS ROAD-RIBEMONT		
3rd Kent Field Co., R.E.	MAMETZ WOOD.		MERI COURT.		
		Orders for march on November 1st will be issued later.			
87TH INFANTRY BDE.GROUP.					
H.Qrs. 87th Brigade.	MERI COURT.				MEAULTE-VILLE-
One Battalion.	"				MERI COURT.
One Battalion.	"			CORBIE.	"
One Battalion.	ALBERT				AMIENS ROAD-
One Battalion.	MERI COURT.				RIBEMONT-MERI COURT
M.G.Coy & T.M.Battery.	"				MEAULTE-VILLE &
1/T.Riding Field Co. R.E.	"				MERI COURT.
87th Field Ambulance.	"				
88TH INFANTRY BDE.GROUP.					
H.Qrs. 88th Brigade.	POMMIERS.	VILLE or MERI COURT			
One Battalion.	MAMETZ VILLAGE.	"			MAMETZ-MEAULTE-
One Battalion.	"	"			VILLE.
One Battalion.	POMMIERS.	VILLE.			
One Battalion.	"	"			
M.G.Coy and T.M.Battery.	"	"			
S/London Field Co., R.E.	MAMETZ VILLAGE.	MEAULTE-VILLE-MERI COURT.			

APPENDICES.

Appendix 1 comprises :-

   (a) 29th Division Order No. 65 re relief by 55th Division commencing October 3rd.
   (b) 29th Division Order No. 66 re move from XIVth to XVth Corps Area on October 10th.
   (c) 29th Division Order No. 67 re moves forward of 86th and 87th Brigades.
   (d) 29th Division Order No. 68 re attack on October 18th.
   (e) 29th Division Order No. 69 re relief of 12th Division on 19th October.
   (f) 29th Division Order No. 70 re attack on 26th October.
   (g) Amendment to 29th Division Order No. 70.
   (h)   -"-   -"-
   (i)   -"-   -"-
   (j) 29th Division Order No. 71 re relief of troops taking part in the attack, by the 88th Brigade.
   (k) 29th Division Order No. 72 re relief of 29th Division by the 1st Australian Division on night 29th/30th October.
   (l) 29th Division Order No. 73 re transfer of 29th Division from XVth to the XIVth Corps on November 1st.
   (m) 29th Division Order No. 74 re move of Division to billets.

Appendix 2 comprises :-

   Reports on raids by the 1st Lancashire Fusiliers and the 1st Border Regiment, on the night of 30th September, 1916.

Appendix 3 comprises :-

   (a) Disposition of 29th Division on morning 5th October.
   (b)   -"-   -"-   on night 5th/6th "
   (c) Locations.   -"-   on   10th   "
   (d)   -"-   -"-   on   13th   "
   (e) Dispositions -"-   on   20th   "
   (f)   -"-   -"-   on   26th   "
   (g)   -"-   -"-   on   28th   "
   (h)   -"-   -"-   on   29th   "
   (i) Locations   -"-   on night 30th/31st "

Appendix 4 comprises :-

   29th Division Daily Summaries from 22nd to 29th October.

Appendix 5.   Map shewing front held by the Division whilst in the line.

----------O----------

SECRET

War Diary
Appendix 1 (b).

HEADQUARTERS,
29th DIVISION.
GENERAL STAFF.
No. G.S. 53/3.
Date 9-11-16.

Headquarters,
  XVth Corps.

605

With reference to your G.119 of the 7th instant, the operations undertaken by the 88th Brigade, whilst under the command of the 12th Division have no doubt already been reported to you through the 12th Division, but I forward herewith a copy of the report by the 88th Brigade for reference.

The only operation undertaken by this Division, whilst holding the Right Sector of the XVth Corps front from the 19th to 29th October, in addition to the consolidation of HILT and GREASE Trenches (captured by the 88th Brigade), and the improvement of the communication trenches to them, was as follows :-

The position of the strong point at the Western end of GREASE TRENCH (N.20.d.80.95) was somewhat unfavourable, and I decided to advance it across the SUNKEN Road to N.20.b.7.1, so as to bring fire to bear on enemy movements in the lower portion of the SUNKEN Road.

The sap was cut through to the above point on the night of the 26th/27th October. While this was being done the working party - 1st Royal Inniskilling Fusiliers - were twice attacked from the direction of LARD TRENCH, once by a force about 30 strong. Both these attacks were beaten off by the covering party, who accounted for 3 of the enemy killed. From identifications made the following night (27th/28th) these men belonged to the 101st Reserve Regiment (23rd Reserve Division).

Work was continued on the night of the 27th/28th on the communication trench across the road, and a "T" head was cut facing N.W. approximately at N.20.b.7.2. The front of the "T" head was constructed as a fire trench and the whole post was wired with concertina wire.

/ Another

Army Form C. 2118.

WAR DIARY - GENERAL STAFF, 29TH DIVISION.

INTELLIGENCE SUMMARY

(Erase heading not required.)

Instructions regarding War Diaries and Intelligence Summaries are contained in F.S. Regs., Part II. and the Staff Manual respectively. Title pages will be prepared in manuscript.

Place	Date	Hour	Summary of Events and Information	Remarks and references to Appendices
	Oct. 29th		Dispositions of the Division on this date attached (App. 3(h)). On 29th/30th night, 1st Australian Division relieved units in the trenches, but owing to the mud, darkness and distance to be marched, 2 Battalions of the 88th Brigade in the Right Sector did not arrive at BERNAFAY CAMP after relief, till 8 a.m. 30th October. A "Locations Table" is attached to this. The Newfoundland Regiment captured a prisoner in the early morning. Orders were issued that the Division would join XIVth Corps vide Operation Order No. 73. Movements Table attached to Operation Order No. 72 was therefore cancelled and that attached to O.O.73 substituted (App. 1(1)). G.S.O.I visited XIV Corps H.Q. in the afternoon.	App. 3(h). App. 1(1).
	Oct. 30th		"Locations Table" attached to App. 3(i). Relief of Division by 1st Australian Division complete by 7 a.m. G.O.C. 1st Australian Division, took over command of the Division Sector at 9 a.m. 86th Brigade moved from MAMETZ WOOD (H.Q. and 3 Bns.) to VILLE and MERICOURT, one Bn. remained at ALBERT. 87th Brigade moved from POMMIERS and MAMETZ Village to FRICOURT (H.Q. and 3 Bns.), one Bn. remained in ALBERT. 88th Brigade moved (after relief 29th/30th night) to POMMIERS (2 Bns. and H.Q.) and MAMETZ village (2 Bns.), from trenches and BERNAFAY Camp. A heavy gale blew all the morning, and heavy rain fell the whole afternoon from 12 midday. Divisional Headquarters moved to CORBIE during the morning, except G.S.O.I and G.S.O.II who remained behind till the evening, to get out orders for the moves to-morrow.	App. 3(i).

Instructions regarding War Diaries and Intelligence
Summaries are contained in F. S. Regs., Part II.
and the Staff Manual respectively. Title pages
will be prepared in manuscript.

WAR DIARY - GENERAL STAFF, 29TH DIVISION.

~~INTELLIGENCE SUMMARY~~

(Erase heading not required.)

Army Form C. 2118.

Place	Date	Hour	Summary of Events and Information	Remarks and references to Appendices
	Oct. 31st		The 86th Brigade moved from VILLE, MERICOURT and ALBERT (1 Battn.) to CORBIE, the 87th Brigade remained at FRICOURT and the 88th Brigade moved from POMMIERS and MAMETZ VILLAGE to VILLE and MERICOURT, vide "Location Table" (App. 1(m)) Operation Order No. 74. G.S.O.II and Major CLARKE visited DAOURS where the Divisional School is to be situated, and inspected the accommodation. Captain ROBERTSON went to XIVth Corps H.Q. to get maps and codes. Eight officers from the Division are allowed to go on leave daily as special cases. Brig-General LUCAS went on leave on night 31stOct./1st Nov. A fine windy day. Daily Intelligence Summaries from 22nd October to 29th October are attached as APP. 4. A map is attached (Appendix 5) showing the front held by the Division whilst in the line.	App. 1(m). App. 4. App. 5

Lieut-Colonel, G.S.,
29th Division.

Army Form C. 2118.

WAR DIARY - GENERAL STAFF, 29TH DIVISION.

~~INTELLIGENCE SUMMARY~~

(Erase heading not required.)

Instructions regarding War Diaries and Intelligence Summaries are contained in F. S. Regs., Part II. and the Staff Manual respectively. Title pages will be prepared in manuscript.

Place	Date	Hour	Summary of Events and Information	Remarks and references to Appendices
	Oct. 27th		The attack was again postponed a further 48 hours till November 1st on account of very heavy rain which fell between 4.15 and 5.15 p.m. The 4 battalions of the 86th and 87th Brigades which are to carry out the attack were relieved during the night 27th/28th by the 4 Battalions of 88th Brigade, the former 4 Battalions coming back to rest at BERNAFAY WOOD. (App.1(j)). Dispositions of the Division on this date are shown in App.3(g). *Corps Commander (Lieut Gen Sir J.D. Crewe) visited Divisional H.Q. in the morning.*	App.1(i). App.1(j). App.3(g).
	Oct. 28th		A fine day, but deep mud, and bad roads. The rearrangements of Battalions between the 88th Brigade and the other Brigades was completed on the night 28th/29th October. The G.O.C. attended a Corps Conference at VIVIER MILL at 10 a.m., also the C.R.E. and C.R.A. Orders were received about noon for the relief of 29th Division by 1st Australian Division to-morrow 29th October, and orders were issued accordingly. App.1(k). There was little artillery activity on either side. The Inniskilling Fusiliers killed 2 Germans of 101st Regiment on 27th/28th night, and captured a man of 64th Regiment on 28th night.	App.1(k)

Army Form C. 2118.

WAR DIARY - GENERAL STAFF, 29TH DIVISION.

INTELLIGENCE SUMMARY.

(Erase heading not required.)

Instructions regarding War Diaries and Intelligence Summaries are contained in F.S. Regs., Part II. and the Staff Manual respectively. Title pages will be prepared in manuscript.

Place	Date	Hour	Summary of Events and Information	Remarks and references to Appendices
	Oct. 25th		Some rain during the morning. The G.O.C. visited the right Brigade front line trenches early returning at 2 p.m. G.S.O.II visited all Brigade Headquarters in afternoon. Drafts arrived for 88th Brigade (Essex and Worcesters). Fairly quiet day.	
	Oct. 26th		The G.S.O.I and G.S.O.II visited the front trenches (west end of GREASE TRENCH) early. A lot of work is being done on the roads which are improving, the trenches are extremely muddy and sticky. Not much shelling on either side. The attack is once more postponed for 48 hours, it will now take place on October 30th, weather permitting. (App. 1(h)). Dispositions of the Division on this date are attached (App.3(f)).	App.1(h). App.3(f).

Instructions regarding War Diaries and Intelligence
Summaries are contained in F. S. Regs., Part II.
and the Staff Manual respectively. Title pages
will be prepared in manuscript.

WAR DIARY - GENERAL STAFF, 29TH DIVISION.

INTELLIGENCE SUMMARY

(Erase heading not required.)

Army Form C. 2118.

Place	Date	Hour	Summary of Events and Information	Remarks and references to Appendices
	Oct. 23rd		The G.O.C. visited 86th Brigade Headquarters at 7 a.m. and afterwards visited Battalion H.Q. in trenches. At 9.30 a.m. he had a conference at 86th H.Q. A very misty morning till 1 p.m. Attack by XIVth Corps on our right was postponed from 11.30 a.m. till 2.30 p.m., it appears to have been satisfactory. Division Operation Order No. 70 was issued in the evening for the attack on 25th October. In the evening a message was received from XVth Corps postponing the attack till 26th Oct. The Corps Commander visited the G.O.C. in the afternoon.	App. 1(f).
	Oct. 24th		A wet day after a wet misty night, roads in a very bad state. The G.S.O.I. visited all Brigade Headquarters during the morning. The Corps Commander visited the G.O.C. at 12.30 p.m. A telephone message was received from XVth Corps about midday to say that the attack was postponed for a further 48 hours and would take place on October 28th. The enemy appears to be actively digging new trenches opposite our front in N.20.b. and d.; the former trench was heavily shelled by our Divisional Artillery yesterday with excellent effect, many Germans were seen running from the trench and were fired on with shrapnel. The 5th Australian Division took over a portion of our front from our left Brigade (the 86th) during the morning, vide map attached to App. 5th Australian Division took over command from 30th Division on our left.	App. 1(g). App.

Army Form C. 2118.

Instructions regarding War Diaries and Intelligence Summaries are contained in F. S. Regs., Part II. and the Staff Manual respectively. Title pages will be prepared in manuscript.

WAR DIARY - GENERAL STAFF, 29TH DIVISION.

INTELLIGENCE SUMMARY.

(Erase heading not required.)

Place	Date	Hour	Summary of Events and Information	Remarks and references to Appendices
	Oct. 21st		G.S.O.II visited Brigade Headquarters of 86th and 87th Brigades, and discussed best methods of using machine guns in the attack. The Machine Gun Coy. Officers of 86th and 87th Machine Gun Coys. accompanied him to the trenches to decide on a suitable position from which to bring indirect fire to bear on BARLEY TRENCH, he visited the forward Battalion H.Q. The G.O.C. held a conference of Brigadiers at 88th Brigade Headquarters at QUARRY (BERNAFAY WOOD) at 3 p.m. The enemy made an unsuccessful attempt to recapture GREASE TRENCH at 5 p.m. A "location of units" statement is attached to App. 3(e). The weather remained cold and fine.	App. 3(e)
	Oct. 22nd		The G.S.O.III visited and reported on the front line trenches in our Right Sector, he reported the GREASE TRENCH good, but the communication trenches are in bad condition. A good deal of shelling took place behind the front line, but not actually on the front line. The G.O.C. and G.S.O.I attended a Corps Conference at VIVIER MILL at 2.30 p.m. with reference to the attack on the 25th instant. Weather still fine and cold. 1 Bde. of 5th Australian Division relieved right Brigade of 30th Division on our left, during night 22nd/23rd October.	

Army Form C. 2118.

WAR DIARY – GENERAL STAFF, 29TH DIVISION.

INTELLIGENCE SUMMARY.

(Erase heading not required.)

Instructions regarding War Diaries and Intelligence Summaries are contained in F. S. Regs., Part II. and the Staff Manual respectively. Title pages will be prepared in manuscript.

Place	Date	Hour	Summary of Events and Information	Remarks and references to Appendices
	Oct. 19th		86th Brigade took over the line from 35th Brigade, 12th Division, vide Operation Order No.69. 87th Brigade moved from FRICOURT CAMP to BERNAFAY CAMP taking over from the 36th Brigade who moved to FRICOURT CAMP. Divisional Headquarters moved from RIBEMONT to POMMIERS REDOUBT CAMP. 2 Battalions 88th Brigade remained in the line. 2 Battalions 87th Brigade moved up in the evening to relieve the 2 front Battalions of the 88th Brigade. G.O.C. 29th Division, took over command from G.O.C. 12th Division, at 5 p.m. Heavy rain during the night 18th/19th. G.s.o.I Divisional H.Q. in DELVILLE VALLEY. The 41st Division Artillery Group covers the Divisional Front under Brig-General LUSHINGTON. 8th Division took over line on our right from 6th Division during night 19th/20th. 8th Division took over command from 6th Division on 20th October.	App.1(e).
	Oct. 20th		The G.O.C. visited Brigade Headquarters in morning. Enemy shelled area north of DELVILLE WOOD a good deal in the evening. Owing to the bad condition of the trenches, the hostile shelling and darkness, it was not possible for the 2 Battalions 87th Brigade to complete relief of the 2 Battalions 88th Brigade, in front line, and their relief was not completed till after dark on the evening of 20th October.	

Army Form C. 2118.

WAR DIARY - GENERAL STAFF, 29TH DIVISION.

~~INTELLIGENCE SUMMARY.~~

(Erase heading not required.)

Instructions regarding War Diaries and Intelligence Summaries are contained in F. S. Regs., Part II. and the Staff Manual respectively. Title pages will be prepared in manuscript.

Place	Date	Hour	Summary of Events and Information	Remarks and references to Appendices
	Oct. 17th		No change. G.O.C. and G.S.O.II went to see *proposed* new Advanced Divisional H.Q. at QUARRY (S.22.d.9.4) G.O.C. also visited 88th Brigade H.Q. A warning order was received from XVth Corps reference probable relief of 35th Brigade (12th Division) by 2 Bns. 29th Division, dependant on result of operations to be carried out early to-morrow morning. F.S.O. ? R.A.M.C. Would H₂ at E.N. Curlue and FRICOURT CAMP ? Orders regarding these operations were issued vide Order No. 68 (App. 1(d)).	~~App.~~ App. 1(d).
	Oct. 18th		Operations carried out successfully by 88th Brigade N. of GUEUDECOURT, both Battalions (2/Hants. and 4/Worcesters) gaining their objective i.e. GREASE TRENCH and part of BAYONET TRENCH. G.O.C. went to see *proposed* Advanced Divl. H.Q. at QUARRY in afternoon. G.S.O.II visited 86th and 87th Brigade H.Q. warning them about move forward to-morrow.	

WAR DIARY - GENERAL STAFF, 29TH DIVISION.

INTELLIGENCE SUMMARY

Army Form C. 2118.

(Erase heading not required.)

Place	Date	Hour	Summary of Events and Information	Remarks and references to Appendices
	Oct. 15th		Nothing to report. G.S.O.I and Divisional Bombing Officer visited 12th Div. H.Q. and dumps at LONGUEVAL.	
	Oct. 16th		A.A. & Q.M.G. and G.S.O.II visited HIGH WOOD in the morning. G.O.C. and G.S.O.I attended a Corps Conference at VIVIERS MILL at 12 noon, and afterwards reconnoitred a site for a road between FRICOURT and MONTAUBAN, which is to be constructed by the Division. 4 platoons are put at disposal of the C.E. XVth Corps for work on the new railways. A new road was started by 87th Brigade from FRICOURT to POMMIERS REDOUBT.	

Army Form C. 2118.

WAR DIARY - GENERAL STAFF, 29TH DIVISION.

~~INTELLIGENCE~~ SUMMARY ~~X~~

(Erase heading not required.)

Instructions regarding War Diaries and Intelligence Summaries are contained in F. S. Regs., Part II. and the Staff Manual respectively. Title pages will be prepared in manuscript.

Place	Date	Hour	Summary of Events and Information	Remarks and references to Appendices
	Oct. 13th		At 8 a.m. the 87th Brigade and 87th Brigade Group moved from BUIRE to FRICOURT Camp, and at 1 p.m. the 86th Brigade and 86th Brigade Group moved from DERNACOURT to MAMETZ Camp. The G.S.O.I visited the trenches, going to the 2 Advanced Battalion H.Q. The G.O.C. visited the XVth and IIIrd Corps H.Q. during the day. Dispositions of the Division on this date attached as App. 3(d).	App. 1(c). App. 3(d).
	Oct. 14th		The G.O.C. Visited HIGH WOOD and Camps of 86th and 87th Brigades at MAMETZ WOOD and FRICOURT respectively. The G.S.O.II visited 88th Bde. Headquarters and all Battalion H.Q. of 88th Bde. Hostile shelling fairly light. The Newfoundland Regt. maintained and consolidated their position.	

Army Form C. 2118.

WAR DIARY - GENERAL STAFF, 29TH DIVISION.

INTELLIGENCE SUMMARY.

(Erase heading not required.)

Instructions regarding War Diaries and Intelligence Summaries are contained in F.S. Regs., Part II. and the Staff Manual respectively. Title pages will be prepared in manuscript.

Place	Date	Hour	Summary of Events and Information	Remarks and references to Appendices
	Oct. 11th		86th and 87th Brigades remained at DERNACOURT and BUIRE respectively, and Divisional Headquarters at RIBEMONT. The 88th Brigade (under the 12th Division) had taken over part of the line north of GUEUDECOURT, during the 10th/11th night, the Newfoundland Regiment being in the front line, the Essex Regiment in support. During the 11th/12th night the Essex Regiment moved up on the left of the Newfoundland Regiment, and prepared for the attack to-morrow. G.S.O. I & II visited Bde. H.Q. and SWITCH TRENCH in the morning.	
	Oct. 12th		The above dispositions remain the same. The 88th Brigade took part in an attack on the German trenches by the XVth Corps, in conjunction with the IIIrd Corps on the left and the 6th Division on the right. The Newfoundland Regiment gained their 1st objective, N. of GUEUDECOURT and captured about 70 prisoners; but the Essex Regiment were counter-attacked and were obliged to withdraw to our original trenches. The weather remained dry. G.O.C. held a Conference at RIBEMONT in the morning	

T2134. Wt. W708—776. 500000. 4/15. Sir J. C. & S.

Army Form C. 2118.

WAR DIARY - GENERAL STAFF, 29TH DIVISION.

INTELLIGENCE SUMMARY.
(Erase heading not required.)

Instructions regarding War Diaries and Intelligence Summaries are contained in F.S. Regs., Part II. and the Staff Manual respectively. Title pages will be prepared in manuscript.

Place	Date	Hour	Summary of Events and Information	Remarks and references to Appendices
	Oct. 9th		In the evening the 88th Brigade moved up to forward area, coming under the orders of the 12th Division. Two battalions were sent up by bus, the remainder following on the morning of the 10th. The G.O.C. rejoined from leave. *Information was received that Division moved to Bouzincourt to XV Corps. G.S.O.I and A.A. & Q.M.G. visited Corps Hd. at HEILLY in the morning.*	App. 1(b).
	Oct. 10th		Divisional Headquarters moved to RIBEMONT, the Division being transferred to the XVth Corps. The 88th Brigade moved to DERNACOURT, and the 87th Brigade to BUIRE. The G.S.O.II rejoined from leave. (For details of move see Division Order No.66). App. 1(b) Several Staff Officers visited the Advanced Headquarters of the 12th Division at the POMMIERS REDOUBT. Dispositions of the Division on this date attached (App. 3(c)).	App. 3(c).

Army Form C. 2118.

WAR DIARY - GENERAL STAFF, 29TH DIVISION.

INTELLIGENCE SUMMARY

(Erase heading not required.)

Instructions regarding War Diaries and Intelligence Summaries are contained in F. S. Regs., Part II. and the Staff Manual respectively. Title pages will be prepared in manuscript.

Place	Date	Hour	Summary of Events and Information	Remarks and references to Appendices
	Oct. 7th		The Division commenced to entrain for the South (see Operation Order No. 65). APP. 1 (a). G.S.O I and A.A.Q.M.G. visited 4th Division at CORBIE, and inspected Camp at CITADEL & SANDPITS	App. 1/1/(a).
	Oct. 8th		Entrainment continued. Brigades, on arrival at their destination, moved to the following villages :- Divl. Headquarters and 88th Brigade to CORBIE, 87th Brigade to ALLONVILLE, 86th Brigade to DAOURS. All these places were some considerable distance from the detraining points, but the men seemed to bear the trying march well. The Division came under the XIVth Corps. G.S.O.I. and A.A. & Q.M.G. visited billets and 6th Division H.Q. in BARNAFAY WOOD.	

Instructions regarding War Diaries and Intelligence
Summaries are contained in F. S. Regs., Part II.
and the Staff Manual respectively. Title pages
will be prepared in manuscript.

WAR DIARY - GENERAL STAFF, 29TH DIVISION.

INTELLIGENCE SUMMARY

(Erase heading not required.)

Army Form C. 2118.

Place	Date	Hour	Summary of Events and Information	Remarks and references to Appendices
	Oct. 5th		The relief of the 88th Bde. was successfully completed at 2 A.M. G.O.C. 29th Division, handed over command of the line to G.O.C. 55th Division, and proceeded on leave. The Corps Commander inspected the various units of the 87th Brigade. G.S.O.I (Division) made Right Sector Survey	
			Dispositions of the Division on this date are attached as App. 3(a).	App. 3(a).
			Dispositions of the Division on the night 5th/6th are attached as App. 3(b).	App. 3(b).
	Oct. 6th		The Corps Commander visited the 88th Brigade in POPERINGHE and the 3 Field Companies R.E. in HOUDTKERQUE. G.S.O.I and A.A. & Q.M.G. motored down to AMIENS, and visited XIV Corps Headquarters near MÉAULTE.	

T2134. Wt. W708—776. 500000. 4/15. Sir J. C. & S.

Army Form C. 2118.

WAR DIARY - GENERAL STAFF, 29TH DIVISION.

INTELLIGENCE SUMMARY

(Erase heading not required.)

Instructions regarding War Diaries and Intelligence Summaries are contained in F. S. Regs., Part II. and the Staff Manual respectively. Title pages will be prepared in manuscript.

Place	Date	Hour	Summary of Events and Information	Remarks and references to Appendices
	Oct. 3rd		General JEUDWINE commanding the 55th Division took up residence with Divisional Headquarters, and visited the line with G.S.O.I, 29th Division. The two reserve Battalions of the 87th Brigade were relieved by the 166th Infantry Brigade. A quiet day.	
	Oct. 4th		G.Os.C. and G.S.Os.I of 29th and 55th Divisions visited the line together during the morning. G.S.O.II, 55th Division visited the line with G.S.O.III during the afternoon. 87th Brigade relieved by 166th Brigade in Left Sector at 9.30 p.m. Two reserve battalions of 88th Brigade relieved by 165th Brigade.	

T/134. Wt. W708—776. 500000. 4/15. Sir J. C. & S.

Army Form C. 2118.

WAR DIARY – GENERAL STAFF, 29TH DIVISION.

~~INTELLIGENCE~~ SUMMARY

(Erase heading not required.)

Instructions regarding War Diaries and Intelligence Summaries are contained in F. S. Regs., Part II. and the Staff Manual respectively. Title pages will be prepared in manuscript.

OCTOBER, 1916.

Place	Date	Hour	Summary of Events and Information	Remarks and references to Appendices
	Oct. 1st		The G.O.C. went to YPRES and C. Camp to congratulate the raiding parties of Lancs. Fus. and Borders, on their successful raids last night. There has been very little retaliation. A quiet day.	
			Orders were issued that the Division would be relieved by the 55th Division on the 5th/6th vide Operation Order No. 65 (App. 1(a)).	App. 1(a).
			Reports on raids carried out by the 1st Lancashire Fusiliers and 1st Border Regiment on the 30th September, are attached as App. 2(a)	App. 2(a).
	Oct. 2nd		The G.O.C. visited Artillery horse lines West of POPERINGHE. Major OVEY (G.S.O.II) proceeded on leave to U.K. General JEUDWINE and several Staff-Officers of the 55th Division came over during the course of the afternoon, and commenced the process of "taking over".	

APPENDICES.

Appendix 1 comprises :-

   (a) 29th Division Order No. 65 re relief by 55th Division commencing October 3rd.
   (b) 29th Division Order No. 66 re move from XIVth to XVth Corps Area on October 10th.
   (c) 29th Division Order No. 67 re moves forward of 86th and 87th Brigades.
   (d) 29th Division Order No. 68 re attack on October 18th.
   (e) 29th Division Order No. 69 re relief of 12th Division on 19th October.
   (f) 29th Division Order No. 70 re attack on 26th October.
   (g) Amendment to 29th Division Order No. 70.
   (h)   -"-   -"-
   (i)   -"-   -"-
   (j) 29th Division Order No. 71 re relief of troops taking part in the attack, by the 88th Brigade.
   (k) 29th Division Order No. 72 re relief of 29th Division by the 1st Australian Division on night 29th/30th October.
   (l) 29th Division Order No. 73 re transfer of 29th Division from XVth to the XIVth Corps on November 1st.
   (m) 29th Division Order No. 74 re move of Division to billets.

Appendix 2 comprises :-

   Reports on raids by the 1st Lancashire Fusiliers and the 1st Border Regiment, on the night of 30th September, 1916.

Appendix 3 comprises :-

   (a) Disposition of 29th Division on morning 5th October.
   (b)   -"-   -"-   on night 5th/6th "
   (c) Locations   -"-   on   10th   "
   (d)   -"-   -"-   on   13th   "
   (e) Dispositions -"-   on   20th   "
   (f)   -"-   -"-   on   26th   "
   (g)   -"-   -"-   on   28th   "
   (h)   -"-   -"-   on   29th   "
   (i) Locations   -"-   on night 30th/31st "

Appendix 4 comprises :-

   29th Division Daily Summaries from 22nd to 29th October.

Appendix 5.   Map shewing front held by the Division whilst in the line.

----------o----------

WAR DIARY

GENERAL STAFF

29TH. DIVISION

FOR THE MONTH

OF

OCTOBER 1916.

VOLUME XX.

	Position Oct. 30th & Oct. 31st	March on November 1st to	Route
Pioneer Batt.	FRAMIERS	Orders regarding march on Nov. 1st will be given direct by XIV Corps.	
Divisional H.Q.	CORBIE		
Div. Reserve Coy.	CORBIE		548
16th Sanitary Sect.	CORBIE		
Divisional Train.	E 10 b	CORBIE	VILLE - MERICOURT
Mob. Vet. Section.	E 10 b	CORBIE	
S.A.A. Section.	E 10 b	Sandpits N of MEAULTE	
88th Field Amblce.) 89th Field Amblce.)	MECORMEL	orders regarding future moves will be given by A.D.M.S.	

Headquarters,

VIIIth Corps.

REPORT ON RAID CARRIED OUT BY THE 1ST LANCASHIRE FUSILIERS ON 30TH SEPTEMBER.

The raiding party under Captain STEVENSON - two officers and 37 rank and file - arrived in the front line at 7 p.m.

7.30 p.m. 2/Lieutenant LOGAN and bangalore torpedo party proceeded to selected point of assembly in NO MANS LAND just North of crater No. 4.

A left flank and right flank guard were also posted in shell holes.

8 p.m. to 8.30 p.m. Four 2" trench mortars opened on the wire; two at selected point of entry and one at selected places to North and South. These mortars fired about 20 rounds each.

Enemy retaliated with a few Minenwerfer only, which fell in the vicinity of S.21 and the SUNKEN ROAD.

8.15 to 8.30 p.m. Twenty four Stokes guns opened, firing a burst 8 rounds and three bursts of 4 a mortar. 4.5 and 13-pdrs also opened, and rifle grenades were showered into the enemy lines.

8.30 p.m. Machine guns opened. Raiding party left our trenches and formed up in NO MANS LAND. No barrage had been opened by the enemy. After 8 p.m. enemy flares were sent up from well behind their front line only.

8.40 p.m. 2/Lieutenant LOGAN'S party moved forward to the enemy wire. The first row was found to be destroyed, but a second row some 8 yards deep was found to be intact.

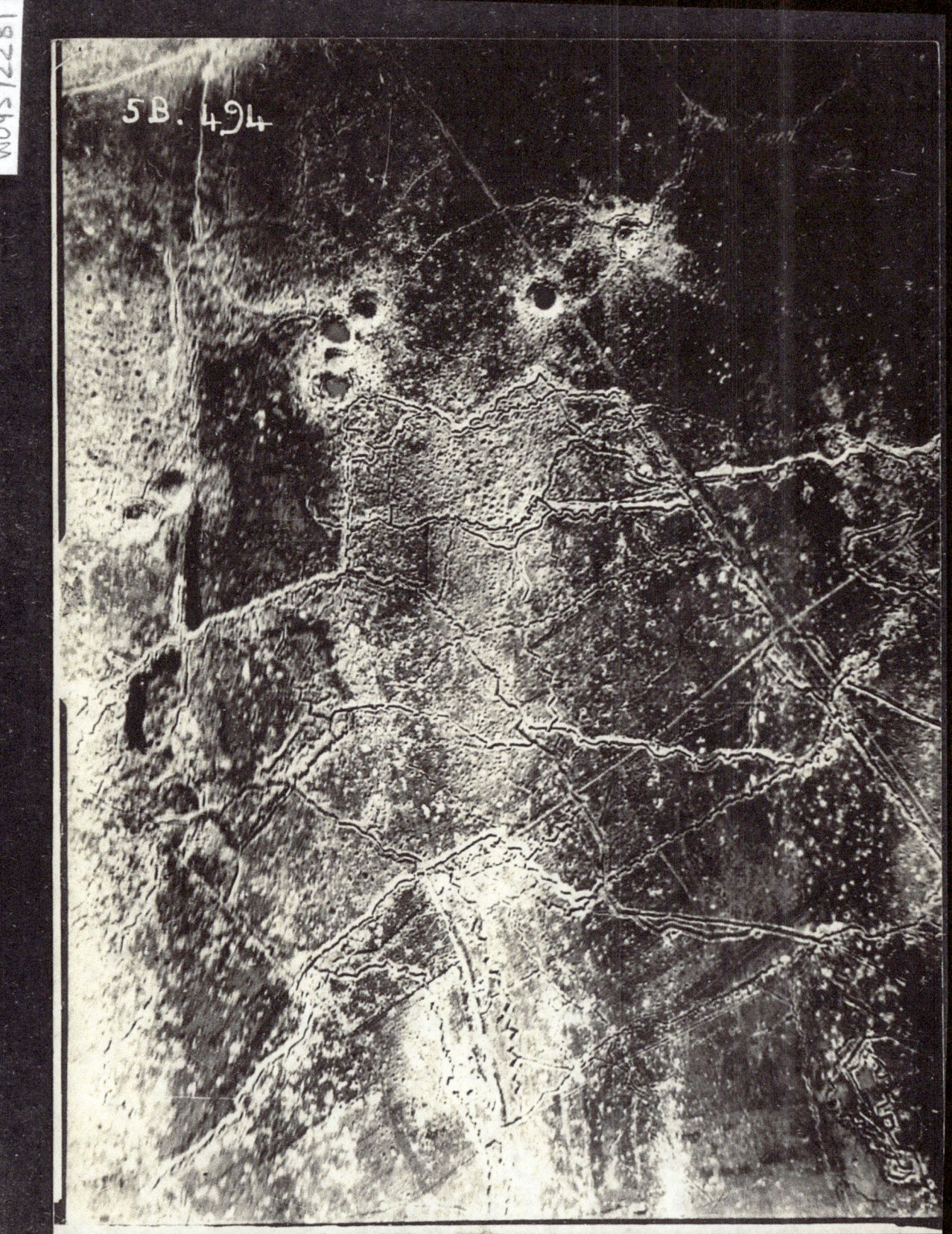

556

R.F.C.
MAP SHEET No. 28
SCALE 20000
SQUARE I

No. 5D494
DATE 3-8-16
HEIGHT 6000
SQUADRON No. 5

a	b	a	b
c	d	c	d
a	b	a	b
c	d	c	d

G.47/
30 Sepr 16.

HQ 29 Divn

The 1/Lanc Fus raiding party entered the enemy trenches tonight and spent some ten minutes there. A few identifications were obtained but no prisoners. No opposition was met with. The trenches entered were apparently held by a small bombing post who fled leaving their rifles behind them. No casualties excepting one man slightly wounded. The trenches were found to be considerably damaged by our Stokes Mortars.
A further report will be sent in tomorrow.

W. J. Williams
Bong/real
86th Bde

Seen by
GOC

By 8.50 p.m. this wire was destroyed by bangalore torpedoes. Two mis fires occurred before this was accomplished.

8.55 p.m. to
9 p.m.   Intensive bombardment. Stokes guns fired 20 rounds a mortar.

9 p.m.   All fire ceased over the area to be raided.

9.5 p.m.   Raiders entered the enemy trenches. A party under 2/Lieutenant DOWNES moved to the right. They met a German post of 4 men who threw away their rifles and ran. They were fired on but apparently escaped unhurt. This party moved about 100 yards down the trench and a short distance up a communication trench, but met with no further signs of the enemy.

2/Lieutenant LOGAN and party moved to the left for 50 yards, passing and blocking a communication trench. They then moved down a second line trench. No enemy were met with.

9.20 p.m.   Regimental call sounded on bugle to collect the raiders.

9.30 p.m.   Entire party back in our lines without casualty.

No opposition of any kind was met with.

Trenches were searched and the following brought in:-

3 rifles.
S.A.A.
Bombs.
A Very pistol.
Periscopes.
Five bundles of kit, greatcoats, etc.

The kit collected was found neatly fastened up in bundles enclosed by waterproof sheets and cartoons strapped to bundles. It looked as if the party had either just reached the trenches, or were packed up ready to be

Appendix 2(a)

HQ 29 Divn

G.1/
2 October 16.

549

Report on raid carried out by 1/Lanc Fus on the night of 30 Sept.

The Raiding party under Capt STEVENSON 9 R.I.F., 2 Officers & 37 R.I.F. arrived in the front line 7 p.m.

7.30 p.m. 2/Lt LOGAN and bangalore torpedo party proceeded to selected point of Assembly in NO MANS LAND just N of Crater No 4.
A left flank & right flank guard were also posted in shell holes.

8 p.m. to 8.30 p.m. Four 2" Trench Mortars opened on the wire; two at selected point of Entry and one at selected places to N & S.
These Mortars fired about 20 rounds each.

550.

Enemy retaliated with a few Minenwerfer only, which fell in vicinity of S.21 & the Sunken road.

8.15–8.30. Twenty four Stokes Guns opened firing a burst of 8 rounds and three bursts of 4. A Mortar, 4.5" + 8p also opened and rifle grenades were showered into the enemy lines.

8.30 p.m. Machine Guns opened. Raiding party left our trenches and formed up in No Mans Land. No barrage had been opened by the enemy. After 8 p.m enemy flares were sent up from well behind their front line only.

8.40 p.m. 2Lt LOGAN's party moved forward to the enemy wire. The first row was found to be destroyed, but a second

row some 8 × 55′
deep was found to
be intact.
by 8.50 p.m this wire was
destroyed by bangalore
torpedoes. Two minor fires
occurred before this was
accomplished.

8.55 p.m – 9 p.m. Intensive
bombardment.
Stokes guns fired 20
rounds a mortar.

9 p.m All fire ceased over
the area to be raided.

9.57 p.m Raiders entered
the enemy trenches.
A party under 2/Lt DOWNES
moved to the right, they
met a German post of
4 men who threw away
their rifles & ran. they
were fired on but apparently
escaped unhurt.
This party moved about 100×
down the trench and a
short distance up a
Comm^t Trench but met with

no further signs
of the enemy. 552

2/Lt LOGAN & party moved
to the left for 50x passing
& blocking a Commt T.
They then moved down a
second line trench. No.
enemy were met with.

9.20 p.m Regimental Call sounded
on bugle to collect the
raiders

9.30 p.m Entire party back in
our lines without
casualty.

No opposition of any kind was
met with.
Trenches were searched and
the following brought in.
 3 rifles.
 S.A.A
 Bombs
 A Very pistol
 Periscopes
 Three Five bundles of Kit
 Great Coats etc

The kit collected 55.3
was found neatly
fastened up in bundles
enclosed by waterproof
sheets & canteens strapped
to bundles.
Looked as if the party
had either just vacated
the trenches or were packed
up ready to be relieved.

Trenches
   Front line
   5' deep, 4' across
   Top 2½' bottom.
Parapet thick & well made.
Towards the North a foot of
water was lying in the
trench.
Brushwood lined dug outs
under the parapet; lined roofed
with timber with central
strut about 6' x 6' and 4'
high. All dug outs empty.
No Deep dug outs.
Second line much the same
               as front line.

Wire between 1st & 2nd line

very thick & strong SSG

The trenches which were entered had been considerably knocked about by our Stokes Mortars.

W J Williams
Brig-Genl
86 B'de

REFERENCES:-
- Machine Gun
- Stokes Gun
- 2" Mortars
- 4.5" Howitzers
- 18 pounders

PROGRAMME

8 pm – 8.30 pm. 2" cut wire.
8.15 pm – 8.30 pm. Stokes, 4.5" 18pdrs and Rifle Grenades.
8.55 pm – 9 pm. Intensive Bombardment as above. Machine guns.
9 pm. Raiders Enter. 86th Stokes mortar cease fire.
9 – 9.30 pm. Stokes (excepting 86th) 4.5", 18 pdr and machine guns.

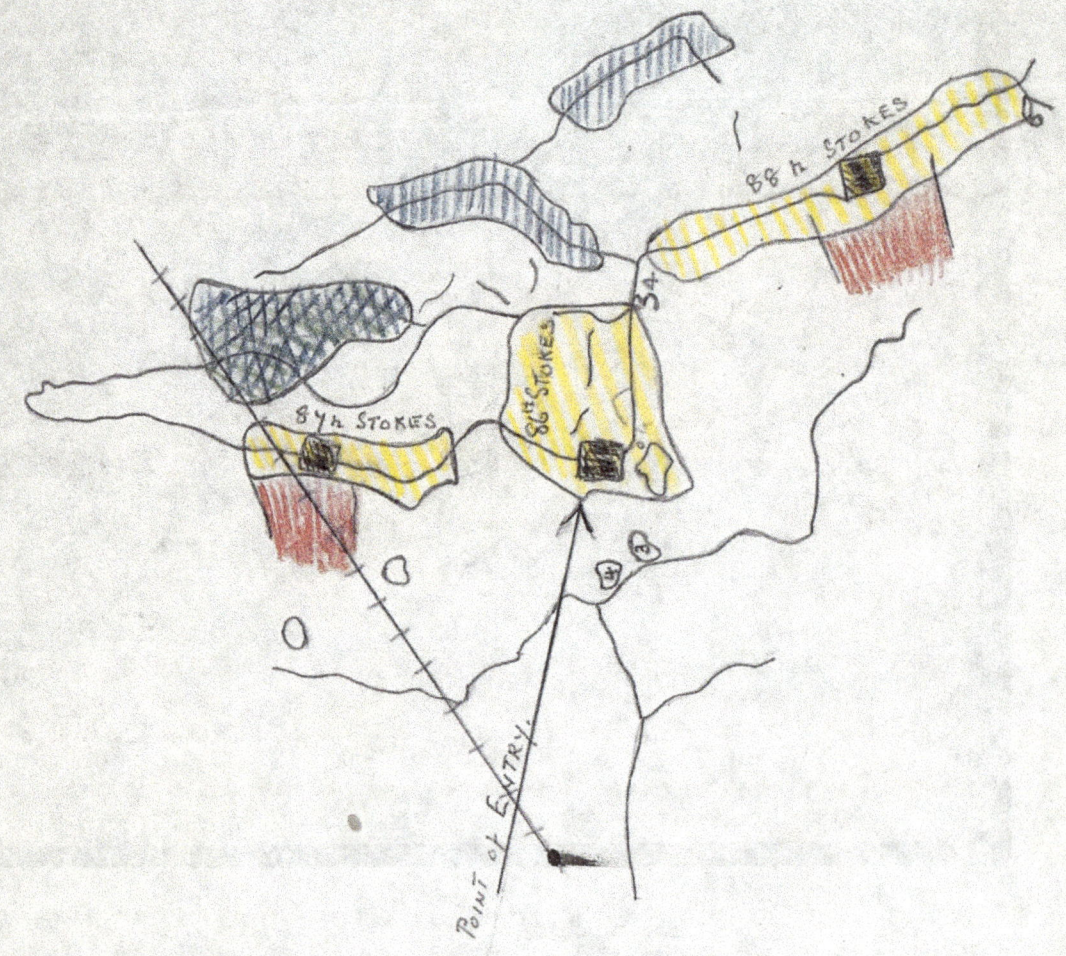

relieved.

Trenches.   Front line 5' deep, 4' across top, 2½' bottom. Parapet thick and well made. Towards the North a foot of water was lying in the trench. Brushwood lined dug-outs under the parapet, (topped with timbers) with centre strut about 6' x 6' and 4' high. All dug-outs empty. No deep dug-outs.

Second line much the same as front line.

Wire between First and Second lines - very thick and strong.

The trenches which were entered had been considerably knocked about by our Stokes Mortars.

2nd October, 1916.

Major-General,
Commanding 29th Division.

Headquarters,

VIIIth Corps.

SECRET

HEADQUARTERS,
29th DIVISION,
GENERAL STAFF.

No. C.G.S.53/10
Date. 1/10/16.

      Herewith report on raid carried out last night by the 1st Border Regiment.

                                        (Signed) G.A.N.Robertson

                                                Captain, G.S.,

                                      for Lieut-Colonel, G.S.,

1st October, 1916.   for G.O.C., 29th Division.

Report on Raid made by 1st Border Regiment on night 30th Sept.1916.

The Covering Party consisting of a Sergeant and 6 riflemen to guard the left flank, a Sergeant and 7 men with Lewis Gun to guard the right flank, were posted at about 7.45 p.m. in the nearer line of trees opposite WILLOW SALIENT. At 8.10 p.m. the raiding party began to leave our trench and were all in position in "NO MANS LAND" as arranged by 8.15 p.m.

During the first 15 minutes of the bombardment the party worked forward to the line of big trees without mishap, and crossed to the line of willows in front of enemy trench by 8.30 p.m. During his second stage of the advance one lance-corporal sustained a slight wound in the hand from a fragment of one of our shells.

At 8.50 p.m. the O.C. Raid left the head of the column by the willows and went forward to reconnoitre the wire. There were a great many enemy flare lights, but there was no firing from the enemy front line and it is probable that enemy were on the flanks or in the support trenches. The wire proved to have been very successfully knocked about by Trench Mortar fire but some inner belts of wire remained too high for easy passage. Accordingly wire-cutters were tried, but this method seemed slow, and at 8.55 p.m. the O.C. returned to party to begin advance through wire prepared to use bangalore torpedoes for any considerable obstructions near parapet. On a roll of concertina wire which remained little damaged in the line of advance, 3 bangalore torpedoes were tried. The fitting of the torpedoes in concertina wire turned out to be quite simple and was well done. Each of the torpedoes failed, however, to detonate owing to the dampness of fuzes. They had evidently been injured in the journey across "NO MANS LAND", as the Very light cases used to protect them had come off.

The O.C. Raid then noticed an easy gap which had been blown in the wire to the right, and the party trampled down what was left of the wire, and made a rush for the parapet. All arrangements worked as they had been planned, the point of entry being only a matter of yards away from that intended. The Right and Left Blocking Parties both experienced some bombing from enemy on flanks. The trench on right of point of entry had been rather badly blown in by our Artillery, and a group of men protected by the blockage sent up Very lights, and brought rifle fire and bombs to bear on right blocking party, from trench in rear of our right. Our bombers retaliated with evident effect, as the enemy party retreated and the sending up of Very lights ceased.

The right searching party found in the main communication trench for some 30 yards to right of the point of entry, 2 dugouts under the parapet. These were securely built, but small, and had merely wooden frames. They were carpeted with straw. In one of these a man was found who was made prisoner. The right communication trench was badly knocked about, and the large dugout shown in the aerial photo, was entirely demolished.

Several dead or unconscious bodies were found in the barbed wire in front of this sector, and several of the enemy who retreated down the communication trenches were fired on and chased, one at least was killed.

Left Blocking Party.

This party got into position opposite the left communication trench noticed in the aerial photo. The enemy threw a large number of bombs at them, but without effect. Our men replied vigorously throwing almost all the bombs they had and kept the enemy on the flank at bay, even if they did no further damage. Four dugouts were found in this section of trench and produced 6 prisoners. The dugouts were of the same pattern as those noted above and all under the parapet. Two of the enemy were killed, one shot and one bayonetted.

All prisoners (8) seemed unwilling to surrender themselves but were obviously frightened.

General.

The trenches were slightly deeper and wider than our

/ front

front line, they had no trench boards but a good wooden firestep. The revetting was for the most part, wooden trellis-work. The floor of the trench was covered with straw. A considerable quantity of bombs, equipment, clothing and papers were found. A large bell for Gas Alarm was found on the parapet at point of entry, and the trench seemed liberally supplied with long-handled bombs. About 25% of the men seen in the trench wore metal helmets. Uniforms and equipment were in a very good state of repair, and everything was noticeably clean and tidy.

The Sap search party.

A recent reconnaissance of the Boche front line by daylight had led us to suppose that this sap was now very little used, and would not produce anything of interest. This was confirmed in fact, and the junction of the sap and the trench had been so blown in by our shells as to be hardly recognisable. Accordingly the sap party which had been sent to search it returned to the main party for work in the front line trench.

29th Divn. Letters - "G" 564
Herewith report on the
raid by 1/Border Regt.
Will you kindly have a
copy made & sent to this
Brigade please -

S Stirling Cookson
Capt
for Brig Gen - Comdg
87th I.B.

1/10/16

Ref: Scheme for
Raid for 1/Border Regt.

Report on Raid made by 1st Berks Regt.
on night 30th Sept. 1916.

561

The Covering Party consisting of a sergeant and 6 riflemen to guard the left flank — a sergeant and seven men with Lewis Gun to guard the right flank were posted at about 19:45 in the nearer line of trees opposite Wieltje Salient.

At 20:10 the raiding party began to leave our trench and were all in position in "No man's Land" as arranged by 20:15.

During the first 15 minutes of the bombardment the party worked forward to the line of big trees without mishap and crossed to the line of willows in front of enemy trench by 20:30.

During this second stage of the advance one lance-corporal sustained a slight wound in the hand from a fragment of one of our shells.

At 20:50 the O.C. Raid left the head of the column by the willows and went forward to reconnoitre the wire. There were a great many enemy flare lights shot but there was no firing from the enemy front line and it is probable that enemy were on the flanks or in the support trenches – The wire proved to have been very successfully knocked about by Trench Mortar fire but some inner belts of wire remained too high for easy passage. Accordingly wire-cutters were tried but this method seemed slow, and at 20:55 the O.C. returned to party to begin advance through wire prepared to use Bangalore torpedoes for any considerable obstruction near parapet. On a roll of concertina wire which remained little undamaged in the line of advance

3 bangalore torpedoes were tried. The fitting of the torpedoes in concertina wire turned out to be quite simple and was well done. Each of the torpedoes however failed to detonate owing to the dampness of fuses. They had evidently been injured in the journey across "No Man's Land" as the Verey light cases used to protect them had come off. The O.C. said then noticed an easy gap which had been blown in the wire to the right, and the party trampled down what was left of wire and made a rush for the parapet. All arrangements worked as they had been planned, the point of entry being only a matter of yards away from that intended.

The Right and Left [4] Blocking Parties both
experienced some bombing from enemy on flanks — [56]
the trench on right of point of entry had been
rather badly ~~beaten~~ blown in by our Artillery and
a group of men protected by the blockage sent
up very lights and brought rifle fire and
bombs to bear on right blocking party from
trench in rear of our ~~system~~ right. Our bombers
retaliated with evident effect as the
enemy party retreated and sending up of Very
lights ceased.

The night searching party found in the main
communication trench for some 30 yds. of right of the point of
entry 2 dugouts under the parapet, these were securely built
but small and had merely wooden frames. They were
carpeted with straw. In one of them a man was found who
was made prisoner. The right communication trench was
badly knocked about & the large dugout shown in the aerial photo.
was entirely demolished. Several dead or unconscious bodies
were found in the barbed wire in front of this sector, and several
enemy who retreated down the communication trenches were fired on
and ?chased, one at least was killed.

5

Left Blocking Party

569

This party got in to position opposite the left communication trench noticed in the aerial photo. The enemy threw a large number of bombs at them but without effect. Our men replied vigorously throwing almost all the bombs they had and kept the enemy on the flank at bay even if they did no further damage.

Left Searching Party

Four dugouts were found in this section of trench and produced 6 prisoners. The dugouts were of the same pattern as those noted above and all under the parapet.

Two of the enemy were killed, one shot & one bayonetted.

All prisoners (*) seemed unwilling to surrender themselves but were obviously frightened.

General.

The trenches were slightly deeper & wider than our front line; they had no trench boards but a good wooden firestep. The revetting was for the most part wooden trellis-work. The floor of the trench was covered with straw. A considerable quantity of bombs, equipment, clothing & papers were found. A large bell for Gas Alarm was found on the parapet at point of entry, and the trench seemed liberally supplied with long-handled bombs. About 25% of men seen in the trench wore metal helmets. Uniforms & equipment were in a very good state of repair and everything was noticeably clean & tidy.

The Sap Search party

A recent reconnaissance of the Boche front line by daylight had led us to suppose that this sap was now very little used & would not produce anything of interest. This was confirmed in fact and the junction of the sap & the trench had been so blown in by

Appendix 3(a)

DISPOSITION OF UNITS OF 29TH DIVISION ON MORNING 5TH OCTOBER

86th Brigade.

Brigade Headquarters	WORMHOUDT
2nd Royal Fusiliers	WORMHOUDT
1st Lancashire Fusiliers	WORMHOUDT
16th Middlesex Regiment	WORMHOUDT
1st Royal Dublin Fusiliers	WORMHOUDT
86th Machine Gun Coy.	WORMHOUDT
86th Trench Mortar Battery	WORMHOUDT

87th Brigade.

Brigade Headquarters	PROVEN
2nd South Wales Borderers	L. Camp
1st K.O.S.Bs.	H. Camp
1st Royal Inniskilling Fusiliers	K. Camp
1st Border Regiment	J. Camp
87th Machine Gun Coy.	J. Camp
87th Trench Mortar Battery	J. Camp

88th Brigade.

Brigade Headquarters	RAMPARTS, YPRES, I.8.d.1.7.
4th Worcester Regiment	Right Sector, right sub-sector.
2nd Hampshire Regiment	" " left "
1st Essex Regiment	POPERINGHE
1st Newfoundland Regiment	POPERINGHE
88th Machine Gun Coy.	POPERINGHE
88th Trench Mortar Battery	POPERINGHE

1/2nd Monmouth Regiment   A. Camp

5th October, 1916.

Captain, G.S.,
29th Division.

Appendix 3 (6).

DISPOSITION OF UNITS OF 29TH DIVISION ON NIGHT 5th/6th OCTOBER.

86th BRIGADE.

    Brigade Headquarters   WORMHOUDT
    2nd Royal Fusiliers   WORMHOUDT
    1st Lancashire Fusiliers   WORMHOUDT
    16th Middlesex Regiment   WORMHOUDT
    1st Royal Dublin Fusiliers   WORMHOUDT
    86th Machine Gun Coy   WORMHOUDT
    86th Trench Mortar Battery   WORMHOUDT

87th BRIGADE.

    Brigade Headquarters   POPERINGHE
    2nd South Wales Borderers   J. Camp
    1st K.O.S.Bs.   M. Camp
    1st Royal Inniskilling Fusiliers   K. Camp
    1st Border Regiment   L. Camp
    87th Machine Gun Company   J. Camp
    87th Trench Mortar Battery   J. Camp

88th BRIGADE.

    Brigade Headquarters   POPERINGHE
    4th Worcestershire Regiment   C. Camp
    2nd Hampshire Regiment   BRANDHOEK
    1st Essex Regiment   POPERINGHE
    1st Newfoundland Reg.   POPERINGHE
    88th Machine Gun Company   POPERINGHE
    88th Trench Mortar Battery   POPERINGHE

    1st/2nd Monmouth Regiment   A. Camp

our shelters as to be hardly recognizable. 5.20
Accordingly the sap party which had been sent to search
it returned to the main party for work in the front line trench.
The O.C. Raid would like to bring to notice the names
of the following officers N.C.O's & men for special
reward.
This report will follow in due course.

W. de H. Robinson
Lieut.

Appendix 3(c).

571

LOCATIONS - 29TH DIVISION - 10th OCTOBER 1916

Divisional Headquarters	RIBEMONT.
86th Brigade Headquarters.-	DERNANCOURT.
2nd Royal Fusiliers	"
1st Lancashire Fusiliers	"
1st Royal Dublin Fusiliers	"
16th Middlesex Regiment	"
86th M. G. Co.,	"
86th T. M. By.,	"
87th Brigade Headquarters.-	BUIRE
2nd South Wales Borderers	"
1st K.O.S.B.s	"
1st Royal Inniskilling Fus.	"
1st Border Regiment	"
87th M. G. Co.,	"
87th T. M. By.,	"
88th Brigade Headquarters.-	
4th Worcester Regiment,	(POMMIERS CAMP
2nd Hants. Regiment,	((S.26.)
1st Essex Regiment,	(temporarily
1st Newfoundland Regiment,	(attached
88th M. G. Co.,	(12th Division.
88th T. M. By.,	(
1/2nd Monmouth Regiment,	MONTAUBAN (S.28.d)
C.R.E. Headquarters.-	RIBEMONT
Royal Engineers.-	
1/2nd London Field Co.,	S.26.c
1/3rd Kent Field Co.,	BUIRE
1/1st West Riding Field Co.	DERNANCOURT
Divisional Train Headquarters	RIBEMONT
No. 1 Company	with Artillery to DAOURS.
No. 2 Company	DERNANCOURT
No. 3 Company	BUIRE
No. 4 Company	S.26.c.
A.D.M.S.	
87th Field Ambulance	RIBEMONT
88th " "	BUIRE
89th " "	CORBIE
16th Sanitary Section	DERNANCOURT
	RIBEMONT
A.D.V.S.	RIBEMONT
18th Mobile Veterinary Section	"
D.A.D.O.S.	RIBEMONT
Divisional R.E. Dump	RIBEMONT
Salvage Dump	MERICOURT
Reinforcement Railhead	DERNANCOURT
Supplies	CORBIE
Refilling Point for 11th instant	BUIRE-DERNANCOURT Main R@

Appendix 3(d)

LOCATIONS - 29TH DIVISION - 13th OCTOBER 1916.

Divisional Headquarters	RIBEMONT.
86th Brigade Headquarters	) S.20.a.0.5
2nd Royal Fusiliers	) S.E. edge of
1st Lancashire Fusiliers	) MAMETZ WOOD
1st Royal Dublin Fusiliers	)
16th Middlesex Regiment	)
86th M. G. Co., ...	)
86th T. M. By., ...	)
87th Brigade Headquarters	)
2nd South Wales Borderers	)
1st K. O. S. B.s	) F.8.c.
1st Royal Inniskilling Fus.	) FRICOURT
1st Border Regiment	) CAMP
87th M. G. Co., ...	)
87th T. M. By., ...	)
88th Brigade Headquarters	) Transport Lines
4th Worcester Regiment	) POMMIERS CAMP
2nd Hants. Regiment, ...	) (S.26.c)
1st Essex Regiment, ...	) temporarily
1st Newfoundland Regiment	) attached
88th M. G. Co., ...	) 12th Division.
88th T. M. By., ...	)
1/2nd Monmouth Regiment, ...	COSY CORNER S.27.c.7.6.
C.R.E. Headquarters.-	RIBEMONT.
Royal Engineers.-	
1/2nd London Field Co.	S.26.c. 3-2
1/3rd Kent Field Co.	S.20.a.0.5
1/1st West Riding Field Co.	F.8.c.
Divisional Train Headquarters.-	RIBEMONT.
No.1 Company	D.18.a.
No.2 Company	E.10.central
No.3 Company	"
No.4 Company	"
A. D. M. S.-	RIBEMONT
87th Field Ambulance	F.8.c.
88th Field Ambulance	RIBEMONT
89th Field Ambulance	S.20.a.0.5.
16th Sanitary Section, ...	RIBEMONT.
A. D. V. S., ...	RIBEMONT.
18th Mobile Veterinary Section.	"
D. A. D. O. S.	RIBEMONT.
Divisional R.E. Dump	RIBEMONT.
Reinforcement Railhead	ALBERT.
Supplies "	"
Refilling Point for 13th inst., less Artillery	E.10.central
" " " " Artillery only	S. of ALBERT D.12.d. on ALBERT-AMIENS Road.

==============================

Appendix 3(e).

SECRET.

HEADQUARTERS.
29th DIVISION.
INTELLIGENCE.
No. S.G. 39
Date 21.10.16

573

DISPOSITIONS.

20 - 10 - 16.

	SITUATION.	HEADQUARTERS.
RIGHT SECTOR.		
Brigade Headquarters.		S.12.b.8.8.
2nd S.W.B.	GREASE TRENCH.	N.26.c.3.0. (PILGRIMS WAY).
1st R. Innis. Fus.	2 Coys. in HILT TRENCH, 2 Coys. in old firing line behind HILT TRENCH with post in gunpits above N.20.c.9.3.	N.26.c.7.3. (GIRD TRENCH).
1st K.O.S.B.	2 Coys. in PIONEER TRENCH. 2 Coys. in BULL'S ROAD.	N.31.b.8.0. (BULL'S ROAD).
1st Border Regt.	SWITCH and GAP TRENCHES.	T.1.d.4.1. (SWITCH TRENCH).
87th M. Gun Coy.	8 Vickers Guns in GREASE TRENCH. 4 " " in HILT TRENCH. 4 " " (reserve) in GIRD TRENCH.	
87th T.M. Battery.	Front Line and GIRD ALLEY.	
LEFT SECTOR.		
Brigade Headquarters.		S.12.b.8.8.
16th Middlesex Regt.	1 Coy. front line from N.20.c.9.1 to N.20.c.4.8. 1 Coy. SUNKEN ROAD and GIRD TRENCH. 2 Coys. in SMOKE TRENCH.	N.31.b.3.1. (BULL'S ROAD).
1st R. Dublin Fus.	1 Coy. front line from N.20.c.4.8 to N.19.b.4.7. 1 Coy. GIRD TRENCH. 2 Coys. in SMOKE TRENCH.	N.31.b.3.1. (BULL'S ROAD).
1st Lanc. Fus.	SWITCH TRENCH.	
2nd Royal Fus.	DELVILLE WOOD.	
86th M.G. Coy.	Trenches.	S.12.b.9.9.
86th T.M. Battery.	Trenches.	S.23.c.2.4.
RESERVE.		
88th Brigade.	N. of BERNAFAY WOOD.	QUARRY. (S.22.d.9.4).

21st October, 1916.

Lieut-Colonel, G.S.,
29th Division.

SECRET Appendix 3

DISPOSITIONS OF THE 29TH DIVISION - 26TH OCTOBER 1916.

No. I.G.39

LEFT SECTOR.

86th Brigade.

16th Middlesex Regiment.	Right Sub-sector.
1st Royal Dub. Fusiliers.	Left Sub-sector.
2nd Royal Fusiliers.	Support (SWITCH TRENCH).
1st Lancashire Fusiliers.	Reserve (DELVILLE WOOD).
86th M.G. Coy.	S.12.b.7.7.
86th T.M. Battery.	S.23.c.2.1.

RIGHT SECTOR

87th Brigade.

2nd S. Wales Borderers.	Right Sub-sector.
1st R. Innis. Fus.	Left Sub-sector.
1st K.O.S.B.	Support (BULLS ROAD).
1st Border Regiment.	Reserve (SWITCH TRENCH).
87th M.G. Coy.	12 guns Front Line. 4 guns Reserve (GIRD TRENCH).
87th T.M. Battery.	Front line and GIRD ALLEY.

88th Brigade

In Divisional Reserve.   BERNAFAY WOOD

Sgd. Robertson
Captain, G.S.,
29th Division.

26th October, 1916.

SECRET Appendix 3(8)

HEADQUARTERS,
29th DIVISION.
INTELLIGENCE.

No. I.G.39

DISPOSITIONS OF 29th DIVISION ON 28th OCTOBER 1916

86th Brigade.

1st Essex Regiment	Right Sub-Sector.
2nd Hampshire Regiment	Left Sub-Sector. 575
16th Middlesex Regiment	2 Coys Switch Trench. 2 Coys N.E.dge TRONES WOOD
1st Royal Dub. Fusiliers	DELVILLE WOOD. Brigade Reserve
2nd Royal Fusiliers) 1st Lancashire Fusiliers)	Divisional Reserve Bernafay Wood.
86th Machine Gun Company	S. 12. b 7.7
86th T. M. Battery	BERNAFAY WOOD.

87th Brigade.

3 Coys 4th Worcesters relieved 2nd S. Wales Borderers	Right Sub-Sector
1st R. Innis. Fus.	Left Sub-Sector
3 Coys Newfoundland Battalion relieved 1st K.O.S.B.	Support, Bulls Road etc.
2nd S. Wales Borderers Relieve 1st Border Regt.	Brigade Reserve Switch Trench.
1st K.O.S.B.) 1st Border Regiment)	BERNAFAY WOOD Divisional Reserve.

28th October 1916.

SN Robertson

Captain, G.S.

29th Division.

DISPOSITIONS OF THE 29TH DIVISION - 29TH OCTOBER, 1916.

Appendix 3 (b).

RIGHT SECTOR.

4th Worcester Regiment.	Right Sub-sector.
Newfoundland Regiment.	Left Sub-sector.
1st R. Innis. Fusiliers.	Support (BULLS ROAD).
2nd South Wales Borderers.	Reserve (SWITCH TRENCH).

LEFT SECTOR.

1st Essex Regiment.	Right Sub-sector.
2nd Hampshire Regiment.	Left Sub-sector.
16th Middlesex Regiment.	Support (SWITCH TRENCH).
1st R. Dublin Fusiliers.	Reserve (DELVILLE WOOD).

Appendix 3(i).

SECRET.

LOCATIONS - 29th DIVISION - Night 30/31st October 1916.

Divisional Headquarters	CORBIE.
1/2nd London Field Co. R.E.	MAMETZ VILLAGE (huts) F.5.c.4.4.
1/3rd Kent Field Co. R.E.	MAMETZ WOOD CAMP. S.20.a.
1/1st West Riding Field Co. R.E.	FRICOURT CAMP.
86th Brigade Headquarters	VILLE & MERICOURT.
3 Battalions, T.M.Battery, and M.G.Company.	-ditto-
16th Middlesex Regiment	ALBERT.
87th Brigade Headquarters	FRICOURT CAMP.
3 Battalions, T.M.Battery, and M.G.Company.	-ditto-
1st Border Regiment	ALBERT.
88th Brigade Headquarters	POMMIER CAMP.
2 Battalions, T.M.Battery, and M.G.Company	-ditto-
1st Essex Regiment and 2nd Hampshire Regiment	MAMETZ VILLAGE (huts)
Pioneer Battalion	POMMIER CAMP.
S.A.A.Sections	E.10.b.
87th Field Ambulance	FRICOURT CAMP.
88th & 89th Field Ambulances	BECORDEL.
Sanitary Section	CORBIE.
Mobile Veterinary Section	E.10.b.
Divisional Train	E.10.b.
Reserve Company	CORBIE & MERICOURT.

C.J. Fuller
Lieut. Colonel, G.S.
29th October 1916. for A.A.&.Q.M.G., 29th Division.

Appendix 4

HEADQUARTERS. 29th DIVISION. INTELLIGENCE.

29TH DIVISION DAILY SUMMARY.

From 12 Noon 28.10.16. to 12 Noon 29.10.16.

OPERATIONS.

Artillery. GUEUDECOURT was shelled intermittently throughout the day, also SWITCH TRENCH and GIRD SUPPORT. FLERS received a little attention, but the shelling in that area below normal.

INTELLIGENCE.

Red rockets were continually sent up throughout the night in the Left Sector.

A prisoner was captured this morning by the Royal Inniskilling Fusiliers at about N.20.b.7.2. He belongs to the 101st Reserve Regiment and to the Class 1917.

The enemy's saps in N.20.d. and along the South-eastern edge of the road in front of PETROL LANE, are all heavily wired.

WORK.

Three saps have now been completed in N.20.c.
One starts from N.20.c.8.3 and runs almost due East to within about 150 yards from the enemy sap at N.20.d.05.40. It is about 30 yards in length, is 3 feet wide and 3 feet deep.
The second sap starts at about N.20.c.5.5 and continues for about 130 yards towards the enemy's sap at N.20.c.95.75. It stops about 100 yards from that point. It is about 3 feet 6 inches deep and 3 feet wide, and is in good condition.
The third sap starts at about N.20.c.3.8½, is about 250 yards in length, and down to within about 100 yards of the enemy sap at N.20.c.9.9. It is 3 feet deep, but wet in places.

HILT TRENCH has been extended in a South-westerly direction and the barricade has been advanced to within about 40 yards of the bend in the road, and erected about 7 feet high.

FLARE ALLEY has been widened to standard dimensions and cleared for a distance of 700 yards from a point at N.26.c.2.4 and running in a Southerly direction.

Communication Trench between SUNKEN ROAD at N.26.a.2.9 and GROVE ALLEY (N.19.d.7.0) was continued in a Westerly direction for 65 yards and cut through to GROVE ALLEY. 150 yards of trench started on the night 27th/28th was deepened to 4 feet 6 inches.

A party of 20 men have continued laying and repairing trench boards on COCOA LANE track through DELVILLE WOOD and North of the Wood to S.12.d.7.6.

GREASE TRENCH has been extended as a Communication Trench across the road and a short length of fire trench cut in far bank facing N.W. This has been wired with hoop wire around the post. Sap has been cut from the post, running North to the bank about 20 yards away.

Captain, G.S.,
29th Division.

29th October, 1916.

29TH DIVISION DAILY SUMMARY.

From 12 Noon 27.10.16. to 12 Noon 28.10.16.

OPERATIONS.

Artillery. GUEUDECOURT was shelled intermittently, also FLERS and the Valley in front of DELVILLE WOOD. A shell was observed to fall near the N.E. corner of DELVILLE and throw up a shower of lights similar to Very Lights, about 4.20 p.m.
There was also considerable reciprocal shooting S.E. of LE TRANSLOY.
Several gas shells landed near SMOKE TRENCH between 1 and 2.30 a.m.

INTELLIGENCE.

Smoke was seen rising from enemy lines about N.20.d.7.8 at 11 a.m. Artillery were informed.

Two Germans were killed last night and identified by shoulder straps as of 101st Regiment. Documents taken from the bodies of these soldiers are enclosed herewith.

Another German killed at the same time has been identified by shoulder straps as belonging to the 64th Regiment.

From these identifications it would appear that the expected relief is at the present moment taking place. The ~~latter~~ Regiment is a Saxon Regiment and belongs to the ~~24th~~ Division of the 12th Reserve Corps. (DRESDEN Depot).

[margin: 161st Reserve Regt / 23rd Reserve Div]

The bodies were found near N.20.b.7.1.

Two enemy machine guns of the 1916 pattern were found in SUNKEN ROAD at N.20.b.8.1. They are being forwarded.

WORK.

GIRD SUPPORT has been deepened a foot and cleared in platoon areas.

Shelters and Dug-outs have been made in SMOKE TRENCH.

FLARE ALLEY. This trench has been widened to standard dimensions and cleared for a distance of 720 yards from the SUNKEN ROAD at N.26.a.2.9 South.

Communication Trench between SUNKEN ROAD and GROVE ALLEY has been dug for a distance of 150 yards, 5 yards South of the Road, to 4 feet wide at the top and 2 feet wide at the bottom.

Notice Boards marked FLARE ALLEY and GROVE ALLEY have been erected at N.26.a.2.9 and N.26.d.7.0.

Captain, G.S.,

28th October, 1916.   29th Division.

I.C.175.

29TH DIVISION DAILY SUMMARY.

From 12 Noon 26.10.16. to 12 Noon 27.10.16.

580

ARTILLERY.

Artillery. Enemy artillery shelled the Left Sector
with shrapnel during the night of the 25th/26th instant.
PIKE, GAP and STORM TRENCHES were shelled intermittently
during the day.
No special heavy firing was reported from the Right
Sector.
At 8.30 p.m. yesterday enemy fired on our front line
West of strong point at N.20.d.7.9.
Our artillery fired on enemy front line.

Aeroplanes. Hostile aeroplanes about 14 strong, flew
over our lines in the Right Sector yesterday.

Patrols. An officer's patrol from the Right Sector
proceeded to reconnoitre the enemy front line. They
proceeded about 100 yards and the officer was killed.
The men who returned stated that the enemy trenches seemed
to be very full of men, and that there was no wire as far
as he had gone. (Direction taken was probably along the
N.E. end of STORMY TRENCH.

INTELLIGENCE.

Enemy was seen this morning near the road from
N.20.b.7.0 to N.20.b.7.5. Our artillery was notified
and the men were seen to hurriedly scatter.

Three Germans were killed last night at approximately
N.20.b.7.2 by one of our covering parties. Identifications
are being forwarded under separate cover.

Patrol reports no wire in front of STORMY TRENCH.

WORK.

Trenches in the front line have been further improved
as far as possible.
Communication trench to strong point at N.20.b.7.1
is now cut, and men can get to it by day.
Communication trench between gun-pits and GREASE TRENCH
deepened as far as small number of men available would
permit.
16 Coils of wire put out in front of GREASE TRENCH.

Patrols. A patrol left our lines at 4 a.m. on the
26th instant at N.20.d.8.9 and advanced along the eastern
edge of the SUNKEN ROAD until coming to the German wire.
A party of about 15 Germans were wiring, besides other
small working parties. Patrol returned safely.

No hostile wire was found by patrols from the Right Sector
on the night of the 26th instant.

LATER INFORMATION.

Note. The identifications recovered from the three Germans
referred to above, show that they belong to the 19th Reserve
Division, 1st Ersatz Battalion of the 88nd Regiment, which
is normal for enemy troops in this sector. This shows
that the expected change has not
yet taken place.
                                        Captain, G.S.,

27th October, 1916.   29th Division.

D.S.174.

29TH DIVISION DAILY SUMMARY.

From 12 Noon 25.10.16. to 12 Noon 26.10.16.

HEADQUARTERS.
29th DIVISION.
INTELLIGENCE.

No. 581
Date.

OPERATIONS.

Artillery. BULL'S ROAD, SWITCH TRENCH, DELVILLE VALLEY, FLERS and GUEUDECOURT, were shelled intermittently throughout the day. Several direct hits were obtained by the enemy, on the road between Brigade Headquarters in S.12.b. and LONGUEVAL.
Previous to the shelling of GUEUDECOURT and FLERS, a strong enemy air reconnaissance was observed, and appeared to direct the fire.
The dump at BULL'S ROAD was damaged at 11 a.m.
Our guns replied by shelling BAYONET TRENCH.

Patrols. A patrol left our line at N.20.c.3.7 and proceeded towards BAYONET TRENCH, along the line of willow trees in a North-easterly direction. The enemy was observed in shell holes in front of his trench. From these, enemy were sending up flares, some towards his own line. Shell holes were very close together, and shelters of iron were found inside them. The patrol proceeded to within 20 yards of BAYONET TRENCH, but could not find any trace of wire in this part of the line. They were occasionally fired at, but returned safely.

~~This corroborates the information of the deserter from the 596th Regiment, referred to in yesterday's summary.~~ (Corps)

INTELLIGENCE.

The expected relief of the 6th (Brandenberg) Division is probably taking place. Men were seen on the 25th opposite the right sector wearing helmets instead of the usual cap.

WORK.

Maintenance work has been carried on in the front trenches as far as circumstances would permit.

26th October, 1916.

San Robertson
Captain, G.S.,
29th Division.

D.S.173.

**HEADQUARTERS.
29th DIVISION.
INTELLIGENCE.**

29TH DIVISION DAILY SUMMARY.

From 12 Noon 24.10.16. to 12 Noon 25.10.16.

OPERATIONS.

Artillery. Hostile artillery showed increased activity during the morning, the principle targets being SUNKEN ROAD and N.26.a. and b., trench and vicinity of Brigade Headquarters in S.12.b.

FLERS was shelled with heavy guns at frequent intervals during yesterday afternoon.

About 3.45 this afternoon 10.5 c.m. shells dropped near BULL'S ROAD, which burst with moderate explosion into white stars resembling Very lights.

Shelling of FLERS, DELVILLE VALLEY and GUEUDECOURT, has been about normal.

Front line in front of GUEUDECOURT was shelled during the afternoon with heavy guns.

Our guns opened all along the line at 2.30 a hurricane bombardment. No direct retaliation was observed.

Snipers. Enemy's snipers have been active in the direction of N.20.central.

Lights. Left Brigade report that the lights sent up the preceeding day which burst into golden rain, resulted in the 5.9" guns lengthening their range.

Patrols. Patrol from GREASE TRENCH reports Listening Post in front of the line from N.20.a.70.75 to N.20.b.95.25.

A patrol went out at 11.20 p.m. from the old strong point at N.20.a.1.1 to about 300 yards N.E., and then moved to the left, but on account of the fog it was difficult to distinguish much. No wire was encountered, and what appeared to be a forward enemy trench about 80 yards in front of the enemy front line was crossed.

Another patrol left the same point at 11.45 p.m. and examined from N.20.central to our right. About 200 yards in front of our line was a single strand of ¼" wire extending for 30 yards, otherwise no wire was encountered.

WORK. An assembly trench 200 yards long was started at N.20.a.1.1 and runs N.W. and S.E. Trench is 3 ft. deep and 2 ft. 6 in. wide.

FLARE ALLEY. Work was continued for 600 yards in a Northerly direction from a point 100 yards North of BULL'S ROAD. No trench boards were found at the bottom of this section of trench.

COMMUNICATION TRENCH to Gun Pits. 420 yards of trench were deepened to 4'6" and widened where necessary.

COMMUNICATION TRENCH from SUNKEN ROAD to GREASE TRENCH. 100 yards of trench from SUNKEN ROAD deepened to 4'3".

Party of one platoon has continued digging sumps during the day.

Visibility has been bad all day.

25.10.16.

Captain, G.S.,
29th Division.

D.S.172.

HEADQUARTERS
29th DIVISION.
INTELLIGENCE.

No. ......
Date. 583

29TH DIVISION DAILY SUMMARY.

From 12 Noon 23.10.16. to 12 Noon 24.10.16.

OPERATIONS.

Artillery. The enemy shelled the road from N.25.a.7.0 to GROVE ALLEY, yesterday morning.
Yesterday afternoon between 2 and 4, he shelled the Left Sector, and between 8 p.m. and 9.30 p.m. put a heavy barrage behind the front line of the left battalion in N.20.c and just in front of reserve trenches.
Between 6 and 8.30 this morning GUEUDECOURT was shelled. Our right front suffered no material damage from the bombardment yesterday afternoon.
During the bombardment last night enemy sent up several red and white flares breaking into golden rain. Red rockets were also seen.

Machine Guns. Machine guns were active on the Left Sector, but flashes could not be spotted.

Patrols. A patrol left the Left Sector and moved towards the junction of SCABBARD and BAYONET Trenches. No wire was seen in front of this part of the line.

Another patrol searched for wire from N.20.a.5.7 to a line of willow trees, but could not find any.

A patrol from N.21.d.3.7 ascertained that the enemy line is about 40 yards distant. Isolated scraps of wire are in front of it.

WORK.

FLARE ALLEY. Work was continued on point N.31.d.2.0 for a distance of 700 yards. No trench boards were found at the bottom of this section of the trench.

COCOA LANE. Work was continued North of T.1.d.5.8 for a distance of 470 yards. Two sump holes and drains (dug) dug into them from the trench. The part of the trench South of SWITCH TRENCH which had been blown in, has been cleared. A day party (one platoon) has continued digging sumps beneath the trench boards.

Captain, G.S.,

24th October, 1916.   29th Division.

29TH DIVISION DAILY SUMMARY.

From 12 Noon 22.10.16. to 12 Noon 23.10.16.

OPERATIONS.

Artillery. On the afternoon of the 21st instant between 4 p.m. and 6 p.m. enemy artillery was active on our front line and supports, and DELVILLE VALLEY.
FLERS was heavily shelled during most of yesterday.
At about 8 p.m. a supposed S.O.S. signal from GUEUDECOURT caused temporary extra activity on the part of our Artillery.
GUEUDECOURT was also shelled consistently yesterday.
Several red rockets were fired by the enemy before they started their barrage at 4.45 p.m.
A large explosion was noticed at N.20.a.2.8 on a line slightly East of BAPAUME Church.
The Valley between SWITCH TRENCH and DELVILLE WOOD has been shelled intermittently during the whole of this morning

Aeroplanes. An aeroplane nationality unknown was destroyed by shell fire at approximately N.19.c. at 9 a.m. yesterday morning.

INTELLIGENCE.

Numerous small groups of men were seen moving about N.14 and 15, and one working party was dispersed by rifle fire from the Right Sector.

Observation has been difficult on account of fog.

WORK.

Trenches in the Left Sector have been deepened where required and cleared of mud.

Repairs have been done on trenches near the junction of GROVE ALLEY and GIRD SUPPORT.

Dug-outs have been made, and dead buried.

FLARE ALLEY. Work has been continued from this trench to a point at N.31.d.2.0. Trench was very muddy and wet, but has been cleared out, and the trench widened to required dimensions. Two sections on which work had been started on the night of the 21st/22nd, have been completed. Total distance cleared 690 yards.

COCOA LANE. Work has been continued on this trench to a point at T.1.d.6.8, 50 yards this side of GAP TRENCH. Distance cleared 450 yards.

A day working party has been employed on both FLARE ALLEY and COCOA LANE making sumps under trench boards at intervals of 50 yards.

23rd October, 1916.

Captain, G.S.,
29th Division.

29TH DIVISION DAILY SUMMARY.

From 12 Noon 21.10.16. to 12 Noon 22.10.16.

OPERATIONS.

Artillery. Enemy's artillery was very active between 3.30 p.m. and 6 p.m. on the Left Sector, and shelled N.31.central to the East of FIERS.
He also was very active in the vicinity of DELVILLE VALLEY, and during the afternoon shelled GREASE TRENCH, and placed a very heavy barrage behind GUEUDECOURT.
Our artillery fired during the day on the enemy front line.

Snipers. Enemy snipers have been active against the western end of GREASE TRENCH, apparently from the trees and small sap in N.20.d.2.5.

INTELLIGENCE.

Enemy Work. Enemy is reported to be working on his trenches at N.20.central.

Lights. About 5 a.m. three red lights followed by three green lights with golden spray, were sent up from about N.20.central, as a result of which, their artillery appeared to lengthen their range.

WORK.

Work is being continued on the front line system of trenches in the Right Sector, and communication trenches have been ~~made~~ worked on.

FLARE ALLEY. Work is continued in a North-easterly direction from SWITCH TRENCH, and 150 yards completed. A further 430 yards were started and made to standard dimensions. The continuation to BULL'S ROAD is in a bad state, but it is hoped to finish that far to-night.

COCOA LANE. This trench is very wet and muddy, but has been cleared out for a distance of 650 yards up to the road at T.1.d.2.3.

Trench boards were found at the bottom of both FLARE ALLEY and COCOA LANE.

22nd October, 1916.

Captain, G.S.,
29th Division.

Appendix 5

Appendix 5

CONFIDENTIAL

587
818

WAR DIARY.

GENERAL STAFF

29TH DIVISION.

FOR THE MONTH

OF

NOVEMBER 1916.

VOLUME XXI.

Army Form C. 2118.

WAR DIARY – GENERAL STAFF, 29TH DIVISION.

INTELLIGENCE SUMMARY.

(Erase heading not required.)

NOVEMBER, 1916.

Instructions regarding War Diaries and Intelligence Summaries are contained in F. S. Regs., Part II. and the Staff Manual respectively. Title pages will be prepared in manuscript.

588

Place	Date	Hour	Summary of Events and Information	Remarks and references to Appendices
	Nov. 1st		A Divisional Conference was held at 10 a.m. to discuss Training and Administrative questions. G.O.C. accompanied by the Commandant Divisional School (Major CLARKE) and the G.S.O.II visited DAOURS and inspected the Divisional School accommodation. Brigades remained in the same locations as yesterday. Lieut. ROSS (A.D.C.) proceeded on leave. Major CLARKE and the Divisional School instructors moved to billets in DAOURS.	
	Nov. 2nd		Heavy rain during the morning. G.S.O.1 and Adjutant RE visited the Div. School. H.R.H. the Duke of Connaught came at 4 p.m. to inspect the Royal Dublin Fusiliers.	

Army Form C. 2118.

WAR DIARY - GENERAL STAFF,
29TH DIVISION.
INTELLIGENCE SUMMARY.

(Erase heading not required.)

Instructions regarding War Diaries and Intelligence Summaries are contained in F. S. Regs., Part II. and the Staff Manual respectively. Title pages will be prepared in manuscript.

589

Place	Date	Hour	Summary of Events and Information	Remarks and references to Appendices
	Nov. 3rd		87th Brigade moved from FRICOURT CAMP to AIRAISNES (H.Q., 2 Bns., T.M. Battery and M.G. Coy.) ALLERY (1 Bn. and 87th Field Amb.) and BETTENCOURT (1 Bn.) they left ALBERT about midday and got to AIRAISNES about midnight 3rd/4th; the advanced parties had not arrived. Communication to Divisional Headquarters difficult, D.Rs. were obliged to take messages to LONG (15th Corps H.Q.). West Riding Field Coy. R.E. moved from FRICOURT to DAOURS in motor lorries. G.S.O.1 & C.R.E. visits Corps H.Qrs.	
	Nov. 4th		A.A. & Q.M.G., G.S.O. II, A.D.M.S. and S.S.O visited the 87th Brigade at AIRAISNES in the morning. The 87th Brigade advanced parties still had not arrived. Fine day. Wet night. G.S.O.1. visits Divl School	

Army Form C. 2118.

WAR DIARY - GENERAL STAFF,
29TH DIVISION.
INTELLIGENCE SUMMARY.
(Erase heading not required.)

Instructions regarding War Diaries and Intelligence Summaries are contained in F. S. Regs., Part II. and the Staff Manual respectively. Title pages will be prepared in manuscript.

590

Place	Date	Hour	Summary of Events and Information	Remarks and references to Appendices
	Nov. 5th		No change in dispositions of Division. G.S.O.I and D.A.Q.M.G. visited the H.Q. 17th Division at BERNAFAY WOOD CAMP. C.R.E., G.S.O.II and Divisional Grenadier Officer went to DaOURS to arrange for accommodation for Grenade School. Capt. ROBERTSON and 2/Lieut. COWAN visited 87th Brigade H.Q. at AIRAISNES.	
	Nov. 6th		The G.S.O.II visited the Divisional School at DaOURS in the morning. The A.P.M. and Attache "Q" Branch visited the Camps in the forward area to find out the accommodation there. The XIVth Corps telephoned to say that we may not go into the line until the 16th instant. Brigades continued training paying special attention to drill, and general smartness.	

Army Form C. 2118.

WAR DIARY - GENERAL STAFF, 29TH DIVISION.

~~INTELLIGENCE SUMMARY.~~

(*Erase heading not required.*)

Instructions regarding War Diaries and Intelligence Summaries are contained in F. S. Regs., Part II. and the Staff Manual respectively. Title pages will be prepared in manuscript.

591

Place	Date	Hour	Summary of Events and Information	Remarks and references to Appendices
	Nov. 7th		Confirmed that the Division will relieve the 8th Division on the right probably on the 16th instant. Work on erection of Nissen huts for the Divisional School at DAOURS progressed. The G.S.O.I visited the 86th and 88th Brigades in the afternoon to explain the G.O.C's. wishes regarding the method of practising an attack and representation of barrages by flags.	
	Nov. 8th		The G.O.C. visited the Divisional School at DAOURS; he also went to Fourth Army Headquarters. The G.S.O.I and **4.D.A.Q.M.G.** rode to TREUX to see the 33rd Division and obtain information about the right sector of the line. The G.S.O.III and Capt. ROBERTSON went to the 87th Brigade at AIRAINES in the afternoon to tell them about the attack practice.	

T/131. Wt. W708—776. 50C000. 4/15. Sir J. C. & S.

Army Form C. 2118.

WAR DIARY – GENERAL STAFF,
29TH DIVISION.
INTELLIGENCE SUMMARY.
(Erase heading not required.)

Instructions regarding War Diaries and Intelligence Summaries are contained in F.S. Regs., Part II. and the Staff Manual respectively. Title pages will be prepared in manuscript.

Place	Date	Hour	Summary of Events and Information	Remarks and references to Appendices
	Nov. 9th		The G.O.C. accompanied by the G.S.O.I inspected two Battalions (2/R.Fus.& 16/Middlesex) of the 86th Brigade in the morning, and witnessed an attack practice in conjunction with an aeroplane. The G.S.O.II took the G.S.Os. I and II of 4th Australian Division round the Divisional School at DAOURS in the afternoon.	App. 1(a)
			A report is attached giving particulars of the operations in which the 88th Brigade took part during the time they were attached to the 12th Division during the month of October. App. 1 (b).	App. 1(b)
	Nov. 10th		The G.O.C. accompanied by the G.S.O.II inspected the Essex Regiment and 2nd Hampshire Regiment (88th Brigade) at MERICOURT, after the parade he presented Military Medals earned during the two attacks recently made by this Brigade on the enemy's trenches North of GUEUDECOURT. A practice attack was afterwards carried out by the above two Battalions, flags representing our artillery barrages. The G.S.O.I, C.R.E. and A.A. & Q.M.G. visited H.Q. 8th Division & Bde H.Qrs. at GUILLEMONT & GINCHY to obtain information concerning our future sector of the line N.E. of LES BOEUFS.	

592

Army Form C. 2118.

WAR DIARY - GENERAL STAFF,
29TH DIVISION.
~~INTELLIGENCE~~ ~~SUMMARY~~

(Erase heading not required.)

Instructions regarding War Diaries and Intelligence Summaries are contained in F.S. Regs., Part II. and the Staff Manual respectively. Title pages will be prepared in manuscript.

593

Place	Date	Hour	Summary of Events and Information	Remarks and references to Appendices
	Nov. 11th		*accompanied by G.S.O. III,* G.O.C. inspected 2 Battalions of the 87th Brigade (K.O.S.Bs. and S.W.Bs.) at AIRAISNES on parade and at an attack practice, in the morning. The G.S.O.I and G.S.O.II visited the Divisional School and Bombing School trenches in the afternoon.	
	Nov. 12th		The G.O.C., G.S.O.I and C.R.E. attended a Corps Conference at MINDEN POST ~~VUVERANNAS~~ at 10 a.m. A Church Service was held in the garden of the Divisional H.Q. chateau, the Lancashire Fusiliers attended. Capt. MORGAN and Lieut. ROSS returned from leave. Operation Order of practice attack to be carried out by the 88th Brigade is attached as App. 1(c) Orders were issued - Operation Order No. 75 - giving dates on which our Brigades would carry out reliefs in the approaching relief of the 8th Division (App.3(a)).	App. 1(c) App. 3(a)

T2134. Wt. W708-776. 500000. 4/15. Sir J.C. & S.

Army Form C. 2118.

WAR DIARY - GENERAL STAFF,
29TH DIVISION.
~~INTELLIGENCE~~ SUMMARY ~~X~~
(Erase heading not required.)

Instructions regarding War Diaries and Intelligence Summaries are contained in F. S. Regs., Part II. and the Staff Manual respectively. Title pages will be prepared in manuscript.

Place	Date	Hour	Summary of Events and Information	Remarks and references to Appendices
	Nov. 13th		The G.O.C. accompanied by the G.S.O.I inspected 2 Battalions (Newfoundland Regt. and Worcester Regt.) of the 88th Brigade at VILLE during the morning. The G.S.O.II, D.A.A. & Q.M.G., and Camp Commandant, visited the 8th Division advanced H.Q. on the MARICOURT - BERNAFAY CORNER road to obtain information and compare orders for the relief. G.S.O.III visited the Divisional School during the afternoon. Orders were issued for the move of the Division to the forward area i.e. CITADEL - SANDPITS - MEAULTE preparatory to the relief. G.H.Q. wire states that BEAUMONT - HAMEL and ST. PIERRE DIVION have been captured by us.	
			Operation Order No. 76 giving full particulars of the relief of the 8th Division by the 29th Division was issued - App. 3(b).	App. 3(b)
	Nov. 14th		87th Brigade moved in French busses from AIRAINES, ALLERY and BETTENCOURT to CITADEL. Students assembled at DAOURS for 1st Course at Divisional School. Signalling Course also commenced at DAOURS, the instructional staff consisting of 1 Officer and 3 N.C.Os. The G.O.C. inspected 2 Battalions (Lancashire Fusiliers and Dublin Fusiliers) on parade and at a practice attack near CORBIE. App. 1(d). The G.S.O.I visited the Divisional School in the afternoon.	App. 1(d)
			Agenda of Conference held at CORBIE at 5p.m. on this date is attached as App. 2(a).	App. 2(a)

394

Army Form C. 2118.

WAR DIARY - GENERAL STAFF, 29TH DIVISION.
~~INTELLIGENCE~~ SUMMARY.
(Erase heading not required.)

Instructions regarding War Diaries and Intelligence Summaries are contained in F. S. Regs., Part II. and the Staff Manual respectively. Title pages will be prepared in manuscript.

Place	Date	Hour	Summary of Events and Information	Remarks and references to Appendices
	Nov. 15th		The 88th Brigade moved from VILLE and MERICOURT to SANDPITS. 2 Battalions and H.Q. 87th Brigade moved from CITADEL to BRIQUETERIE. Divisional Headquarters moved from CORBIE to TREUX. Capt. FIRTH (Signalling Officer) returned from leave. Capt. ROBERTSON (attache G.S.) returned from leave. (to Paris) The G.S.O.I visited left sector of 8th Division trenches leaving CORBIE at 4 a.m., he was accompanied by Brigade Major 88th Brigade. The A.A.&.Q.M.G., D.A.Q.M.G., C.R.E. and Adjutant visited 87th Brigade Headquarters at BRIQUETERIE and R.E. Dumps.	
	Nov. 16th		The G.O.C. and G.S.O.I, A.A.&.Q.M.G. and C.R.E. went to Conference at Guards Division Headquarters at 10.0 am. The Corps Commander stated that the Corps front was to be considerably extended, the Guards Division to take over a portion of the French line to the South of our present line and the 29th Division to extend some hundreds of yards to the South of their present line. The G.O.C. afterwards - at 2.30 pm. - went to a discussion at Fourth Army School FLIXECOURT, on the various methods of attack. The G.S.O. II visited the Right Sector of 8th Division front. The 88th Brigade moved from SANDPITS to BRIQUETERIE and CARNOY CAMPS. 87th Brigade took over Right Sector of 8th Division line during the night of 16th/17th November. 86th Brigade moved from CORBIE to MEAULTE. Extremely cold, but fine and dry weather.	App. 3(c) App. 3(c)

T2134. Wt. W708—776. 500000. 4/15. Sir J.C. & S.

Army Form C. 2118.

WAR DIARY - GENERAL STAFF, 29TH DIVISION.
INTELLIGENCE SUMMARY.
(Erase heading not required.)

Instructions regarding War Diaries and Intelligence Summaries are contained in F. S. Regs., Part II. and the Staff Manual respectively. Title pages will be prepared in manuscript.

596

Place	Date	Hour	Summary of Events and Information	Remarks and references to Appendices
	Nov. 17th		G.S.O.III visited 8th Division Headquarters in morning. Capt. ROBERTSON visited 14th Corps H.Q. to obtain information about the boundaries of our future line after taking over from the French, but they could give him no information. G.O.C. visited 86th Brigade H.Q. at MEAULTE in morning, and the Divisional School at DAOURS in the afternoon. Still very cold weather. 88th Brigade took over left sector of 8th Division line during the night 17th/18th November.	
	Nov. 18th		Divisional Headquarters moved from TREUX to A.4.d.5.2 (Advanced H.Q.) and A.2.d.9.7. (Rear H.Q.). General de LISLE took over command from G.O.C. 8th Division at 10 a.m. The G.O.C. and G.S.O.II visited the two forward Brigade Headquarters at GUILLEMONT (87th and 88th Brigades) in the morning. H.Q. lorries did not arrive till 3 p.m. owing to traffic difficulty. Rained hard at night.	

Army Form C. 2118.

WAR DIARY - GENERAL STAFF, 29TH DIVISION.
INTELLIGENCE SUMMARY
(Erase heading not required.)

Instructions regarding War Diaries and Intelligence Summaries are contained in F. S. Regs., Part II. and the Staff Manual respectively. Title pages will be prepared in manuscript.

597

Place	Date	Hour	Summary of Events and Information	Remarks and references to Appendices
	Nov. 19th		G.O.C. went round support and reserve trenches in right sector with Brigadier-General LUCAS early. G.S.O.II accompanied by the O.C. Monmouths and Brigade Major, 88th Brigade, reconnoitred site for continuation of OZONE TRENCH from COW TRENCH to the rear, he visited the two forward Battalion Headquarters in the left sector. The G.S.O.I visited the right sector in the afternoon, and of French Brin HQrs The Corps Commander visited the G.O.C. in the afternoon. Night of 18th/19th was windy and wet.	18½
	Nov. 20th		The G.S.O.I laid a tape for a new intermediate line trench in T.10.a. The G.O.C. visited the CARNOY CAMPS in the afternoon. The Corps Commander visited the G.O.C. at 12.30 p.m. A fine day.	

Army Form C. 2118.

WAR DIARY - GENERAL STAFF, 29TH DIVISION.
INTELLIGENCE SUMMARY
(Erase heading not required.)

Instructions regarding War Diaries and Intelligence Summaries are contained in F. S. Regs., Part II. and the Staff Manual respectively. Title pages will be prepared in manuscript.

Place	Date	Hour	Summary of Events and Information	Remarks and references to Appendices
	Nov. 21st		The G.O.C. went round the whole Divisional front line early with Brigadier-General CAYLEY. A very foggy day. G.S.O.1 and C.R.E. visited MANSEL CAMP in the afternoon. The G.S.O.II visited the Pioneers and 1st Essex Camps and inspected the Drying Rooms near TRONES WOOD.	598
	Nov. 22nd		The G.S.O.II visited the left sector with Brigade Major, 88th Brigade early. Corps Commander visited G.O.C. in the evening. The G.S.O.III inspected the French Communication trenches on our right in view of our soon taking over part of their line. A foggy morning and afternoon till 2 p.m. fine. The Pioneer Battalion continued work on OZONE TRENCH and the right Communication Trench to GERMAN TRENCH. A Warning Order was received in the evening from XIV Corps saying 29th Division will be prepared to take over a portion of the French front on the night of 1st/2nd December.	

T 2134. Wt. W708-776. 500000. 4/15. Sir J.C. & S.

Army Form C. 2118.

WAR DIARY - GENERAL STAFF, 29TH DIVISION.
INTELLIGENCE SUMMARY
(Erase heading not required.)

Instructions regarding War Diaries and Intelligence Summaries are contained in F. S. Regs., Part II. and the Staff Manual respectively. Title pages will be prepared in manuscript.

599

Place	Date	Hour	Summary of Events and Information	Remarks and references to Appendices
	Nov. 23rd		The G.S.O.I accompanied by the O.C. Monmouths (Pioneer Bn) visited the communication trench on our right (FLANK TRENCH) in course of construction. The G.S.O.II visited 9th French Corps H.Q. to obtain information about the line which we shall take over from them. Capt. ROBERTSON visited the 5th Anzac Division on our left, they have no objection to our left Brigade Headquarters and left Advanced Battalion Headquarters remaining in their present positions although not now in our area. An uneventful day, some shells were fired at BERNAFAY CORNER during the morning. A fine cold day.	
	Nov. 24th		The G.S.O.II visited the right of our line where BENNETT TRENCH connects with the French left, he also looked at the new Communication Trench (FLANK AVENUE). 86th Brigade Headquarters took over from the 87th Brigade Headquarters the command of the right sector.	

Army Form C. 2118.

WAR DIARY - GENERAL STAFF, 29TH DIVISION.

~~INTELLIGENCE SUMMARY~~

(Erase heading not required.)

Instructions regarding War Diaries and Intelligence Summaries are contained in F. S. Regs., Part II. and the Staff Manual respectively. Title pages will be prepared in manuscript.

600

Place	Date	Hour	Summary of Events and Information	Remarks and references to Appendices
	Nov. 25th		The G.S.O.I visited the French line on our right to try and locate certain trenches. He also visited the right of our line (BENNETT TRENCH etc.). The G.O.C. had a conference with Brigadiers of 86th and 88th Brigades at 86th Brigade Headquarters at 3.30 p.m. It rained practically all day. Three prisoners of 81st Reserve Regiment were taken by our left Brigade (88th). Warning Order issued with regard to taking over a certain portion of the French line - App. 3(d).	App.3(d)
	Nov. 26th		A very wet day. The G.S.O.II and A.A. & Q.M.G. went to left of the line. The trenches were in a very bad condition after the rain. The G.O.C., G.S.O.I and A.A. & Q.M.G. attended a Conference at Corps Headquarters at 2.30 p.m. The 88th Brigade took 2 more prisoners in the early morning.	

T1234. Wt. W708—776. 50C090. 4/15. Sir J. C. & S.

Army Form C. 2118.

WAR DIARY - GENERAL STAFF,
29TH DIVISION.
INTELLIGENCE SUMMARY.
(Erase heading not required.)

Instructions regarding War Diaries and Intelligence Summaries are contained in F.S. Regs., Part II. and the Staff Manual respectively. Title pages will be prepared in manuscript.

601

Place	Date	Hour	Summary of Events and Information	Remarks and references to Appendices
	Nov. 27th		The G.S.O.III visited the French trenches on our immediate right in the early morning, they appear to be very bad. The G.S.O.I visited the Headquarters of the 5th Australian Division in the afternoon to arrange about liaison between our left and their right. The G.O.C. visited GUILLEMONT and TRONES WOOD Camps during the day. Operation Order No. 78 giving dates etc. on which we should take over from the French was issued on this date - App. 3(e)	App.3 (e)
	Nov. 28th		The G.S.O.II reconnoitred machine gun positions in the FLERS line and COW and JOHN BULL TRENCHES with the O.C. 88th Machine Gun Coy. during the morning. The G.O.C. visited the IXth French Corps Headquarters in the afternoon. The G.S.O.I visited the French (152nd) Divisional Headquarters in the afternoon. Capt. ROBERTSON (S.W.B.) attached to General Staff was evacuated sick.	

Army Form C. 2118.

WAR DIARY - GENERAL STAFF,
29TH DIVISION.
~~INTELLIGENCE~~ SUMMARY.
(Erase heading not required.)

Instructions regarding War Diaries and Intelligence Summaries are contained in F. S. Regs., Part II. and the Staff Manual respectively. Title pages will be prepared in manuscript.

Place	Date	Hour	Summary of Events and Information	Remarks and references to Appendices
	Nov. 29th		The G.S.O.I visited the left of the line early. The G.O.C. reconnoitred a site for the Brigade Transport lines South of MONTAUBAN. A very cold day, slight frost early. The Newfoundland and 4th Worcesters each captured a German of 104th Reserve Regiment, 24th Reserve Division, opposite FALL TRENCH. The Corps Commander visited the Divisional School at DAOURS and expressed his approval of all he saw.	
	Nov. 30th		The G.S.O.III visited FLANK AVENUE and the Intermediate line between MORVAL and the Sunken Road at T.3.d.4.1., he also looked at the machine guns in ANTELOPE TRENCH. G.S.O.II visited the two Brigade Headquarters at GUILLEMONT during the afternoon. with G.S.O.I The G.O.C. visited the 256th Tunnelling Coy. in the morning, and GINCHY. A cold, dull, but dry day.	
			Daily Summaries from 18th to 30th November inclusive are attached as App. 4. Location Reports from 19th to 30th November inclusive are attached as App. 5.	App.4 App.5

J.P. Fuller
Lieut-Colonel, G.S.,
29th Division.

LIST OF APPENDICES.

Appendix 1 comprises :-

  (a) Programme of 86th Brigade Inspection and Attack.

  (b) Report on Operations by the 88th Brigade while attached to the 12th Division.

  (c) Operation Order No. 41 for practice attack by 88th Brigade.

  (d) Programme of 86th Brigade Inspection and Attack.

Appendix 2 comprises :-

  (a) Agenda for 29th Division Conference No. 13 held at CORBIE on 14th November, 1916.

Appendix 3 comprises :-

  (a) 29th Division Order No. 75 re probable dates of relief of 8th Division. Moves carried out as per March Table.

  (b) 29th Division Order No. 76 re relief of 8th Division on night 16th/17th and 17th/18th November.

  (c) 29th Division Order No. 77 readjustment of XIV Corps front.

  (d) 29th Division Warning Order for relief of 9th French Corps.

  XXX Amendment to above Order.

  (e) 29th Division Order No. 78 for relief of 9th French Corps.

Appendix 4 comprises :-

  Daily Intelligence Summaries from 18th to 30th November.

Appendix 5 comprises :-

  Location Reports from 19th to 30th November.

-o-o-o-o-o-o-

Appendix 1 (a)
War Diary.

PROGRAMME OF 86TH BRIGADE INSPECTION AND ATTACK.

603

I. The G.O.C. will inspect the 2nd Royal Fusiliers and the 16th Middlesex Regt on the 9th November at the following times:-
        10-0 a.m.   16th Middlesex Regt.
        10.30.a.m. 2nd Royal Fusiliers.

II. At the conclusion of the inspection the following attack scheme will be carried out:-

1. **OBJECTIVES.**
The 86th Brigade less two Battalions will attack the line A - B, marked on the ground by a line of red flags and spitlocked.
The 16th Middlesex Regt will attack on the right and the 2nd Royal Fusiliers on the left.
Each Battalion has a frontage of 300 yards.

2. **PLAN OF ATTACK.**
(a) Battalions will attack with four companies in line of Company Columns, i.e. in four waves.
(b) The first three waves will carry 120 rounds S.A.A. No bombs will be carried.
(c) Lewis Guns will accompany the third wave and this wave will be detailed to protect the flanks and fill in gaps on either side of the Battalion.
(d) Battalion Bombing platoons will accompany the fourth wave; every man in this wave will carry an entrenching tool. 6 men per platoon to carry buckets of bombs.
(Bombs will be represented by sandbags rolled up.)
(e) A Company of the 2nd Royal Fusiliers will be specially detailed to cover the right of the Zth Brigade.
(f) Before Zero, Battalions will be formed up in forward lines and imaginary shell holes well closed up, prepared to move forward at the Zero hour.

3. The attack will be preceded by a heavy artillery bombardment. There will be no intense fire before Zero. The heavy artillery barrage on the trenches will be represented by blue flags.
The creeping barrage and the fixed barrage carried out by the 18 pdr. will be represented by white flags.
The assault will be carried out under cover of a creeping artillery barrage, which will lift as follows:-
(a) From Zero to 0.3 a heavy barrage will be placed on the objectives and on a line 150 yards short of the enemy's front trench. The Infantry will advance and get as close to it as possible.
(b) At 0.3 the barrage will creep forward at the rate of 50 yards per minute until at 0.9 it has reached a line 150 yards beyond the first objective, where it will halt while the objective is being consolidated.
At 0.6 the barrage passes over the objective and the Infantry will enter the trench.
During the attack the Divisional Artillery Howitzers and Heavy Artillery will engage the further objectives and lift off them when the assault is launched.

4. **MACHINE GUNS.**
(a) Two guns will move forward on the left flank of the 2nd Royal Fusiliers.
(b) Before Zero four guns will take up forward positions in NO MAN'S LAND, their special task being to deal with hostile machine gun fire as soon as the Infantry advance.

(c)   Eight guns will open at Zero on the enemy's second line (imaginary) continuing their fire until masked.

Four of these guns will remain in position to hold our present front line. The remaining four will occupy positions, prepared to open on any signs of counter attack.

5.   Stokes Mortars.

Before Zero four Stokes Mortars will take up positions as far forward in NO MAN'S LAND as possible, prepared to open on any hostile machine guns within range.

These guns will move into the enemy's trench when it is captured.

6.   As soon as the objective is gained strong points must be constructed at once by special parties told off for the purpose.

These will subsequently be joined up, every effort being made to make the defence as strong as possible.

NOTE:-   Strong points during consolidation will be spitlocked only.

Army Form C. 2121

...ES AND SIGNALS.

| Prefix... Code... | ...ds | Charge. | This message is on a/c of:— | Recd. at ... m. |
| Office of Origin and Service Instructions. | Sent | At ... m. To ... By ... | Service | Date From By |

TO 86 Bde

| Sender's Number. | Day of Month. | In reply to Number. | AAA |
| * G.O. 74 | 29/10/10 | | |

The march table attached to 29th Div Order no 74 is cancelled as regards movements on Nov 1st and units will remain in the billets they will occupy tonight until they receive further orders.

D. My...
B.

From SOME
Place
Time 10.15 am

SECRET.

Appendix 1(e) Copy No 5
War Diary

OPERATION ORDER NO. 41

By

Brigadier General D.E. Cayley, C.M.G. Commanding 88th Brigade.

****

12th November, 1916.

1. The 4th Worcestershire Regt. and 1st Newfoundland Regt. will attack the hostile trenches about K.1 B.20 tomorrow. The Newfoundland Regt. on the right and the 4th Worcestershire Regt. on the left.

    The frontage to be attacked is about 700 yards.

2. The attack will be made by each Battalion in four lines on a frontage of 2 Companies with 2 platoons of each Company in each line.

3. At ZERO the time of which will be notified later, a barrage will be established on the hostile trench and on ground 150 yards in front of our trench. At this time the attackers will leave the trench and get as close up to the barrage as possible, which will lift at + 2 minutes and move back at the rate of 50 yards a minute on to the hostile trench. The barrage will be followed up as closely as possible.

    At + 5 minutes the barrage will lift off the hostile trench, which will be at once assaulted.

4. When the trench has been captured, the Worcestershire Regt. will detach men to form a defensive flank to the left.

    The 2 Battalions will send out covering parties of Lewis Gunners and rifles about 50 yards to the front and on the flanks to cover the working parties.

    As far as men are available the consolidation of the whole trench will be taken in hand.

5. Special parties of bombers will be detailed to deal with deep dugouts. The Newfoundland Regt. will detail a special bombing party on their right to ensure getting into touch with the Battalion on their right.

6. 120 rounds ammunition and 2 sandbags will be carried by each man. Waterbottles will be full. Iron rations will be carried.

(2)

611

50% of the men will carry tools in the proportion of 2 shovels to 1 pick.

Aeroplane flares, and screens and 4 artillery boards per battalion will be carried.

Carrier pigeons will be taken forward.

Relays of runners will be arranged. Attempt will be made to get forward telephones with the advance.

7. Battalion Headquarters will be established in the forming up trenches.

                                                 Captain,
                             Brigade Major, 88th Brigade.

Copy 1 - 2 Staff
       3 Worcestershire Regt.
       4 Newfoundland
       5 29th Division

Appendix 1(d)

612

O.C., 2nd Royal Fusiliers.
    1st Lancashire Fusiliers.
    16th Middlesex Regt.
    1st Royal Dublin Fusiliers.
    86th Machine Gun Company.
    86th Trench-Mortar Battery.

----

1. The G.O.C. will inspect the 1st Lancashire Fusiliers and the 1st Royal Dublin Fusiliers on Tuesday, November 14th at the following times:-
    1st Lancashire Fusiliers.   10.a.m.
    1st Royal Dublin Fusiliers.   10.30.a.m.

2. At the conclusion of the inspection he will inspect these Battalions in the attack.
    Each Battalion will first assault the blue line shewn on the attached map. It will then advance and assault the green line.

3. The attack will be preceded by a heavy artillery bombardment. There will be no intense fire before Zero. (The heavy artillery barrage on the trenches will be represented by blue flags.)
    The creeping barrage and fixed barrage carried out by the 18 pdrs. will be represented by white flags.
    The assault will be carried out under cover of a creeping artillery barrage which will lift as follows:-
    (a) From Zero to 0.5 a heavy barrage will be placed on the first objective and on a line 50 yards short of the enemy's front trench. The infantry will advance and get as close to it as possible.
    (b) At 0.5 the barrage will creep forward at the rate of 25 yards per minute until at 0.9 it has reached a line 100 yards beyond the first objective where it will halt till 0.13.
    At 0.5 the barrage passes over the first objective and the infantry will enter the trench.
    (c) At 0.10 the infantry less clearing up parties previously detailed will leave the first objective and get close under the barrage which will commence to creep at 0.13 at the rate of 25 yards per minute until it reaches a line 150 yards beyond the second objective where it will halt whilst the second objective is being consolidated.
    During the attack the Divisional Artillery Howitzers and Heavy Artillery will engage the further objectives and lift off them when the assault is launched.

                                                          Captain,

13th November 1916.   Brigade Major, 86th Brigade.

613

Magnetic North →

Rough Trench Map

Scale 1" = 100x

Assembly Trenches

Suspected Machine Guns

SECRET.   War Diary.   Appendix 2(a)

Agenda for 29th Division Conference No. 13
to be held at CORBIE at 5 p.m. on 14th Nov. 1916.
---

(1) Future policy of the Corps is :-

    (a) To harass the enemy and approach LE TRANSLOY line with a view to its assault.

    (b) The immediate objectives are the occupation of the gunpits in T.5.b.9.9 and SLEET Trench, on the right, and the capture of the Sunken Road in N.35.a and ORION Trench in the centre.

(2) With this in view, troops in the front line, should :-

    (a) Take every opportunity of connecting up and advancing the front line, so as to get as close to the objective as possible.

    (b) Make exit steps (with sandbag treads) in every bay of the front line to facilitate the assault.

    (c) Assist the Heavy Artillery by bringing to notice good Observation Posts for the observation of the enemy's trenches. Divisions have to keep the Corps informed of the targets they wish the Heavy Artillery to deal with.

(3) Troops when at rest should also be trained :-

    (a) to advance to within 30 or 40 yards of the barrage;

    (b) to fix bayonets on the move and after leaving our trenches;

    (c) to advance without any cheering or shouting of orders;

    (d) to have Lewis Gunners and bombers (about 1 bomber per 10 yards) in the first wave, to deal immediately with any opposition encountered.

    (e) The formation for attack is under consideration, and instructions will be issued shortly.

    (f) The tactical training of Company and Platoon Commanders requires attention (vide 4th Army 414.G.).

(4) The defensive policy of the Corps, consists in the construction of :-

    (a) A well organised front line system, with support and reserve trenches, supported by strong points and defended localities.

    (b) An intermediate line - BOVRIL - OX - COW - NEEDLE Trench.

    (c) A second line - STRAIGHT Trench - SERPENTINE - FLERS Line, the exact siting of which will be settled by XIV Corps.

(5) These lines can only be improved, if all troops living in them, devote their attention to the work (vide Corps G.61/2).
This work includes :-

    (a) Positions for machine guns in support and reserve trenches, and the intermediate and second lines. The emplacements in the second line to be occupied when made.

/ b.

- 2 -

(b) The wiring of the intermediate and second lines.

(c) Construction of deep dug-outs in support and reserve trenches. All available men of the 256th Tunnelling Coy. will be attached to the Right Division for this purpose.

(d) Completion of forward Duck-board tracks.

(e) Communication Trenches.

(f) Erection of Notice-boards
vide also 4th Army No. 379(G).

In view of the intention to keep the Division in the Right Sector for 8 days only, and then ultimately transfer the Division to the Left Sector, all work commenced by the 8th Division will be continued.

(6) Reduction of wastage in personnel.

(a) Saving of life on days when there is no attack can be effected :-
  (i) by the construction of traverses in the trenches;
  (ii) by making deep dug-outs;
  (iii) by insisting on troops not exposing themselves needlessly, and observing reasonable precautions.

(b) No man should remain in the front line more than 48 hours.
To enable the reliefs entailed by this to be carried out, the Brigades holding the line will each be allotted two Battalions from the Reserve Brigade, to draw upon when required. Normally a Battalion should remain 48 hours only in the front line system.

(c) The defence of the line should be entrusted chiefly to Machine gun fire from the flanks and rear, with Lewis Guns in the front line itself, the maximum garrison of which should be 1 man to two yards.

(d) Zones continually shelled, should only be lightly held, and their defence entrusted to flanking machine gun fire.

(e) Carrying parties should be organised in short stages.

(f) Trench feet should be avoided by the use of gum-boots, dry socks and hot meals. Drying Rooms are under construction West of TRONES WOOD, a tea-house has been established just East of GINCHY, and solidified alcohol and wood should be taken by troops up to the front trenches. Macintoshes have been received, and allotted, 2000 to each Brigade in the front line to be handed over as trench stores, and receipts of taking over sent to D.H.Q. Losses to be paid for.

(g) The number of Officers, accompanying a Battalion in the trenches should be limited to the O.C., 2nd in command, Adjutant, Specialists, Company and Platoon Commanders. The remainder of the Officers should remain at CARNOY CAMP.

(7) Brigades after an attack must ascertain the situation early, by sending forward one of the Brigade Staff to make a personal reconnaissance, instead of relying entirely on the reports sent in by Battalions.

Appendix 3(a).

S E C R E T.   Copy No.............

29TH DIVISION ORDER NO. 75.

Ref. Map ALBERT   12th November, 1916.
(Combined Sheet) 1/40,000.

1. In view of the approaching relief of the 8th Division by the 29th Division, moves will be carried out in accordance with the attached March Table.

2. Reliefs will probably take place as follows :-

   The 87th Brigade will relieve the 25th Brigade in the Right Sector on the 16th/17th. night.

   The 88th Brigade will relieve the 23rd Brigade in the Left Sector on the 17th/18th. night.

   The 86th Brigade will relieve the 24th Brigade in Reserve.

3. Troops marching East of MEAULTE will march in file with 200 yards interval between Companies and 500 yards between Battalions.

4. Divisional Headquarters will close at CORBIE at 10 a.m. on 15th instant and reopen at TREUX at the same hour.

5. Please acknowledge.

                                              C.G. Fuller
                                         Lieut-Colonel, G.S.,
                                              29th Division.

Issued at ..... 8 p.m. .....

```
                     Copies 1 - 5  General Staff.
                            6      86th Brigade.
20  8th Division.          7      87th Brigade.
21  17th      "            8      88th Brigade.
22  20th      "            9      C.R.A.
23  Guards    "            10     C.R.E.
                            11     Officer i/c Signals.
                            12     O.C. 1/2nd Monmouth Regt.
                         13-17    A.A. & Q.M.G.
                            18     XIV Corps "G".
                            19     XIV Corps "Q".
```

MARCH TABLE "A".

Unit.	Date.	Road or bus.	From.	To.	Route.	Remarks.
Personnel 87th Inf. Bde. Group.	14th Nov.	Bus.	Area 5.	CITADEL (F.21.b.)	S. of SOMME - ALLENS - QUERRIEUX at D.20.b.6.2. - RIENCONT - BUIRE - VILLE.	Busses will rendezvous area 5 at 9 a.m. under arrangements "Q" 4th Army. On debusing at VILLE troops will march to CITADEL via MEAULTE and CARCAILLOT FARM.
Transport 87th Bde. Group.	14th Nov.	Road.	CORBIE	CITADEL	CORBIE - FERICOURT - VILLE - MEAULTE - CARCAILLOT FARM.	To start at 10 a.m.
89th Inf. Bde. Group.	15th Nov.	Road.	VILLE and FERICOURT	SANDPITS	MEAULTE	To start at 9 a.m.
Div.H.Q. Reserve Coy. Mob.Vet. Sect. Sanitary Sect. S.A.A. Sect.	}15th }Nov. }16th }Nov.	Road.	CORBIE	TREUX	FERICOURT	Taking over from corresponding units of 8th Division who will move out the same day.
		Road.	CORBIE	F.17.b. near CARNOY. A.2.d.9.7 Rear D.H.Q. F.18.c.2.8 CARNOY.	MEAULTE	
88th Inf. Bde. Group.	16th Nov.	Road.	CORBIE	MEAULTE	FERICOURT - VILLE	Head to start at 11.30 a.m.

NOTE. The West Riding Field Coy. will probably move by bus from DAOURS to MEAULTE on 16th November and march thence to S.30.a.7.7. Further orders will be issued. The 1/3rd Kent Field Coy. and 1/2nd London Field Coy. will move from MEAULTE to SANDPITS and MANSEL Camp respectively on 13th November and will remain there till they receive further orders.

"A" Form
MESSAGES AND SIGNALS.

Army Form C. 2121
No. of Message: 33

TO: 86th Bde. ~~87th Bde.~~ ~~88th Bde.~~ ~~8th Divn.~~

Sender's Number.	Day of Month.	In reply to Number.	
G.R.127	14/11		A A A

Reference 29th Division Order No. 76 para. 10 please amend Half teams of the 88th and 86th Machine Gun Companies to read AAA Half teams of the 87th and 88th Machine Gun Companies.

J. Fuller
Lieut-Col
~~Captain~~, G.S.

From: 29th Division.
Place:
Time: 12.45 p.m.

Appendix 3(4)

S E C R E T.   Copy No.........

29TH DIVISION ORDER NO. 76.

Reference ALBERT combined sheet 1/40,000)
 Sheet 57 C S.W. 1/20,000   )   13th November, 1916.

1. The 29th Division (less Artillery) will relieve the 8th Division (less Artillery) in the front line from approx. T.5.d.2.8 to N.34.b.7.3 on the nights of 16th/17th, 17th/18th November. Relief to be completed by 6 a.m. 18th November.

2. Reliefs will be carried out as follows :-
87th Bde. will relieve the 25th Bde. in the Right Sector
　　　　　　　　　　　　　on the night of 16th/17th.
88th Bde. "   "   " 24th Bde. in the Left Sector
　　　　　　　　　　　　　on the night of 17th/18th.
86th Bde. will move into Divisional Reserve on the 18th inst.

3. The reliefs will be carried out in accordance with the attached March Table.

4.(a) East of MEAULTE, infantry will move by cross country tracks as far as possible. They will march with 200 yards intervals between Companies and 500 yards between Battalions.
 (b) Transport will use the MEAULTE - MAMETZ - MONTAUBAN road and intervals of 200 yards will be kept between the transport of units.

5. Details of the relief will be arranged between Brigadiers concerned. Completion of all reliefs will be reported to Divisional Headquarters.

6. Brigades will arrange for 1 Officer and 1 N.C.O. per Company to visit the trenches beforehand, to make themselves acquainted with their sections.

7. Relief of the Field Companies R.E. will be arranged direct between the Cs.R.E.
　　The Pioneer Battalion will be relieved by the Pioneer Battalion of the 8th Division and will come under the command of the G.O.C. 29th Division at 10 a.m. on the 18th instant.

8. Field Ambulances will carry out the relief under the orders of the A.D.M.S.

9. All units not mentioned in these orders will move under the orders of the A.A. & Q.M.G.

10. Half teams of the 88th and 86th Machine Gun Companies will go into the line on the nights of 15th/16th, 16th/17th respectively and will take over from the 25th and 24th Machine Gun Companies on the nights of the 16th/17th, 17th/18th November respectively. Tripods and ammunition, and Stokes Mortars will be exchanged in the line.

11. All S.A.A., grenades and trench stores in the line will be taken over and receipts given.

12. Troops proceeding to the front line will take with them 2 days rations, wood, and 1 petrol tin of water (per 2 men). They will leave their greatcoats in CARNOY CAMP.

/ 13.

- 2 -

619

13. The line on the right is held by the 135th French Regiment (152nd French Division) with Headquarters at T.10.c.8.7.
    The line on the left is held by the 1st Guards Brigade (Guards Division) with Headquarters at T.8.Central.

14. The G.O.C. 29th Division will assume command of the Right Sector at 10 a.m. 18th instant.
    Divisional Headquarters will close at TREUX and reopen with Advanced Headquarters at A.4.d.6.2 and Rear Headquarters at A.2.d.9.7 at the same time.

15. Acknowledge by wire.

C.P. Fuller.
Lieut-Colonel, G.S.,
29th Division.

Issued at ...9 p.m.......

```
Copies  1 - 5    General Staff.
            6    86th Brigade.
            7    87th Brigade.
            8    88th Brigade.
            9    C.R.A.
           10    C.R.E.
           11    Officer i/c Signals.
           12    O.C. 1/2nd Monmouth Regt.
        13-17    A.A. & Q.M.G.
           18    XIV Corps "G".
           19    XIV Corps "Q".
           20    8th Division.
           21    Guards Division.
           22    152nd French Division.
```

S E C R E T.   Copy No............

Appendix 3(c)

620

29TH DIVISION ORDER NO. 77.

17th November, 1916.

1. A readjustment of the front of the XIV Corps will take place in the immediate future.

2. The 5th Australian Division (1st ANZAC Corps) will relieve the XIV Corps as far South as the SUNKEN ROAD at N.35.a.e.8 (inclusive to the 5th Australian Division).

3. The new tactical Northern boundary of the XIV Corps will run as follows :- N.35.a.05.80 - N.34.b.1.0 - N.34.c.0.4 - N.33.d.4.0 - T.3.c.0.8.

4. The relief will be carried out as follows :-
Night 20th/21st November - Relief of Left Brigade of Guards Division.
Night 21st/22nd November - Relief of Right Brigade of Guards Division.
Night 22nd/23rd November - Adjustment of the left boundary between 29th Division and 5th Australian Division.

5. In order to enable reliefs to be carried out during the further adjustment of the Corps front, the 29th Division front will be held by two Brigade Groups, each consisting of six Battalions. For this purpose the 86th Brigade will detail two Battalions to be attached to each of the 87th and 88th Brigades.

6. The reliefs of the Brigade Headquarters will take place as follows :-
86th Brigade Headquarters - In Reserve till 24th/25th November, in Right Sector from 24th/25th November till 10th/11th December.
87th Brigade Headquarters - In Right Section from 16th/17th to 24th/25th November - Reserve from 24th/25th November to 3rd/4th December - Left Section from 3rd/4th December to 11th/12th December.
88th Brigade Headquarters - In Left Section till 3rd/4th December, then in Reserve.

7. Accommodation for an additional three battalions of the 29th Division will be available in MANSEL CAMP (F.11.c.4.4) from Noon 21st November onwards. This accommodation will be divided equally between the two Brigade Groups.

8. From the 21st November until further orders, Brigadiers Commanding Brigade Groups will hold the line with three Battalions in the forward area, and three Battalions in the BRIQUETERIE, CARNOY and MANSEL CAMPS.

9. Battalions in Camps mentioned in para. 8, will act as Divisional Reserve, and will not be utilised to reinforce the line without reference to these Headquarters.

/ 10.

(2)

10. It is intended that the 29th Division be relieved by the 20th Division, commencing on December 10th, and that the 29th Division be then moved to the CAVILLON Area for rest.

11. Acknowledge by wire.

C.F. Fuller
Lieut-Colonel, G.S.,
29th Division.

Issued at ..7 p.m.

```
Copies  1 - 5  General Staff.
            6  86th Brigade.
            7  87th Brigade.
            8  88th Brigade.
            9  C.R.A.
           10  C.R.E.
           11  O.C. 1/2nd Monmouth Regt.
           12  Officer i/c Signals.
        13-17  A.A. & Q.M.G.
           18  XIV Corps "G".
           19  XIV Corps "Q".
           20  Guards Division.
           21  8th Division.
           22  .............Division.
                           20th
```

Appendix. 3(d)

622

SECRET.   Copy No.........
                                      29th Division No.C.G.S.71.

29TH DIVISION WARNING ORDER.

25th November, 1916.

1. The 29th Division will be prepared to relieve the 9th French Corps on the front as far as T.6.b.8.2, on the night December 1st/2nd, relief to be completed by 6 a.m. on December 2nd.

2. The Guards Division will be prepared to relieve the remainder of the 9th French Corps on the nights 2nd/3rd and 3rd/4th December.

3. The boundary between the 29th Division and Guards Division will then be as follows :-   T.6.b.8.2 - T.6.c.5.3 - T.11.b.2.3 - thence along road to T.11.c.7.3 - thence through MORVAL and along road to T.21.c.3.8.
    Instructions regarding the boundary in the back area will be issued later.

4. Consequent on the above, the Boundary between the Right and Left Brigades will be as follows :-   T.5.b.3.7 - T.5.c.2.8 - T.10.a.7.3 - T.9.d.0.3.

5. The adjustment of the boundary between the Right and Left Brigades will be arranged between the Brigadiers concerned, but the rearrangement will be completed by 6 a.m. on December 2nd.

6. The Artillery allotted at present to cover our present front will continue to cover the new Divisional frontage.

7. The Right Brigade will get into touch with the French on their right with a view to arranging details of the relief.
    The Headquarters of the French formations on our right are as follows :-
    H.Q. 152nd Division (Gen. AUDRIEN) - BOIS DORÉ   T.20.d.3.0.
    H.Q. 34th Brigade (Gen. FRAYSSE)   - T.21.d.5.3.
    H.Q. 125th Regiment (Colonel OUDRY) - T.6.c.6.0.

8. There will be no alteration of the present Headquarters of the Brigades holding the line, nor any augmentation of the troops allotted to the forward area.

9. ACKNOWLEDGE BY WIRE.

                                     D. Okey, Major
                                  for Lieut-Colonel, G.S.,
                                       29th Division.

Issued at ..Mam...

Copies 1 - 5 G.S.   11 O.C. Monmouths. 21 XIV Corps "G".
        6 86th Bde.   12 Off. i/c Sigs.   22 XIV Corps "Q".
        7 87th Bde.   13 - 17 A.A. & Q.M.G.
        8 88th Bde.   18 - 19 French Liaison
        9 C.R.A.   Officer.
       10 C.R.E.   20 5th Aust. Divn.

S E C R E T.   29th Division No. C.G.S.71A.

86th Brigade.
87th Brigade.
88th Brigade.
C.R.A.
C.R.E.
O.C. 1/2nd Monmouth Regt.
Officer i/c Signals.
A.A. & Q.M.G.
French Liaison Officer.
5th Australian Division.
XIVth Corps "G".
XIVth Corps "Q".

Amendment to 29th Division No. C.G.S.71 dated 25.11.16.

Para. 7, line 7 - H.Q., 34th Brigade (Gen. FRAYSSE) are at HAIE WOOD (T.23.b.8.4) and not at T.21.d.5.3 as therein stated.

25th November, 1916

(signed) D. O'Key, Major p.s.
for Lieut-Colonel, G.S.,
    29th Division.

Appendix 3(e)

6/4

S E C R E T.   Copy No...........

29TH DIVISION ORDER NO. 78.

Reference Trench Maps   27th November, 1916.
1/10,000 and 1/20,000.

1. The 29th Division will relieve the IX French Corps as far South as T.6.b.90.45. on the night of December 1st/2nd. Relief to be completed by 6 a.m. on December 2nd.

2. The Guards Division will relieve the remainder of the IX French Corps on the nights December 2nd/3rd and 3rd/4th. This relief will be completed by 6 a.m. on December 4th.

3. The boundaries between the 29th Division and Guards Division will then be as follows - T.6.b.90.45 - T.6.c.5.3 - T.11.b.2.3 - thence along road to T.11.c.7.3 - thence through MORVAL and along road to T.21.c.3.8. Instructions regarding the back area will be issued later.

4. The boundary between the right and left Brigade Groups will be as follows :- T.5.b.5.6 - T.5.c.1.7 - T.9.b.55.30 - T.14.c.2.4,.. The duckwalk from GINCHY to OX TRENCH will be used by both Brigade Groups.

5. The Right Brigade will get into touch with the French on their right, with a view to arranging details of the relief.

6. The 17th Divisional Artillery Group will cover the new Divisional frontage; no alteration will be made in the present disposition of batteries and Artillery Group Headquarters.

7. There will be no alteration of the present Headquarters of the Brigade Groups holding the line.

8. Completion of reliefs to be reported to these Headquarters.

9. Divisional Headquarters will remain in their present positions at A.4.d.5.2 and A.2.d.9.7 respectively.

10. Acknowledge by wire.

C.P. Fuller.
Lieut-Colonel, G.S.,
29th Division.

Issued at ...6.p.m....

Copies 1 - 5	General Staff.	13 - 17	A.A. & Q.M.G.
6	86th Brigade.	18	Guards Division
7	87th Brigade.	19 - 20	French Liaison Officer.
8	88th Brigade.		
9	C.R.A.	21	5th Aust. Divn.
10	C.R.E.	22	XIV Corps "G".
11	Officer i/c Sigs.	23	XIV Corps "G".
12	O.C. 1/2nd Monmouths.		

Appendix 4

D.S.178.

HEADQUARTERS.
29th DIVISION.
INTELLIGENCE.

No. 625
Date.

29TH DIVISION DAILY SUMMARY.

From 8.30 a.m. 17.11.16. to 8.30 a.m. 18.11.16.

OPERATIONS.

Artillery. Enemy artillery activity normal in the front areas. Slightly more active in the back area. About 3.30 p.m. GINCHY cross roads was shelled causing several casualties. There was a good deal of counter battery work against the French left.

Aircraft. Hostile aircraft were again active on the morning of the 17th. Occasionally Machine Gun fire was opened by them on our front line system.

Infantry. During the day hostile infantry has been inactive. There has been no sniping and no movement seen.

INTELLIGENCE.

Enemy's Order of Battle. A prisoner of 1st Coy. 104th R.I.R. was captured about N.29.c. last night. He stated that he moved into the front line three days ago. This confirms relief of Bavarian Ersatz Division by 24th Reserve Division.

Strong Points. Enemy appear to be making a strong point at about N.35.d.6.2. This can be dealt with by our Trench Mortars.

Wire. Enemy are putting out wire in front of SLEET TRENCH.

Patrols. Our patrols encountered no enemy patrols but ran into an enemy working party - evidently working on their new strong point N.35.d.6.2. There was a covering party out in front of the working party.

Signals. Enemy appeared to be using a much larger golden rain rocket last night - no apparent action followed the signal.

WORK DONE.

The trench connecting North end of AUTUMN TRENCH with sap on S. side of SUNKEN ROAD is now complete. It is reported that this so called SUNKEN ROAD is not sunken. In reality that portion of the road beside which the sap from SUMMER TRENCH runs is flush with the surface of the ground.

L. Carden Roe

Captain, G.S.,

18th November, 1916.   29th Division.

29TH DIVISION DAILY SUMMARY.
From 8.30 a.m. 18.11.16. to 8.30 a.m. 19.11.16.

OPERATIONS.

Artillery. On the Right Section nothing of importance occurred during the day. As a result of the French attack on the gun pits on our right, our support and reserve trenches were bombarded, but little damage was done. LES BOEUFS was shelled during the afternoon with heavy guns. On the left front there was continued intermittent enemy shelling chiefly on the rear of DEWDROP TRENCH. THISTLE and WINDY TRENCHES and the communication trench from THISTLE to DEWDROP were also shelled with Field Guns (4.2's and 5.9's) some damage was done.
The area behind WINTER TRENCH was shelled between 2 p.m. and 3 p.m. and between 8.0 a.m. and 8.30 a.m. with light high explosives, but no damage was done.
The front line was practically unshelled during the day.

Snipers. Enemy snipers were active on the left front from the direction of ORION TRENCH, and 3 men belonging to a covering party of a working party in front of SUMMER TRENCH, were killed. No other sniping has taken place along the front.

Patrols. Two officer's patrols went out from the Left Section last night. One proceeded from the left of the Section and found no trace of the enemy. On returning to our lines the patrol was followed in by a German who gave himself up. He belongs to the 10th Company 81st R.I.R.

Strong Point. The Strong Point mentioned in yesterday's Summary, is now located at N.36.c.5.1. It is suspected that the enemy is working from that point to N.35.a.6.1, as patrols have been in contact with enemy working parties.

Prisoners. Besides the man of the 10th Company 81st R.I.R. captured last night, a deserter came into the left of BENNETT TRENCH this morning. He belonged to No. 6 Company 104th R.I.R. These men captured in their normal sectors give the order of battle North to South - 133rd R.I.R. - 107th R.I.R. - 104th R.I.R. - 81st R.I.R. - 193rd I.R.
The second battalion 104th R.I.R. relieved the first battalion, on the night of the 18th/19th.

INTELLIGENCE.

Enemy movement was observed yesterday afternoon, and small parties of twos and threes were seen running between shell holes about 500 yards in front of BENNETT TRENCH. Lewis Gun fire was brought to bear on them with some success.

Flares were being continuously put up opposite the Left Section throughout the night. It was impossible to locate the exact trenches from which they were fired, but opposite the left front of the Section, the number was abnormal.

WORK DONE.

Work has been continued along the whole line.
The New Trench which has been dug from FALL TRENCH to connect with the sap in SUNKEN ROAD is incomplete, but when finished will give a good field of view as it is on the top of a ridge. The whole area, on its front and flanks, is very confused being nothing but a mass of shell holes, and

/ it

- 2 -

627

it is extremely difficult to locate enemy trenches.
Work has been continued on TAN LANE, on the FLERS Line,
and fire steps have been worked on in DEWDROP and SUMMER
TRENCHES.
Work has been done on the fire steps in the New Trench
in front of SUMMER TRENCH.
WINTER TRENCH was also worked on, but it was impossible
to keep pace with the weather and this Trench is still
impassible.
A Platoon Commander's dug-out was commenced in AUTUMN TRENCH,
and mud cleared from the bottom of this trench.
A considerable amount of work that was done in the trenches
during the night in making fire steps etc. was obliterated
by the rain.

Ian Robertson

Captain, G.S.,
29th Division.

19th November, 1916.

29TH DIVISION DAILY SUMMARY.
From 8.30 a.m. 19.11.16. to 8.30 a.m. 20.11.16.

OPERATIONS.

Artillery. On the right front enemy activity was normal. MORVAL and LES BOEUFS were shelled with heavies.
The enemy was very quick in getting on to any movement in the vicinity of ANTELOPE TRENCH.
On the Left Section DEWDROP and THISTLE TRENCHES and the SUNKEN ROAD were continuously shelled throughout the day. The shelling was particularly heavy between 1700 and 1930.
AUTUMN TRENCH was shelled with 5.9's incessantly.
WINTER TRENCH was barraged at 1600 for half an hour. It was intense for about 15 minutes.

Snipers. Sniping has quietened down.

Signals. At 4 a.m. this morning golden rain rockets were sent up opposite the right front, which resulted in a light gun barrage behind BENNETT TRENCH. No damage was done.
On the left many enemy flares were sent up, but it could not be observed whether they were sent from the firing line or shell holes.

Patrols. An officer's patrol proceeded from the Left Section to get into touch with the Guards right, but without success. The distance from our left is estimated to be about 400 yards.

INTELLIGENCE.

An enemy observation post has been observed from SUMMER TRENCH to the left of Cemetery at LE TRANSLOY.

At 10 a.m. on the 19th enemy plane flew low over the centre of BENNETT TRENCH. After being there for a short time it fired a single white flare and withdrew towards BAPAUME. No enemy action appeared to follow this signal.

Little enemy movement was observed along the front.

Enemy Work. The enemy has put out a line of wire 400 yards in front of the centre of BENNETT TRENCH. This is most probably in front of the suspected line from N.36.c.5.1 towards N.35.a.6.1, reported in yesterdays summary.

WORK.

Firing line has been widened and deepened in parts, and saps pushed out preparatory to the proposed new firing line in front of BENNETT TRENCH.
Work has been continued on communication trenches and the trench from BENNETT to FROSTY TRENCH is completed except for duckboards.
The trench between FROSTY and SNOW TRENCH has also been completed.
On the left front TAN TRENCH, THISTLE and SUMMER TRENCHES, and DEWDROP TRENCH have all been worked on. These trenches have been deepened, widened and fire steps made.
WINTER TRENCH has been cleaned and Trench floored with timber.
One latrine per Company has been constructed.

Captain, G.S.,
20th November, 1916.   29th Division.

29TH DIVISION DAILY SUMMARY.
From 8.30 a.m. 20.11.16. to 8.30 a.m. 21.11.16.

OPERATIONS.

Artillery. Shelling on the right front was normal throughout the day.
Early this morning a few gas shells fell in and behind GERMAN TRENCH.
On the left section a heavy barrage was put between DEWDROP TRENCH and LES BOEUFS between 1700 and 1800., the Battalion Headquarters in the neighbourhood being consistently shelled. 5.9's, 4.2's and field guns, shrapnel and H.E. shrapnel were used in shelling the preceding area.
A carrying party going along the FLERS Line towards LES BOEUFS were heavily shelled during the afternoon.

INTELLIGENCE.

Enemy sniping comparatively inactive over the whole front.

No movements have been observed. At 17.15 a party of 3 men appeared in front of the left section, and one was believed to have been killed by one of our snipers.

Aircraft. Five hostile machines flew over our line during yesterday afternoon. They are believed to have been photographing the trenches. One machine on the left dropped a flare consisting of a red and white ball on our front line, and a single red flare on SUMMER TRENCH. This was repeated during the night, but nothing is reported to have occurred as a result of these signals.

Patrols. A patrol from the Guards Battalion on our left established touch with the Left Brigade last night.

WORK.

The sap from Point 9211 (T.5.b.8.9) to 9511 (T.16.a.5.9) was continued, and about 100 yards completed. It is hoped to get into touch with the French tonight.

Work has been continued on Communication trenches in SUNKEN ROAD to Battalion Headquarters, although duckboards have not yet been laid.

The firing line and support trenches have been deepened and improved, and wire is being put in front of BENNETT TRENCH.

In the reserve area work has also been continued, and trenches and drains dug. FLERS Line, TAN TRENCH, SUMMER TRENCH, DEWDROP TRENCH, THISTLE TRENCH, THISTLE Communication Trench, and OZONE TRENCH, have all been worked on and improved, and a large amount of R.E. Stores have been carried to the front area from the rear.

Sam Robertson

Captain, G.S.,

21st November, 1916.   29th Division.

29TH DIVISION DAILY SUMMARY.
From 8.30 a.m. 21.11.16. to 8.30 a.m. 22.11.16.

OPERATIONS.

Artillery. Enemy artillery was normal along the whole front with the exception of a heavy barrage between 3.30 to 5.30 p.m. on FROSTY, ANTELOPE and GERMAN Trenches. Some casualties were caused in the last named trench owing to a direct hit.

Machine Gun fire was quiet, and no snipers were active.

INTELLIGENCE.

No aircraft were observed on the front.

On the extreme left of the Right Section, a hostile patrol was discovered, but did not succeed in approaching close to our lines.

An officer's patrol went out from the Right Section, but reported no signs of the enemy.

A thick haze has prevailed throughout the last 24 hours except for a few minutes at sunrise, which has stopped any observation of enemy movements.

A prisoner was taken by the French yesterday at N.36.c.6.1. He belongs to the 81st Regiment, 222nd Division. He was examined at these Headquarters, and a copy of the information extracted from him is attached hereto.

WORK.

The sap running from point 9211 referred to in yesterday's summary was continued, and 180 yards are now completed. A small gap still exists between us and the French, which it is hoped will be completed to-night.

Half of the front of BENNETT Trench has been wired, and a fire step has been dug in this trench.

FLANK Trench and OZONE Avenue have both been worked on by the Pioneer Company, and parts of the latter trench were cleared of mud 18 inches deep.
On FLANK Trench work was continued to within about 100 yards of ANTELOPE Trench. This trench has been widened and deepened, and drained in many places.

During the day work was continued laying trench boards in both of these trenches.

NOTE. Reference yesterday's summary, heading WORK, the first line should read :-
"The sap from point 9211 (T.5.b.8.9) to 9511 (T.6.a.5.9.)"

Captain, G.S.,
22nd November, 1916.   29th Division.

29TH DIVISION DAILY SUMMARY.

From 8.30 a.m. 22.11.16. to 8.30 a.m. 23.11.16.

OPERATIONS.

Artillery. At 7.15 p.m. a German bombardment started on our left towards GUEUDECOURT; a light barrage was opened at the same time on WINTER Trench and FALL and AUTUMN Trenches; little damage was done.

Between midnight and 2 a.m. some gas shells with a smell somewhat like aniseed, fell near the centre of our line. It only seemed to affect the eye.

Patrols. A listening patrol went out from FALL Trench last night, and reports that the enemy could be heard working about 500 yards away.

A hostile patrol was observed opposite our centre just before dawn.

Aeroplanes. A hostile machine was brought down about 1.30 p.m. yesterday, North of our sector in the direction of GUEUDECOURT.

Aeroplanes were heard in the air before dawn to-day, and at 7 a.m. both British and German planes were out scouting.

INTELLIGENCE.

Signals. Two white rockets were observed to go up from the enemy lines opposite BENNETT TRENCH. They were white and each broke into 12 white stars. No result was observed.

WORK.

A hazy mist prevented observation of enemy movements.

The trench joining up our line with that of the French has been completed, and we are now in touch.

The Communication Trench running from the Right Battalion Headquarters to GERMAN TRENCH, has been extended to about 100 yards beyond ANTELOPE TRENCH.

ANTELOPE TRENCH has been deepened and improved, and is being provided with a fire step.

Trenches damaged by shell fire have been repaired, and the erection of fire steps along the whole firing line is well in hand.

The new defensive line in front of OX TRENCH has been commenced.

Captain, G.S.,

23rd November, 1916.   29th Division.

HEADQUARTERS.
29th DIVISION.
INTELLIGENCE.
D.S.184.

29TH DIVISION DAILY SUMMARY.

From 8.30 a.m. 23.11.16. to 8.30 a.m. 24.11.16.

OPERATIONS.

Artillery.   Yesterday morning (23rd) BERNAFAY Cross Roads and the vicinity were shelled.
GINCHY, the GUILLEMONT – COMBLES Road, and the vicinity of T.20.d. were shelled during the day.
ZENITH TRENCH and ANTELOPE TRENCH were shelled during the night.
Yesterday evening about 8 p.m. in response to red flares, the enemy barraged FALL, WINTER and ANTELOPE TRENCHES. This continued until about 9.20 p.m.   Shells used were mostly 5.9's both H.E. and shrapnel.   FALL and WINTER TRENCHES were damaged in places, but repaired during the night.   This shelling is believed to have been caused by the enemy observing a wiring party in front of FALL TRENCH, as the flares were sent up at this point.   The flares burst into 4 red balls.

INTELLIGENCE.

There was considerable aerial activity during the morning, and both sides were active throughout the day, several decisive combats being witnessed on the Divisional front.

Some sniping has taken place, just before dark and during the night, area affected being the left of the Battalion in support on the Right Section.   Distance is estimated at about 800 yards.

Patrols report that the enemy during the evening came out to the track near MAIL TRENCH at N.35.b.3.1.   From here listening patrols apparently proceed close up to our line. One of these listening posts sent up a flare on discovering a covering party in front of one of our wiring parties. This flare was followed by a red rocket fired from a point further back.

As a result of red and yellow parachute flares, it has been observed the enemy's barrage appears to increase.

On a yellow star shell being sent up a short bombardment followed.
        X see below

WORK.

Work has been continued on all trenches, and a gap of about 200 yards on the left of ZENITH TRENCH has been connected up

SUMMER and DEWDROP TRENCHES have been reclaimed.

Work has been continued on fire step in SUMMER TRENCH.

SHAMROCK and GERMAN TRENCHES have been deepened and improved.

Trench boards have been carried up for use in PLANK AVENUE, this has been extended another 200 yards.

Communication Trench between BENNETT and SNOW TRENCHES has been deepened.

Work on the defensive line in front of OX TRENCH was carried out.

X Intelligence.   Enemy has been observed doubling across the open in small parties between his front and support lines. This would seem to show that he is without serviceable communication trenches.

24.11.16.
                                                            Captain, G.S.,
                                                            29th Division.

29TH DIVISION DAILY SUMMARY.

From 8.30 a.m. 24.11.16. to 8.30 a.m. 25.11.16.

OPERATIONS.

Artillery. On the Right Brigade front enemy artillery activity was about normal.
Several shells fell near SUMMER TRENCH and OZONE AVENUE.
A little damage was done.

Machine gun fire was inactive during the period.

Snipers were again active on the East end of FROSTY TRENCH.

INTELLIGENCE.

Signals. There were no signals observed throughout the night on either front.

WORK.

Work has been continued on fire and communication trenches on the whole front system.

Captain, G.S.,

25.11.16.
29th Division.

29TH DIVISION DAILY SUMMARY.

From 8.30 a.m. 25.11.16. to 8.30 a.m. 26.11.16.

D.S.186.

HEADQUARTERS.
29th DIVISION.
INTELLIGENCE.

No.
Date 639

OPERATIONS.

Artillery. Operations have been below normal probably due to bad weather conditions.
On the support and reserve trenches in the Left Section there was slight activity, but no damage was done.

INTELLIGENCE.

Three prisoners gave themselves up last night on the left front. They belong to the 81st R.I.R., showing that the expected relief has not yet taken place. They give the order of battle from North to South - 81st R.I.R. - 193rd Regiment.

Two prisoners gave themselves up this morning near SUMMER TRENCH. They belong to the 6th Company, 133rd Regiment, of the 24th Reserve Division. This Regiment has apparently come into the line on the left of its Division instead of its old position on the right. These two prisoners have the initials "W.R." on their shoulder straps, besides the numerals of their Regiment.

WORK.

Weather has precluded much work being done during the last 24 hours, and what work was done, was chiefly confined to rebuilding trenches which had subsided owing to heavy rain.

San Robertson

Captain, G.S.,

26th November, 1916.   29th Division.

29TH DIVISION DAILY SUMMARY.

From 8.30 a.m. 26.11.16. to 8.30 a.m. 27.11.16.

No. 635

OPERATIONS.

Artillery. Opposite the Left Brigade the enemy's artillery was more active on support and reserve trenches.
SUMMER TRENCH was heavily shelled between 5.30 p.m. and 6 p.m. with 77 mm. shrapnel.
Between 10 a.m. and 12 Noon OZONE AVENUE and GOT TRENCH were shelled, but no damage was done.
The usual continuous shelling was maintained on LES BOEUFS throughout the day.
At 5 a.m. the approaches to our Right Brigade were shelled at random, enemy evidently searching tracks to the firing line.

Machine Guns. Enemy machine guns showed no activity except for two short bursts of machine gun fire during the night against our Right Brigade.

Snipers. The enemy's snipers have been much more active during the last two days, but our snipers continue to maintain their supremacy.

INTELLIGENCE.

When the enemy's artillery were shooting short yesterday evening, two red rockets were sent up by the enemy, and their guns immediately lifted.

Bad weather interfered with observation.

WORK DONE.

Right Brigade. 100 yards of new trench dug 30 yards behind ANTELOPE TRENCH 6 feet deep and 5 feet wide, as the existing trench is uninhabitable.
Work was done maintaining fire trenches, and building fire steps.

Left Brigade. All available men engaged in clearing and rebuilding trenches.
The trench between ZENITH TRENCH and OZONE AVENUE was considerably deepened.

L. Carden Roe

Captain, G.S.,
27th November, 1916.   29th Division.

29TH DIVISION DAILY SUMMARY.

From 8.30 a.m. 27.11.16. to 8.30 a.m. 28.11.16.

OPERATIONS.

Artillery. Enemy activity normal.
The GINCHY - LES BOEUFS Road about Right Battalion Headquarters of the Left Brigade was shelled intermittently all day, more especially between 11 a.m. and 1 p.m.
FROSTY and ANTELOPE TRENCHES were shelled during the afternoon.
About 3 p.m. a barrage was put on the French front line for nearly an hour.
About 4 p.m. some shrapnel shells burst between the Right Battalion Headquarters and the end of the duck walk.
LES BOEUFS was shelled in the usual manner, but at 7 p.m. a barrage was put by the enemy in that neighbourhood, for a few minutes and considerably hampered the relief.

Snipers. Considerable trouble was given by a hostile sniper at about N.35.c.9.9. Rifle grenade fire was opened on him, and he has not fired since.

INTELLIGENCE.

A few of the enemy seen yesterday proceeding across the open towards their rear in ones and twos. When fired on they continued to run in the open, having apparently no communication trenches.

Patrols. An identification patrol sent out last night reports that no enemy were encountered.

Aeroplanes. At about 12.30 p.m. one of our aeroplanes was brought down by an enemy plane. The aeroplane dropped at GINCHY, the pilot being killed and the observer badly shaken.

WORK DONE.

Right Brigade. Trench joining our right with the French line has been considerably improved.
Front line Companies have been employed clearing mud out of the trenches and generally improving them.
T's have been commenced, but so far it has been impossible to do much work on them.
New trench in rear of ANTELOPE TRENCH has been improved, latrines made and dump constructed.
SUNKEN ROAD at Battalion Headquarters improved and drained.

Left Brigade. All labour devoted to rebuilding trenches that have fallen in, especially OZONE AVENUE and SUMMER TRENCH.

L. Carden Roe
Captain, G.S.,

28th November, 1916.   29th Division.

HEADQUARTERS.
29th DIVISION.
INTELLIGENCE

No. 697
Date.

29TH DIVISION DAILY SUMMARY.

From 6.30 a.m. 29.11.16. to 6.30 a.m. 30.11.16.

OPERATIONS.

Artillery. The enemy artillery activity on the whole below normal.
Between 2 p.m. and 4 p.m. a few shells were dropped about the end of the duck-walk.
At 6 p.m. the enemy opened a heavy barrage on the front line trench and supports of the left Brigade.
Between 6 p.m. and 10 p.m. a few shells fell in the vicinity of TRIPLE [TREE].
The usual intermittent shelling took place both by day and night.
Our own artillery were very active on our left between 5.30 p.m. and 6.30 p.m.

Infantry. Enemy snipers were quieter than usual throughout the day.

INTELLIGENCE.

Enemy Defences. Barbed wire has been put up by the enemy straight in front of FILL TRENCH about 150 yards distant.

There is an unnamed enemy trench plainly visible in aeroplane photographs about this point.

Identification. During the night a German was seen about 60 yards in front of the left battalion of the left Brigade. He was shot at and wounded and brought in a prisoner. He belongs to the 104th [Reserve] Regiment (normal). His identity disc and purse are forwarded herewith. The purse contains a mechanical drawing which does not, however, appear to be of military importance.

Signals. At 6 p.m. when the enemy opened a heavy barrage on our front line, _was fired_ a white rocket breaking into 4 red stars, whereupon his artillery immediately shortened their range.

Once more a heavy fog greatly hindered observation of the enemy's movements.

[WORK].

All labour was devoted to rebuilding and improving existing trenches in the front line system.

L. Carden Roe
Captain, G.S.,
29th Division.

30th November, 1916.

HEADQUARTERS.
29th DIVISION.
INTELLIGENCE.

No. 658
Date.

29TH DIVISION DAILY SUMMARY.

From 8.30 a.m. 29.11.16. to 8.30 a.m. 30.11.16.

OPERATIONS.

Artillery. Heavy artillery much less active both on our front system and back areas.

Snipers. A hostile sniper gave trouble opposite our extreme left. Our snipers have not yet succeeded in silencing him.

Machine Guns. Our own machine guns were very active last night on account of supposed relief of German battalion opposite our front.

Rifle Grenades. We are continuing to harass the enemy with rifle grenade fire.

INTELLIGENCE.

Enemy defences. Enemy appears to be working in the vicinity of T.5.b.9.9 (gun pits). Newly dug earth can be seen at this point, and early yesterday morning smoke was noticed rising from behind this earth. Flares which were fired from this position last night fell behind SUNKEN TRENCH. This point is also believed to be used by the enemy as a sniper's post.

An officer who visited the French front line yesterday, reports that men can be seen using the newly dug German front line trench in T.6.a. and b. This trench is not yet connected up with the gun pits at T.5.b.9.9, as men could be seen running across the open between the two.

Observation. Smoke was seen coming from a point about 300 yards directly in front of WHITE TRENCH, and between the two Sunken Roads running over the HILL at about R.35.a.4.7 (this is probably FINCH TRENCH).

Patrols. The following intelligence was gained by reconnoitring patrols.

(1) A patrol of one officer and two men went out in front of SUNKEN TRENCH to a distance of about 40 yards. They remained out some time but had nothing to report except that Germans could be seen in Sunken Road R.35.a.4.4, and flares could be seen fired from just behind them.

(2) Another patrol which went out from HALL TRENCH, report as follows:-
 (i) Distance between HALL TRENCH and enemy front line 250 to 300 yards.
 (ii) An enemy sap runs out to within 80 yards of our left sap in HALL TRENCH.
 (iii) There are several similar saps running out from enemy trench about 30 to 40 yards apart. These saps are covered by two or three strands of barbed wire.
 (iv) The enemy have a sniper's post about 60 yards in front of our left sap.
 (v) In front of the trench and between the saps they have good barbed wire and concertina wire, with gaps where the saps run forward. Their wire is estimated to be 4 feet high.
 (vi) All the saps are occupied and very lights are sent up from them.

- 2 -

Identification. Effects collected from the body of a German in front of our line, are forwarded herewith. From the condition of the body the man had been dead only a short time.

WORK DONE.

Fire trenches generally improved.
Work continued on dug-outs in THISTLE and TENNY TRENCHES; duckboards in same; parados repaired and sandbagged.

L. Carden Roe
        Captain, G.S.,
30th November, 1916.   29th Division.

Appendix 5

S E C R E T.

640

I.G.39.

29TH DIVISION DAILY DISPOSITION REPORT.

10 a.m. 19th Nov. 1916.

Unit.	Code Name.	Locality.	Remarks.
29th Division H.Q.	ROSSLARE	A.4.d.5.2.	Headquarters (Advd)
29th Division H.Q.	ROSSLARE	A.2.d.9.7.	Headquarters (Rear-Adm)
86th Inf. Bde.	RAKE		
2nd Royal Fus.	RANDOM	BRIQUETERIE	
1st Lancs. Fus.	RECESS	Camp at BRIQUETERIE	
16th Middx. Regt.	RAMROD	Camp at CARNOY	
1st R. Dub. Fus.	RAPIER	-"-	
87th Inf. Bde.	REACH		
2nd S.W.Bs.	RAZOR	GUILLEMONT QUARRIES	H.Q. T.19.c.2.3
		"C" Bn. FLERS Line.	H.Q. T.9.central (FLERS)
1st K.O.S.Bs.	READY	"A" Bn. Right Bde.	H.Q. T.10.a.7.6.
1st R. Innis. Fus.	REALM	"D" Bn. GUILLEMONT.	H.Q. T.19.c.8.7.
1st Border Regt.	RASHER	"B" Bn. Right Bde.	H.Q. T.10.a.7.6.
88th Inf. Bde.	RECITE		
4th Worcester Regt.	RECKON	GUILLEMONT STATION	H.Q. S.24.b.7.4.
2nd Hants Regt.	RECORD	"A" Bn. Left Bde.	H.Q. T.3.d.7.8.
1st Essex Regt.	REDAN	"C" Bn. FLERS Line	H.Q. T.8.d.3.9.
Newfld. Regt.	REFORM	"D" Bn. TRONES WOOD	H.Q. S.29.c.6.3.
		"B" Bn. Left Bde.	H.Q. N.34.c.2½.9.
29th Div. R.E. H.Q.	RAJAH	A.4.d.5.2.	
29th Div. A.D.M.S.		A.2.d.9.7.	

S.N. Robertson

Captain, G.S.,

29th Division.

19th November, 1916.

Copies to :-

G.O.C.
G.S. (3)
"Q" (4)
C.R.A.
C.R.E.
86th Bde.
87th Bde.
88th Bde.

A.D.M.S.
Officer i/c Sigs.
XIV Corps "G"
XIV Corps "Q"
French Liaison Officer (2)
Guards Division.

S E C R E T.

[Stamp: HEADQUARTERS. 29th DIVISION. INTELLIGENCE. No. I.G.39.] 641

29TH DIVISION DAILY DISPOSITION REPORT.

10 a.m. November 21st, 1916.

Unit.	Code Name.	Locality.	Remarks.
29th Div. H.Q.	ROSLARE	A.4.d.5.2.	H.Q. Advanced.
29th Div. H.Q.	ROSLARE	A.2.d.9.7.	H.Q. Rear (Adm).
86th Inf. Bde.	RAKE	Camp at BRIQUETERIE.	
2nd Royal Fus.	RANDOM	-"-	
1st Lancs. Fus.	RECESS	Camp at CARNOY.	
16th Middx. Regt.	RAMROD	"D" Bn. GUILLEMONT.	T.19.c.8.7.
1st R. Dub. Fus.	RAPIER	Camp at CARNOY.	
87th Inf. Bde.	REACH	GUILLEMONT QUARRIES.	H.Q. T.19.c.2.3.
2nd S.W.B.	RAZOR	"B" Bn. Right Bde.	H.Q. T.10.a.7.6.
1st K.O.S.B.	READY	Camp at CARNOY.	
1st R. Innis. Fus.	REALM	"A" Bn. Right Bde.	H.Q. T.10.a.7.6.
1st Border Regt.	RASHER	"C" Bn. FLERS Line.	H.Q. T.9.Central (FLERS).
88th Inf. Bde.	RECITE	GUILLEMONT STATION.	H.Q. S.24.b.7.4.
4th Worcester Regt.	RECKON	"A" Bn. Left Bde.	H.Q. T.3.d.7.8.
2nd Hants. Regt.	RECORD	"C" Bn. FLERS Line.	H.Q. T.8.d.3.9.
1st Essex Regt.	REDAN	"D" Bn. TRONES WOOD.	H.Q. S.29.c.6.3.
Newfoundland Regt.	REFORM	"B" Bn. Left Bde.	H.Q. N.34.c.2½.9.
Pioneer Bn.			
1/2nd Monmouth Regt.	RAFT	A.4.c.Central.	A.4.c.Central.
29th Div. R.E. H.Q.	RAJAH	A.4.d.5.2.	
29th Div. A.D.M.S.		A.2.d.9.7.	

_____

20th November, 1916.

(signed) G.N. Robertson
Captain, G.S.,
29th Division.

Copies to :-

G.O.C.
G.S. (3)
"Q" (4)
C.R.A.
C.R.E.
86th Bde.
87th Bde.
88th Bde.

A.D.M.S.
Officer i/c Signals.
O.C. 1/2nd Monmouth Regt.
XIV Corps "G".
XIV Corps "Q".
French Liaison Officer (2).
Guards Division.
49th Group Heavy Artillery.

SECRET.   I.G.39. 642

29TH DIVISION DAILY DISPOSITION REPORT.

10 a.m. November 22nd, 1916.

Unit.	Code Name.	Locality.	Remarks.
29th Div. H.Q.	ROSLARE	A.4.d.5.2.	H.Q. Advanced.
29th Div. H.Q.	ROSLARE	A.2.d.9.7.	H.Q. Rear (Adm).

Right Brigade Group.
Unit	Code	Locality	Remarks
1st R. Innis. Fus.	REALM	"A" & "B" Battn. R. Bde. Front.	H.Q. T.10.a.7.6.
2nd S.W.B.	RAZOR	"C" Battn. FLERS line.	H.Q. T.9.Central.
16th Middx. Regt.	RAMROD	"D" Battn. GUILLEMONT.	H.Q. T.19.c.8.7.
1st K.O.S.B.	READY	Camp at CARNOY.	H.Q. CARNOY.
1st Lanc. Fus.	RECESS	-"-	-"-
1st Border Regt.	RASHER	MANSELL Camp.	H.Q. F.11.c.4.4.

Left Brigade Group.
Unit	Code	Locality	Remarks
1st Essex Regt.	REDAN	"A" Battn.	H.Q. T.3.d.7.8.
2nd Hants. Regt.	RECORD	"B" Battn. (less 1 Coy. FLERS line)	H.Q. N.34.c.1.8.
1st R. Dub. Fus.	RAPIER	"C" Battn. TRONES WOOD.	H.Q. S.29.c.6.3.
2nd Roy. Fus.	RANDOM	"D" Battn. BRIQUETERIE (less 1 Coy. FLERS line)	H.Q. A.4.b.5.4.
4th Worcester Regt.	RECKON	Camp at CARNOY.	H.Q. CARNOY.
Newfoundland Regt.	REFORM	MANSEL Camp.	H.Q. F.11.c.4.4.

Right Brigade Group.
Unit	Code	Locality	Remarks
87th Inf. Bde. H.Q.	REACH	GUILLEMONT QUARRIES.	T.19.c.2.3.

Left Brigade Group.
Unit	Code	Locality	Remarks
88th Inf. Bde. H.Q.	RECITE	GUILLEMONT STATION.	S.29.b.7.4.
86th Inf. Bde. H.Q.	RAKE	Camp at BRIQUETERIE.	

Pioneer Battn.
Unit	Code	Locality	Remarks
1/2nd Monmouth Regt.	RAFT	A.4.c.Central.	A.4.c.Central.
29th Div. R.E. H.Q.	RAJAH	A.4.d.5.2.	
29th Div. A.D.M.S.		A.2.d.9.7.	

L. Carden Roe
Captain, G.S.,
29th Division.

21st November, 1916.

Copies to :-

G.O.C.
G.S. (3)
"Q" (4)
C.R.E.
C.R.A.
86th Bde.
87th Bde.
88th Bde.
A.D.M.S.

Officer i/c Signals.
O.C. 1/2nd Monmouth Regt.
XIV Corps "G".
XIV Corps "Q".
French Liaison Officer (2).
Guards Division.
49th Group Heavy Artillery.
Reinforcement Officer, ALBERT.

SECRET.   I.G.39.

29TH DIVISION DAILY DISPOSITION REPORT.

10 a.m. 24th November, 1916.

Unit.	Code Name.	Locality.	Remarks.
29th Div. H.Q.	ROSLARE	A.4.d.5.2.	H.Q. Advanced.
29th Div. H.Q.	ROSLARE	A.2.d.9.7.	H.Q. Rear (Adm).
87th Inf. Bde. H.Q.	REACH	GUILLEMONT QUARRIES	T.19.c.2.3.

Right Brigade Group.

16th Middlesex Regt.	RAMROD	"A" & "B" Battn.	H.Q. T.10.a.7.6.
1st Lancs. Fus.	RECESS	"C" Battn. FLERS Line.	H.Q. T.9.Central.
1st K.O.S.B.	READY	"D" Battn. GUILLEMONT.	H.Q. T.19.c.8.7.
1st Border Regt.	RASHER	MANSEL CAMP.	H.Q. F.11.c.4.4.
2nd S.W.B.	RAZOR	CARNOY CAMP.	H.Q. CARNOY.
1st R. Innis. Fus.	REALM	-"-	-"-
88th Inf. Bde. H.Q.	RECITE	GUILLEMONT STATION.	S.24.b.7.4.

Left Brigade Group.

1st Essex Regt.	REDAN	"A" Battn.	H.Q. T.3.d.7.8.
2nd Hants. Regt.	RECORD	"B" Battn. less ½ Coy. DEWDROP and THISTLE TRENCHES. ½ Coy. FLERS LINE.	H.Q. N.34.c.1½.8.
1st R. Dub. Fus.	RAPIER	"C" Battn. TRONES WOOD.	H.Q. S.29.c.6.3.
2nd Royal Fus.	RANDOM	"D" Battn. BRIQUETERIE (less 1 Coy. FLERS LINE)	H.Q. A.4.b.5.4.
4th Worcester Regt.	RECKON	Camp at CARNOY.	H.Q. CARNOY.
Newfoundland Regt.	REFORM	Camp at MANSEL.	H.Q. F.11.c.4.4.
86th Inf. Bde. H.Q.	RAKE	BRIQUETERIE	A.4.b.Central.

Pioneer Battn.

1/2nd Monmouth Regt.	RAFT	A.4.c.Central.	A.4.c.Central.
29th Div. R.E. H.Q.	RAJAH	A.4.d.5.2.	
29th Div. A.D.M.S.		A.2.d.9.7.	

23rd November, 1916.   L Carden Roe   Captain, G.S.,
                                                            29th Division.

Copies to :-

G.O.C.   Officer i/c Signals.
G.S. (3)   O.C 1/2nd Monmouth Regt.
"Q" (4)   XIV Corps "G".
C.R.A.   XIV Corps "Q".
C.R.E.   French Liaison Officer (2)
86th Bde.   Guards Division.
87th Bde.   49th Group Heavy Artillery.
88th Bde.   Reinforcement Officer, ALBERT.
A.D.M.S.

S E C R E T.   I.G.39.

29TH DIVISION DAILY DISPOSITION REPORT.

10 a.m. Nov. 25th, 1916.

Unit.	Code Name.	Locality.	Remarks.
29th Div. H.Q.	ROSLARE	A.4.d.5.2.	H.Q. Advanced.
29th Div. H.Q.	ROSLARE	A.2.d.9.7.	H.Q. Rear (Adm).
86th Inf.Bde.H.Q.	RAKE	GUILLEMONT QUARRIES	T.19.c.2.3.
Right Bde. Group.			
16th Middx. Regt.	RAMROD	"A" & "B" Battn.	H.Q. T.10.a.7.6.
1st Lancs. Fus.	RECESS	"C" Bn. FLERS Line.	H.Q. T.9.Central.
1st K.O.S.B.	READY	"D" Bn. GUILLEMONT.	H.Q. T.19.c.8.7.
1st Border Regt.	RASHER	MANSEL Camp.	H.Q. F.11.c.4.4.
2nd S.W.B.	RAZOR	CARNOY Camp.	H.Q. CARNOY.
1st R. Innis. Fus.	RIALA	-"-	-"-
88th Inf.Bde.H.Q.	RECITE	GUILLEMONT STATION	H.Q. S.24.b.7.4.
Left Bde. Group.			
1st R. Dub. Fus.	RAPIER	"A" Battn.	H.Q. T.3.d.7.8.
2nd Royal Fus.	RANDOM	"B" Battn. less ½ Coy. DEWDROP and THISTLE TRENCHES. ½ Coy. FLERS LINE.	H.Q. N.34.c.1½.8.
4th Worcester Regt.	RECKON	"C" Battn. TRONES WOOD.	H.Q. S.29.c.6.3.
Newfoundland Regt.	REFORM	"D" Battn. BRIQUETERIE. less 1 Coy. FLERS LINE.	H.Q. A.4.b.5.4.
1st Essex Regt.	REDAN	CARNOY CAMP.	H.Q. CARNOY.
2nd Hants. Regt.	RECORD	MANSEL CAMP.	H.Q. F.11.c.4.4.
87th Inf.Bde.H.Q.	REACH	BRIQUETERIE.	A.4.b.Central.
Pioneer Battn.			
1/2nd Monmouth Regt.	RAFT	A.4.c.Central.	A.4.c.Central.
29th Div. R.E. H.Q.	RAJAH	A.4.d.5.2.	
29th Div. A.D.M.S.		A.2.d.9.7.	

Signature

Captain, G.S.,
29th Division.

24th November, 1916.

Copies to :-

G.O.C.
G.S. (3)
"Q" (4)
C.R.A.
C.R.E.
86th Bde.
87th Bde.
88th Bde.
A.D.M.S.

Officer i/c Signals.
O.C. 1/2nd Monmouth Regt.
XIV Corps "G".
XIV Corps "Q".
French Liaison Officer. (2)
5th Australian Division.
49th Group Heavy Artillery.
Reinforcement Officer, ALBERT.

S E C R E T.

29TH DIVISION DAILY DISPOSITION REPORT.

10 a.m. Nov. 27th, 1916.

Unit.	Code Name.	Locality.	Remarks.
29th Div. H.Q.	ROSLARE	A.4.d.5.2.	H.Q. Advanced.
29th Div. H.Q.	ROSLARE	A.2.d.9.7.	H.Q. Rear.
86th Inf.Bde.H.Q.	RAKE	GUILLEMONT QUARRIES	T.19.c.2.3.
Right Bde. Group.			
1st K.O.S.B.	READY	"A" & "B" Bn.	H.Q. T.10.a.7.6.
16th Middx. Regt.	RAMROD	"C" Bn.	H.Q. T.9.Central.
1st Lanc. Fus.	RECESS	"D" Bn. GUILLEMONT	H.Q. T.19.c.8.7.
1st Border Regt.	RASHER	MANSEL Camp.	H.Q. F.11.c.4.4.
2nd S.W.B.	RAZOR	CARNOY Camp.	H.Q. CARNOY.
1st R. Innis. Fus.	REALM	-"-	-"-
88th Inf.Bde.H.Q.	RECITE	GUILLEMONT STATION	H.Q. S.24.b.7.4.
Left Bde. Group.			
4th Worc. Regt.	RECKON	"A" Bn.	H.Q. T.3.d.7.8.
Newfoundland Regt.	REFORM	"B" Bn. less ½ Coy. DEWDROP and THISTLE TRENCHES. ½ Coy. FLERS LINE.	H.Q. N.34.c.1½.8.
1st Essex Regt.	REDAN	"C" Bn. TRONES WOOD.	H.Q. S.29.c.6.3.
2nd Hants. Regt.	RECORD	"D" Bn. BRIQUETERIE.	H.Q. A.4.b.5.4.
1st R. Dublin Fus.	RAPIER	CARNOY Camp.	H.Q. CARNOY.
2nd Royal Fus.	RANDOM	MANSEL Camp.	H.Q. F.11.c.4.4.
87th Inf.Bde.H.Q.	REACH	BRIQUETERIE	A.4.b.Central.
Pioneer Bn.			
1/2nd Monmouth Regt.	RAFT	A.4.c.Central	A.4.c.Central.
29th Div. R.E. H.Q.	RAJAH	A.4.d.5.2.	
29th Div. A.D.M.S.		A.2.d.9.7.	

W. Cardew Roe
Captain, G.S.,
29th Division.

26th November, 1916.

Copies to :-

G.O.C.
G.S. (3)
"Q" (4)
C.R.A.
C.R.E.
86th Bde.
87th Bde.
88th Bde.
A.D.M.S.

Officer i/c Signals.
O.C. 1/2nd Monmouth Regt.
XIV Corps "G".
XIV Corps "Q".
French Liaison Officer (2).
5th Australian Division.
49th Group Heavy Artillery.
Reinforcement Officer, ALBERT.

S E C R E T.

29TH DIVISION DAILY DISPOSITION REPORT.

646

10 a.m. 28th Nov. 1916.

Unit.	Code Name.	Locality.	Remarks.
29th Div. H.Q.	ROSLARE	A.4.d.5.2.	H.Q. Advanced.
29th Div. H.Q.	ROSLARE	A.2.d.9.7.	H.Q. Rear.
86th Inf.Bde.H.Q.	RAKE	GUILLEMONT QUARRIES.	T.19.c.2.3.
Right Bde.Group.			
1st K.O.S.B.	READY	"A" & "B" Bn.	H.Q. T.10.a.7.6.
1st Border Regt.	RASHER	"C" Bn.	H.Q. T.9.Central.
2nd S.W.B.	RAZOR	"D" Bn. GUILLEMONT.	H.Q. T.19.c.8.7.
1st Lanc. Fus.	RECESS	MANSEL CAMP.	H.Q. F.11.c.4.4.
16th Middx. Regt.	RAMROD	CARNOY CAMP.	H.Q. CARNOY.
1st R. Innis.Fus.	REALM	-"-	-"-
88th Inf.Bde.H.Q.	RECITE	GUILLEMONT STATION.	S.24.b.7.4.
Left Bde. Group.			
4th Worc. Regt.	RECKON	"A" Bn.	H.Q. T.3.d.7.8.
Newfoundland Regt	REFORM	"B" Bn. less ½ Coy. DEWDROP and THISTLE TRENCHES. ½ Coy. FLERS LINE.	H.Q. N.34.c.1½.8.
1st Essex Regt.	REDAN	"C" Bn. TRONES WOOD.	H.Q. S.29.c.6.3.
2nd Royal Fus.	RANDOM	"D" Bn. BRIQUETERIE.	H.Q. A.4.b.5.4.
1st R. Dub. Fus.	RAPIER	CARNOY CAMP.	H.Q. CARNOY.
2nd Hants. Regt.	RECORD	MANSEL CAMP.	H.Q. F.11.c.4.4.
87th Inf.Bde.H.Q.	REACH	BRIQUETERIE	A.4.b.Central.
Pioneer Bn.			
1/2nd Monmouth Regt.	RAFT	A.4.c.Central.	A.4.c.Central.
29th Div.R.E. H.Q.	RAJAH	A.4.d.5.2.	
29th Div. A.D.M.S.		A.2.d.9.7.	

L. Carden Roe
Captain, G.S.,
29th Division.

27th November, 1916.

Copies to :-

G.O.C. Officer i/c Sigs.
G.S. (3) O.C. 1/2nd Monmouth Regt.
"Q" (4) XIV Corps "G".
C.R.A. XIV Corps "Q".
C.R.E. French Liaison Officer (2)
86th Bde. 5th Australian Divn.
87th Bde. 49th Group Heavy Artillery.
88th Bde. Reinforcement Officer, ALBERT.
A.D.M.S.

S E C R E T.

I.G.39.   647

29TH DIVISION DAILY DISPOSITION REPORT.

10 a.m. 29th Nov. 1916.

Unit.	Code Name.	Locality.	Remarks.
29th Div. H.Q.	ROSLARE	A.4.d.5.2.	H.Q. Advanced.
29th Div. H.Q.	ROSLARE	A.2.d.9.7.	H.Q. Rear.
86th Inf.Bde.H.Q.	RAKE	GUILLEMONT QUARRIES.	T.19.c.2.3.
Right Bde. Group.			
1st Border Regt.	RASHER	"A" & "B" Bn.	H.Q. T.10.a.7.6.
1st R. Innis. Fus.	REALM	"C" Bn. FLERS line.	H.Q. T.9.Central.
2nd S.W.B.	RAZOR	"D" Bn. GUILLEMONT.	H.Q. T.19.c.8.7.
1st Lanc. Fus.	RECESS	MANSEL CAMP.	H.Q. F.11.c.4.4.
16th Middx. Regt.	RAMROD	CARNOY CAMP.	H.Q. CARNOY.
1st K.O.S.B.	READY	-"-	-"-
88th Inf.Bde.H.Q.	RECITE	GUILLEMONT STATION.	S.24.b.7.4.
Left Bde. Group.			
4th Worc. Regt.	RECKON	"A" Bn.	H.Q. T.3.d.7.8.
Newfoundland Regt.	REFORM	"B" Bn. less ½ Coy. DEWDROP and THISTLE TRENCHES. ½ Coy. FLERS line.	H.Q. N.34.c.1½.8.
1st Essex Regt.	REDAN	"C" Bn. TRONES WOOD.	H.Q. S.29.c.6.3.
2nd Hants. Regt.	RECORD	"D" Bn. BRIQUETERIE.	H.Q. A.4.b.5.4.
1st R. Dub. Fus.	RAPIER	CARNOY CAMP.	H.Q. CARNOY.
2nd Royal Fus.	RANDOM	MANSEL CAMP.	H.Q. F.11.c.4.4.
87th Inf.Bde.H.Q.	REACH	BRIQUETERIE	A.4.b.Central.
Pioneer Bn.			
1/2nd Monmouth Regt.	RAFT	A.4.c.Central.	A.4.c.Central.
29th Div. R.E. H.Q.	RAJAH	A.4.d.5.2.	
29th Div. A.D.M.S.		A.2.d.9.7.	

L. Carden Roe   Captain, G.S.,
28th November, 1916.   29th Division.

Copies to :-
    G.O.C.   Officer i/c Sigs.
    G.S. (4)   O.C. 1/2nd Monmouth Regt.
    "Q" (3)   XIV Corps "G".
    C.R.A.   XIV Corps "Q".
    C.R.E.   French Liaison Officer (2).
    86th Bde.   5th Australian Division.
    87th Bde.   49th Group Heavy Artillery.
    88th Bde.   Reinfcemnt. Officer, ALBERT.
    A.D.M.S.

S E C R E T.

29th Division No. I.G.39.

86th Brigade.
87th Brigade.
88th Brigade.
C.R.A. 17th Division.
C.R.E.
A.D.M.S.
"Q"
Officer i/c Signals.
O.C. 1/2nd Monmouth Regt.
XIV Corps "G".
XIV Corps "Q".
French Liaison Officer.
5th Australian Division.
49th Group Heavy Artillery.
Reinforcement Officer, ALBERT.

----

10 a.m. 30th November, 1916.

Dispositions unchanged except that 2nd South Wales Borderers relieve 1st Border Regiment in the front line; the 1st Border Regiment becoming "D" Battalion in GUILLEMONT.

Carden Roe Captain, G.S.,

29th November, 1916.   29th Division.

MARCH TABLE "A".

Date.	86th Brigade.	88th Brigade.	87th Brigade.
Nov. 14th	CORBIE	VILLE and MERICOURT	Moves to CITADEL.
Nov. 15th	At CORBIE	At SANDPITS	Moves from CITADEL at 9 a.m. to CARNOY and BRIQUETERIE. H.Q. & 2 Bns. at BRIQUETERIE.
Nov. 16th	At MEAULTE	2 Bns. at SANDPITS. Bde. H.Q. and 2 Bns. move from SANDPITS at 12 noon to BRIQUETERIE.	Relieves 25th Inf. Bde. in Right Section. 2 Bns. in line, 1 Bn. FLERS line, 1 Bn. GUILLEMONT. H.Q. from BRIQUETERIE to GUILLEMONT (quarries).
Nov. 17th	At MEAULTE	Relieves 24th Inf. Bde. in Left Section. 2 Bns. in line, 1 Bn. FLERS line, 1 Bn. TRONES WOOD. Bde. H.Q. to GUILLEMONT STATION. To be clear of SANDPITS by 11.30 a.m.	In Right Section.
Nov. 18th	Moves from MEAULTE to BRIQUETERIE (Bde. H.Q. and 1 Bn.) and CARNOY (3 Bns.). To be clear of MEAULTE by 11 a.m. DIVNL. RESERVE.	In LEFT SECTION.	In RIGHT SECTION.

MARCH TABLE "B".

Date.	23rd Inf. Bde. Reserve CARNOY and BRIQUETERIE.	24th Inf. Bde. LEFT SECTION.	25th Inf. Bde. RIGHT SECTION.	Remarks.
Nov. 14th				
Nov. 15th	Moves from CARNOY and BRIQUETERIE at 9 a.m. to CITADEL.	2 Bns. in the line Left Section. 1 Bn. FLERS line. 1 Bn. TRONES WOOD. H.Q. GUILLEMONT.	2 Bns. in the line Right Section. 1 Bn. FLERS line. 1 Bn. GUILLEMONT. H.Q. GUILLEMONT STATION. (quarries).	87th Inf. Bde. becomes Divl. Res. to 8th Divn.
Nov. 16th	At CITADEL	In left section.	On relief by 87th Inf. Bde. H.Q. at BRIQUETERIE to SANDPITS. 2 Bns. to CARNOY. 2 Bns. from FLERS line and GUILLEMONT move to SANDPITS.	2 Bns. of 88th Bde. at BRIQUETERIE come under the orders of the G.O.C. 8th Div. and with 2 Bns. of 25th Bde. at CARNOY will form 8th Divl. Reserve.
Nov. 17th	At CITADEL	On relief by 88th Inf. Bde. 2 Bns. to SANDPITS. Bde. H.Q. and 2 Bns. from line to BRIQUETERIE. 2 Bns. from FLERS and TRONES WOOD to CARNOY.	2 Bns. already at SANDPITS.	
Nov. 18th	At CITADEL	Moves to MEAULTE. To be clear of Camps by 12 noon.	At SANDPITS.	

NOTE :-
1. CARNOY Camps are in A.8.a. and A.8.c. both East of MONTAUBAN - CARNOY Road. BRIQUETERIE Camp is at A.4.b.
2. If cross country tracks are not passable for infantry on account of the weather, they will move by the MEAULTE - MAMETZ - MONTAUBAN Road.
3. 1st Line Transport lines will be taken over by Brigades as follows :-
   86th Brigade take over from 24th Brigade.
   87th   "   "   "   " 23rd   "
   88th   "   "   "   " 25th   "

S E C R E T.

HEADQUARTERS, 29th DIVISION. INTELLIGENCE.
I.G.39.
No. 180

29TH DIVISION DAILY DISPOSITION REPORT

10 a.m. 19th Nov. 1916.

Unit.	Code Name.	Locality.	Remarks.
29th Division H.Q.	ROSSLARE	A.4.d.5.2.	Headquarters (Advd)
29th Division H.Q.	ROSSLARE	A.2.d.9.7.	Headquarters (Rear-Adm)
86th Inf. Bde.	RAKE		
2nd Royal Fus.	RANDOM	BRIQUETERIE	
1st Lancs. Fus.	RECESS	Camp at BRIQUETERIE	
16th Middx. Regt.	RAMROD	Camp at CARNOY	
1st R. Dub. Fus.	RAPIER	-"-	
87th Inf. Bde.	REACH		
2nd S.W.Bs.	RAZOR	GUILLEMONT QUARRIES	H.Q. T.19.c.2.3
		"C" Bn. FLERS Line	H.Q. T.9.central (FLERS)
1st K.O.S.Bs.	READY	"A" Bn. Right Bde.	H.Q. T.10.a.7.6.
1st R. Innis. Fus.	REALM	"D" Bn. GUILLEMONT.	H.Q. T.19.c.8.7.
1st Border Regt.	RASHER	"B" Bn. Right Bde.	H.Q. T.10.a.7.6.
88th Inf. Bde.	RECITE	GUILLEMONT STATION	H.Q. S.24.b.7.4.
4th Worcester Regt.	RECKON	"A" Bn. Left Bde.	H.Q. T.3.d.7.8.
2nd Hants Regt.	RECORD	"C" Bn. FLERS Line	H.Q. T.8.d.3.9.
1st Essex Regt.	REDAN	"D" Bn. TRONES WOOD	H.Q. S.29.c.6.3.
Newfld. Regt.	REFORM	"B" Bn. Left Bde.	H.Q. N.34.c.2½.9.
29th Div. R.E. H.Q.	RAJAH	A.4.d.5.2.	
29th Div. A.D.M.S.		A.2.d.9.7.	

S.N. Ricketts
Captain, G.S.,
29th Division.

19th November, 1916.

Copies to :-

G.O.C.
G.S. (3)
"Q" (4)
C.R.A.
C.R.E.
86th Bde.
87th Bde.
88th Bde.

A.D.M.S.
Officer i/c Sigs.
XIV Corps "G"
XIV Corps "Q"
French Liaison Officer (2)
Guards Division.

SECRET.

> HEADQUARTERS,
> 29th DIVISION,
> INTELLIGENCE.
> I.G.39.

29TH DIVISION DAILY DISPOSITION REPORT.

10 a.m. November 21st, 1916.

Unit.	Code Name.	Locality.	Remarks.
29th Div. H.Q.	ROSLARE	A.4.d.5.2.	H.Q. Advanced.
29th Div. H.Q.	ROSLARE	A.2.d.9.7.	H.Q. Rear (Adm).
86th Inf. Bde.	RAKE	Camp at BRIQUETERIE.	
2nd Royal Fus.	RANDOM	-"-	
1st Lancs. Fus.	RECESS	Camp at CARNOY.	
16th Middx. Regt.	RAMROD	"D" Bn. GUILLEMONT.	T.19.c.8.7.
1st R. Dub. Fus.	RAPIER	Camp at CARNOY.	
87th Inf. Bde.	REACH	GUILLEMONT QUARRIES.	H.Q. T.19.c.2.3.
2nd S.W.B.	RAZOR	"B" Bn. Right Bde.	H.Q. T.10.a.7.6.
1st K.O.S.B.	READY	Camp at CARNOY.	
1st R. Innis. Fus.	REALM	"A" Bn. Right Bde.	H.Q. T.10.a.7.6.
1st Border Regt.	RASHER	"C" Bn. FLERS Line.	H.Q. T.9.Central (FLERS).
88th Inf. Bde.	RECITE	GUILLEMONT STATION.	H.Q. S.24.b.7.4.
4th Worcester Regt.	RECKON	"A" Bn. Left Bde.	H.Q. T.3.d.7.8.
2nd Hants. Regt.	RECORD	"C" Bn. FLERS Line.	H.Q. T.8.d.3.9.
1st Essex Regt.	REDAN	"D" Bn. TRONES WOOD.	H.Q. S.29.c.6.3.
Newfoundland Regt.	REFORM	"B" Bn. Left Bde.	H.Q. N.34.c.2½.9.
Pioneer Bn.			
1/2nd Monmouth Regt.	RAFT	A.4.c.Central.	A.4.c.Central.
29th Div. R.E. H.Q.	RAJAH	A.4.d.5.2.	
29th Div. A.D.M.S.		A.2.d.9.7.	

[signed] N Robertson
Captain, G.S.,
29th Division.

20th November, 1916.

Copies to :-

G.O.C.   A.D.M.S.
G.S. (3)   Officer i/c Signals.
"Q" (4)   O.C. 1/2nd Monmouth Regt.
C.R.A.   XIV Corps "G".
C.R.E.   XIV Corps "Q".
86th Bde.   French Liaison Officer (2).
87th Bde.   Guards Division.
88th Bde.   49th Group Heavy Artillery.

SECRET.

[HEADQUARTERS 29th DIVISION INTELLIGENCE. I.G.39.]

29TH DIVISION DAILY DISPOSITION REPORT.

10 a.m. November 22nd, 1916.

Unit.	Code Name.	Locality.	Remarks.
29th Div. H.Q.	ROSLARE	A.4.d.5.2.	H.Q. Advanced.
29th Div. H.Q.	ROSLARE	A.2.d.9.7.	H.Q. Rear (Adm).
Right Brigade Group.			
1st R. Innis. Fus.	REALM	"A" & "B" Battn. R. Bde. Front.	H.Q. T.10.a.7.6.
2nd S.W.B.	RAZOR	"C" Battn. FLERS line.	H.Q. T.9.Central.
16th Middx. Regt.	RAMROD	"D" Battn. GUILLEMONT.	H.Q. T.19.c.8.7.
1st K.O.S.B.	READY	Camp at CARNOY.	H.Q. CARNOY.
1st Lanc. Fus.	RECESS	-"-	-"-
1st Border Regt.	RASHER	MANSELL Camp.	H.Q. F.11.c.4.4.
Left Brigade Group.			
1st Essex Regt.	REDAN	"A" Battn.	H.Q. T.3.d.7.8.
2nd Hants. Regt.	RECORD	"B" Battn. (less 1 Coy. FLERS line)	H.Q. N.34.c.1½.8.
1st R. Dub. Fus.	RAPIER	"C" Battn. TRONES WOOD.	H.Q. S.29.c.6.3.
2nd Roy. Fus.	RANDOM	"D" Battn. BRIQUETERIE (less 1 Coy. FLERS line)	H.Q. A.4.b.5.4.
4th Worcester Regt.	RECKON	Camp at CARNOY.	H.Q. CARNOY.
Newfoundland Regt.	REFORM	MANSEL Camp.	H.Q. F.11.c.4.4.
Right Brigade Group.			
87th Inf. Bde. H.Q.	REACH	GUILLEMONT QUARRIES.	T.19.c.2.3.
Left Brigade Group.			
88th Inf. Bde. H.Q.	RECITE	GUILLEMONT STATION.	S.29.b.7.4.
86th Inf. Bde. H.Q.	RAKE	Camp at BRIQUETERIE.	
Pioneer Battn.			
1/2nd Monmouth Regt.	RAFT	A.4.c.Central.	A.4.c.Central.
29th Div. R.E. H.Q.	RAJAH	A.4.d.5.2.	
29th Div. A.D.M.S.		A.2.d.9.7.	

L. Carden Roe

Captain, G.S.,

21st November, 1916.   29th Division.

Copies to :-

G.O.C.   Officer i/c Signals.
G.S. (3)   O.C. 1/2nd Monmouth Regt.
"Q" (4)   XIV Corps "G".
C.R.E.   XIV Corps "Q".
C.R.A.   French Liaison Officer (2).
86th Bde.   Guards Division.
87th Bde.   49th Group Heavy Artillery.
88th Bde.   Reinforcement Officer, ALBERT.
A.D.M.S.

S E C R E T.

29TH DIVISION DAILY DISPOSITION REPORT.

10 a.m. 24th November, 1916.

Unit.	Code Name.	Locality.	Remarks.
29th Div. H.Q.	ROSLARE	A.4.d.5.2.	H.Q. Advanced.
29th Div. H.Q.	ROSLARE	A.2.d.9.7.	H.Q. Rear (Adm).
87th Inf. Bde. H.Q.	REACH	GUILLEMONT QUARRIES	T.19.c.2.3.
Right Brigade Group.			
16th Middlesex Regt.	RAMROD	"A" & "B" Battn.	H.Q. T.10.a.7.6.
1st Lancs. Fus.	RECESS	"C" Battn. FLERS Line.	H.Q. T.9.Central.
1st K.O.S.B.	READY	"D" Battn. GUILLEMONT.	H.Q. T.19.c.8.7.
1st Border Regt.	RASHER	MANSEL CAMP.	H.Q. F.11.c.4.4.
2nd S.W.B.	RAZOR	CARNOY CAMP.	H.Q. CARNOY.
1st R. Innis. Fus.	REALM	-"-	-"-
88th Inf. Bde. H.Q.	RECITE	GUILLEMONT STATION.	S.24.b.7.4.
Left Brigade Group.			
1st Essex Regt.	REDAN	"A" Battn.	H.Q. T.3.d.7.8.
2nd Hants. Regt.	RECORD	"B" Battn.	H.Q. N.34.c.1½.8.
		less ½ Coy. DEWDROP and THISTLE TRENCHES. ½ Coy. FLERS LINE.	
1st R. Dub. Fus.	RAPIER	"C" Battn. TRONES WOOD.	H.Q. S.29.c.6.3.
2nd Royal Fus.	RANDOM	"D" Battn. BRIQUETERIE (less 1 Coy. FLERS LINE)	H.Q. A.4.b.5.4.
4th Worcester Regt.	RECKON	Camp at CARNOY.	H.Q. CARNOY.
Newfoundland Regt.	REFORM	Camp at MANSEL.	H.Q. F.11.c.4.4.
86th Inf. Bde. H.Q.	RAKE	BRIQUETERIE	A.4.b.Central.
Pioneer Battn.			
1/2nd Monmouth Regt.	RAFT	A.4.c.Central.	A.4.c.Central.
29th Div. R.E. H.Q.	RAJAH	A.4.d.5.2.	
29th Div. A.D.M.S.		A.2.d.9.7.	

23rd November, 1916.   L Carden Roe   Captain, G.S.,
29th Division.

Copies to :-

G.O.C.   Officer i/c Signals.
G.S. (3)   O.C 1/2nd Monmouth Regt.
"Q" (4)   XIV Corps "G".
C.R.A.   XIV Corps "Q".
C.R.E.   French Liaison Officer (2)
86th Bde.   Guards Division.
87th Bde.   49th Group Heavy Artillery.
88th Bde.   Reinforcement Officer, ALBERT.
A.D.M.S.

S E C R E T. I.G.39.

29TH DIVISION DAILY DISPOSITION REPORT.

10 a.m. Nov. 25th, 1916.

Unit.	Code Name.	Locality.	Remarks.
29th Div. H.Q.	ROSLARE	A.4.d.5.2.	H.Q. Advanced.
29th Div. H.Q.	ROSLARE	A.2.d.9.7.	H.Q. Rear (Adm).
86th Inf.Bde.H.Q.	RAKE	GUILLEMONT QUARRIES	T.19.c.2.3.
Right Bde. Group.			
16th Middx. Regt.	RAMROD	"A" & "B" Battn.	H.Q. T.10.a.7.6.
1st Lancs. Fus.	RECESS	"C" Bn. FLERS Line.	H.Q. T.9.Central.
1st K.O.S.B.	READY	"D" Bn. GUILLEMONT.	H.Q. T.19.c.8.7.
1st Border Regt.	RASHER	MANSEL Camp.	H.Q. F.11.c.4.4.
2nd S.W.B.	RAZOR	CARNOY Camp.	H.Q. CARNOY.
1st R. Innis. Fus.	RUALA	-"-	-"-
88th Inf.Bde.H.Q.	RECITE	GUILLEMONT STATION	H.Q. S.24.b.7.4.
Left Bde. Group.			
1st R. Dub. Fus.	RAPIER	"A" Battn.	H.Q. T.3.d.7.8.
2nd Royal Fus.	RANDOM	"B" Battn.	H.Q. N.34.c.1½.8.
		less ½ Coy. DEWDROP and THISTLE TRENCHES.	
		½ Coy. FLERS LINE.	
4th Worcester Regt.	RECKON	"C" Battn. TRONES WOOD.	H.Q. S.29.c.6.3.
Newfoundland Regt.	REFORM	"D" Battn. BRIQUETERIE.	H.Q. A.4.b.5.4.
		less 1 Coy. FLERS LINE.	
1st Essex Regt.	REDAN	CARNOY CAMP.	H.Q. CARNOY.
2nd Hants. Regt.	RECORD	MANSEL CAMP.	H.Q. F.11.c.4.4.
87th Inf.Bde.H.Q.	REACH	BRIQUETERIE.	A.4.b.Central.
Pioneer Battn.			
1/2nd Monmouth Regt.	RAFT	A.4.c.Central.	A.4.c.Central.
29th Div. R.E. H.Q.	RAJAH	A.4.d.5.2.	
29th Div. A.D.M.S.		A.2.d.9.7.	

S.N. Robertson

Captain, G.S.,
29th Division.

24th November, 1916.

Copies to :-

G.O.C.
G.S. (3)
"Q". (4)
C.R.A.
C.R.E.
86th Bde.
87th Bde.
88th Bde.
A.D.M.S.

Officer i/c Signals.
O.C. 1/2nd Monmouth Regt.
XIV Corps "G".
XIV Corps "Q".
French Liaison Officer. (2)
5th Australian Division.
49th Group Heavy Artillery.
Reinforcement Officer, ALBERT.

S E C R E T.

> HEADQUARTERS.
> 29th DIVISION.
> INTELLIGENCE.
> No. I.G.89.

29TH DIVISION DAILY DISPOSITION REPORT.

10 a.m. Nov. 27th, 1916.

Unit.	Code Name.	Locality.	Remarks.
29th Div. H.Q.	ROSLARE	A.4.d.5.2.	H.Q. Advanced.
29th Div. H.Q.	ROSLARE	A.2.d.9.7.	H.Q. Rear.
86th Inf.Bde.H.Q.	RAKE	GUILLEMONT QUARRIES	T.19.c.2.3.
Right Bde. Group.			
1st K.O.S.B.	READY	"A" & "B" Bn.	H.Q. T.10.a.7.6.
16th Middx. Regt.	RAMROD	"C" Bn.	H.Q. T.9.Central.
1st Lanc. Fus.	RECESS	"D" Bn. GUILLEMONT	H.Q. T.19.c.8.7.
1st Border Regt.	RASHER	MANSEL Camp.	H.Q. F.11.c.4.4.
2nd S.W.B.	RAZOR	CARNOY Camp.	H.Q. CARNOY.
1st R. Innis. Fus.	REALM	-"-	-"-
88th Inf.Bde.H.Q.	RECITE	GUILLEMONT STATION	H.Q. S.24.b.7.4.
Left Bde. Group.			
4th Worc. Regt.	RECKON	"A" Bn.	H.Q. T.3.d.7.8.
N'foundland Regt.	REFORM	"B" Bn.	H.Q. N.34.c.1½.8.
		less ½ Coy. DEWDROP and THISTLE TRENCHES.	
		½ Coy. FLERS LINE.	
1st Essex Regt.	REDAN	"C" Bn. TRONES WOOD.	H.Q. S.29.c.6.3.
2nd Hants. Regt.	RECORD	"D" Bn. BRIQUETERIE.	H.Q. A.4.b.5.4.
1st R. Dublin Fus.	RAPIER	CARNOY Camp.	H.Q. CARNOY.
2nd Royal Fus.	RANDOM	MANSEL Camp.	H.Q. F.11.c.4.4.
87th Inf.Bde.H.Q.	REACH	BRIQUETERIE	A.4.b.Central.
Pioneer Bn.			
1/2nd Monmouth Regt.	RAFT	A.4.c.Central	A.4.c.Central.
29th Div. R.E. H.Q.	RAJAH	A.4.d.5.2.	
29th Div. A.D.M.S.		A.2.d.9.7.	

W. Carden Roe
Captain, G.S.,
29th Division.

26th November, 1916.

Copies to :-

G.O.C. Officer i/c Signals.
G.S. (3) O.C. 1/2nd Monmouth Regt.
"Q" (4) XIV Corps "G".
C.R.A. XIV Corps "Q".
C.R.E. French Liaison Officer (2).
86th Bde. 5th Australian Division.
87th Bde. 49th Group Heavy Artillery.
88th Bde. Reinforcement Officer, ALBERT.
A.D.M.S.

SECRET

**HEADQUARTERS.
29th DIVISION.
INTELLIGENCE.
No. I.G.39.**

29TH DIVISION DAILY DISPOSITION REPORT.

10 a.m. 28th Nov. 1916.

Unit.	Code Name.	Locality.	Remarks.
29th Div. H.Q.	ROSLARE	A.4.d.5.2.	H.Q. Advanced.
29th Div. H.Q.	ROSLARE	A.2.d.9.7.	H.Q. Rear.
86th Inf.Bde.H.Q.	RAKE	GUILLEMONT QUARRIES.	T.19.c.2.3.
Right Bde.Group.			
1st K.O.S.B.	READY	"A" & "B" Bn.	H.Q. T.10.a.7.6.
1st Border Regt.	RASHER	"C" Bn.	H.Q. T.9.Central.
2nd S.W.B.	RAZOR	"D" Bn. GUILLEMONT.	H.Q. T.19.c.8.7.
1st Lanc. Fus.	RECESS	MANSEL CAMP.	H.Q. F.11.c.4.4.
1/ Middx. Regt.	RAMROD	CARNOY CAMP.	H.Q. CARNOY.
1st R. Innis.Fus.	REALM	-"-	-"-
88th Inf.Bde.H.Q.	RECITE	GUILLEMONT STATION.	S.24.b.7.4.
Left Bde. Group.			
4th Worc. Regt.	RECKON	"A" Bn.	H.Q. T.3.d.7.8.
Newfoundland Regt	REFORM	"B" Bn.	H.Q. N.34.c.1½.8.
		less ½ Coy. DEWDROP and THISTLE TRENCHES.	
		⅔ Coy. FLERS LINE.	
1st Essex Regt.	REDAN	"C" Bn. TRONES WOOD.	H.Q. S.29.c.6.3.
2nd Royal Fus.	RANDOM	"D" Bn. BRIQUETERIE.	H.Q. A.4.b.5.4.
1st R. Dub. Fus.	RAPIER	CARNOY CAMP.	H.Q. CARNOY.
2nd Hants. Regt.	RECORD	MANSEL CAMP.	H.Q. F.11.c.4.4.
87th Inf.Bde.H.Q.	REACH	BRIQUETERIE	A.4.b.Central.
Pioneer Bn.			
1/2nd Monmouth Regt.	RAFT	A.4.c.Central.	A.4.c.Central.
29th Div.R.E. H.Q.	RAJAH	A.4.d.5.2.	
29th Div. A.D.M.S.		A.2.d.9.7.	

L. Carden Roe
Captain, G.S.,
29th Division.

27th November, 1916.

Copies to :-

G.O.C.   Officer i/c Sigs.
G.S. (3)   O.C. 1/2nd Monmouth Regt.
"Q" (4)   XIV Corps "G".
C.R.A.   XIV Corps "Q".
C.R.E.   French Liaison Officer (2)
86th Bde.   5th Australian Divn.
87th Bde.   49th Group Heavy Artillery.
88th Bde.   Reinforcement Officer, ALBERT.
A.D.M.S.

SECRET.

[Stamp: HEADQUARTERS. 29th DIVISION. INTELLIGENCE. I.G.39.]

29TH DIVISION DAILY DISPOSITION REPORT.

10 a.m. 29th Nov. 1916.

Unit.	Code Name.	Locality.	Remarks.
29th Div. H.Q.	ROSLARE	A.4.d.5.2.	H.Q. Advanced.
29th Div. H.Q.	ROSLARE	A.2.d.9.7.	H.Q. Rear.
86th Inf.Bde.H.Q. Right Bde. Group.	RAKE	GUILLEMONT QUARRIES.	T.19.c.2.3.
1st Border Regt.	RASHER	"A" & "B" Bn.	H.Q. T.10.a.7.6.
1st R. Innis. Fus.	REALM	"C" Bn. FLERS line.	H.Q. T.9.Central.
2nd S.W.B.	RAZOR	"D" Bn. GUILLEMONT.	H.Q. T.19.c.8.7.
1st Lanc. Fus.	RECESS	MANSEL CAMP.	H.Q. F.11.c.4.4.
16th Middx. Regt.	RAMROD	CARNOY CAMP.	H.Q. CARNOY.
1st K.O.S.B.	READY	-"-	-"-
88th Inf.Bde.H.Q. Left Bde. Group.	RECITE	GUILLEMONT STATION.	S.24.b.7.4.
4th Worc. Regt.	RECKON	"A" Bn.	H.Q. T.3.d.7.8.
Newfoundland Regt.	REFORM	"B" Bn. less ½ Coy. DEWDROP and THISTLE TRENCHES. ½ Coy. FLERS line.	H.Q. N.34.c.1½.8.
1st Essex Regt.	REDAN	"C" Bn. TRONES WOOD.	H.Q. S.29.c.6.3.
2nd Hants. Regt.	RECORD	"D" Bn. BRIQUETERIE.	H.Q. A.4.b.5.4.
1st R. Dub. Fus.	RAPIER	CARNOY CAMP.	H.Q. CARNOY.
2nd Royal Fus.	RANDOM	MANSEL CAMP.	H.Q. F.11.c.4.4.
87th Inf.Bde.H.Q.	REACH	BRIQUETERIE	A.4.b.Central.
Pioneer Bn. 1/2nd Monmouth Regt.	RAFT	A.4.c.Central.	A.4.c.Central.
29th Div. R.E. H.Q.	RAJAH	A.4.d.5.2.	
29th Div. A.D.M.S.		A.2.d.9.7.	

L. Carden Roe
Captain, G.S.,
29th Division.

28th November, 1916.

Copies to :-
G.O.C. Officer i/c Sigs.
G.S. (4) O.C. 1/2nd Monmouth Regt.
"Q" (3) XIV Corps "G".
C.R.A. XIV Corps "Q".
C.R.E. French Liaison Officer (2).
86th Bde. 5th Australian Division.
87th Bde. 49th Group Heavy Artillery.
88th Bde. Reinfcemnt. Officer, ALBERT.
A.D.M.S.

S E C R E T.

29th Division No. I.G.39.

> HEADQUARTERS.
> 29th DIVISION.
> INTELLIGENCE.
> No.............
> Date............

86th Brigade.
87th Brigade.
88th Brigade.
C.R.A. 17th Division.
C.R.E.
A.D.M.S.
"Q"
Officer i/c Signals.
O.C. 1/2nd Monmouth Regt.
XIV Corps "G".
XIV Corps "Q".
French Liaison Officer.
5th Australian Division.
49th Group Heavy Artillery.
Reinforcement Officer, ALBERT.

----

10 a.m. 30th November, 1916.

Dispositions unchanged except that 2nd South Wales Borderers relieve 1st Border Regiment in the front line; the 1st Border Regiment becoming "D" Battalion in GUILLEMONT.

L. Carden Roe Captain, G.S.,

29th November, 1916.   29th Division.

CONFIDENTIAL.
----------oOo----------

WAR   DIARY   of

GENERAL STAFF,
29th Division.

from

1st DECEMBER, 1916 - 31st DECEMBER, 1916.

VOLUME XXII

Army Form C. 2118.

WAR DIARY – GENERAL STAFF
29TH DIVISION.
INTELLIGENCE SUMMARY.
(Erase heading not required.)

Instructions regarding War Diaries and Intelligence Summaries are contained in F. S. Regs., Part II. and the Staff Manual respectively. Title pages will be prepared in manuscript.

December 1916.

DECEMBER 1916.

Place	Date	Hour	Summary of Events and Information	Remarks and references to Appendices
	Dec. 1st		The G.O.C. reconnoitred the Intermediate Line in the morning. The G.S.O.II showed the Corps Machine Gun Officer round the machine gun positions in the Intermediate Line and Second Line but it was difficult to see owing to the fog. During the night 30th Nov./1st Dec. the 86th Brigade Group took over the portion of French line from our existing right to the SUNKEN ROAD at T.6.a.6.8.) The Corps Commander called at Divisional H.Q. during the morning. G.S.O.I visited 5t Hast Div 16 Gns (on the left) in the afternoon. Weather still fine and cold.	
	Dec. 2nd		The G.S.O.II accompanied by the O.C. 86th Machine Gun Coy. reconnoitred positions for machine guns in the Intermediate and Second Lines. During the night 1st/2nd Dec, the relief of the French as far as T.6.b.90.45 was completed without incident. 3 prisoners (2 of 193rd Regiment, 1 of 397th Regiment) were captured during the relief. A moderate hostile barrage was put on SLUSH TRENCH and to the right of it about 7 p.m. but it had little effect. The map attached to App. 1(a) shows the new boundaries between Divisions and Brigades. A frosty fine day. FLANK AVENUE was completed to BENNETT TRENCH during the night 1st/2nd Dec. The G.O.C. lectured on "Horsemastership" at the Divisional School, DAOURS, at 11 a.m. He afterwards visited the G.O.C. 20th Division.	App. 1 (a)

Army Form C. 2118.

WAR DIARY GENERAL STAFF
29TH DIVISION.
INTELLIGENCE SUMMARY.
(Erase heading not required.)

Instructions regarding War Diaries and Intelligence Summaries are contained in F. S. Regs., Part II. and the Staff Manual respectively. Title pages will be prepared in manuscript.

651

Place	Date	Hour	Summary of Events and Information	Remarks and references to Appendices
	Dec. 3rd		The G.S.O.I accompanied by an R.E. officer taped out a portion of the Intermediate line S.W. of MORVAL early in the morning. The G.O.C. 20th Division and his G.S.O.II visited H.Q. at 11 a.m. They went up to GUILLEMONT with the G.O.C. to inspect accommodation there. Drafts of Div. Defence Scheme were sent to Bdes.	
	Dec. 4th		G.S.O.II visited the right of the line early. The French Liaison Officer left to join the Guards Divn H.Qrs. The G.O.C. went up FLANK AVENUE and to right Battalion H.Q. in the morning. A fine frosty day, clear morning.	

Army Form C. 2118.

WAR DIARY – GENERAL STAFF
29TH DIVISION.
~~INTELLIGENCE~~ SUMMARY.
(Erase heading not required.)

Instructions regarding War Diaries and Intelligence Summaries are contained in F. S. Regs., Part II. and the Staff Manual respectively. Title pages will be prepared in manuscript.

Place	Date	Hour	Summary of Events and Information	Remarks and references to Appendices
	Dec. 5th		A Corps Conference was held at 29th Division H.Q. at 11.45 a.m. attended by Division Commanders and Cs.R.A. only. The G.S.O.I of 20th Division visited H.Q. to arrange about relief of 29th by 20th Division on 10th – 13th inst. A warmer day, some rain. XIVth Corps state that the Division will only be out till January 13th instead of February 10th.	
	Dec. 6th		The G.O.C. and G.S.O.I went round the whole front line from right to left during the morning. The Army Commander visited the G.O.C. in the afternoon. The G.O.C. had a conference with Brigadiers of 86th and 87th Bdes. at 4 p.m. A fire occurred in the Advanced Divl. H.Q. at 6.45 a.m. the officers' mess hut and 2 other huts being burnt to the ground. A warmer day, no rain. 29th Division Order No.79 re relief of 29th Division by 20th Division was issued. (Appendix 2 (a)	App. 2 (a)

652

Army Form C. 2118.

WAR DIARY – GENERAL STAFF
29TH DIVISION.
INTELLIGENCE SUMMARY

(Erase heading not required.)

Instructions regarding War Diaries and Intelligence Summaries are contained in F.S. Regs., Part II. and the Staff Manual respectively. Title pages will be prepared in manuscript.

653

Place	Date	Hour	Summary of Events and Information	Remarks and references to Appendices
	Dec. 7th		The G.O.C. accompanied by the G.S.O.II inspected the class on conclusion of the course at the Divisional School at DAOURS during the morning. The G.O.C. visited the G.O.C. 20th Div. at CORBIE on the way back and the Corps Commander at MEAULTE later. A damp day but no rain. Orders were received for the relief of 29th Division by 20th Division to be carried out one day earlier i.e. on 9th/10th, 10th/11th, 11th/12th nights instead of 10th/11th, 11th/12th, 12th/13th nights. Amendment to Div. Order No.79 and attached Tables was issued.(Appendix 2 (b)	App. 2 (b)
	Dec. 8th		The G.O.C. went round Intermediate Line and selected positions for "strong points" which were pegged out: he also met the G.O.C. Guards Div. on our right and decided on the point of junction of 29th and Guards Divisions in the Intermediate Line. The G.S.O.I of 20th Div. visited the left of the line with G.S.O.I 29th Div. in the morning. The A.A. & Q.M.G. visited CAVILLON (H.Q. in Rest Area) during the day. Major Middleton was appointed to command the new Labour Bn. to be formed on 9th and 10th.	

T.I34. Wt. W708-776. 500090. 4/15. Sir J.C. & S.

Army Form C. 2118.

WAR DIARY – GENERAL STAFF
29TH DIVISION.

INTELLIGENCE SUMMARY.
(Erase heading not required.)

Instructions regarding War Diaries and Intelligence Summaries are contained in F. S. Regs., Part II. and the Staff Manual respectively. Title pages will be prepared in manuscript.

654

Place	Date	Hour	Summary of Events and Information	Remarks and references to Appendices
	Dec. 9th		The G.S.O.II took the G.O.C. 20th Div. and his G.S.O.I round the right of the line via FLANK AVENUE. Rain all day. The G.S.O.III visited and reported on Strong Points dug last night. Three Battalions 87th Brigade moved to VILLE and MERICOURT. The 20th Division commenced moving up.	
	Dec. 10th		G.O.C. visited the "strong points" in the afternoon, it rained most of the day. Two Battalions 59th Brigade, 20th Division, took over the right sector during the night 10th/11th. The moves of other units were carried out in accordance with March Table attached to Division Order No.79.(App. 2 (a) Operation Order No. 80 giving particulars of move of the Division to Corps Back Area issued on this date (Appendix 2 (c)	App. 2 (a) App. 2 (c)

Army Form C. 2118.

655

WAR DIARY GENERAL STAFF
29TH DIVISION.
INTELLIGENCE SUMMARY.
(Erase heading not required.)

Instructions regarding War Diaries and Intelligence Summaries are contained in F. S. Regs., Part II. and the Staff Manual respectively. Title pages will be prepared in manuscript.

Place	Date	Hour	Summary of Events and Information	Remarks and references to Appendices
	Dec. 11th		The G.O.C. visited the forward Bde. H.Qs (59th and 87th) during the afternoon and the G.S.O.I visited them in the morning. G.S.O.II visited the Pioneer Bn. Camp in the afternoon. The Pioneer Bn. will not move with the Division into Rest Area, but will remain working under the C.E. XIVth Corps. H.Q. 20th Div. Artillery relieved H.Q. 17th Div. Artillery.	
	Dec. 12th		The G.O.C. 20th Div. took over command of the Div. Sector at 10 a.m. at which hour 29th Div. H.Q. closed at A.4.d.5.2 and reopened at CORBIE. The relief of the 2 Battalions 88th Bde. in the left sector was carried out last night without incident. The weather was bad, heavy rain and snow all night. Movements of units were carried out in accordance with March Table attached to Division Orders Nos.79 and 80. 86th Bde. H.Q. at MEAULTE, 87th Bde. H.Q. at CITADEL, 88th Bde. H.Q. at VILLE. Capt. CARDEN ROE proceeded on leave to England. The 4 Bns. of 87th Bde. left CORBIE by train for PICQUIGNY, NEUNCOURT and LE MESGE. RIENCOURT	

Army Form C. 2118.

WAR DIARY
GENERAL STAFF 29TH DIVISION
INTELLIGENCE SUMMARY.
(Erase heading not required.)

Instructions regarding War Diaries and Intelligence Summaries are contained in F.S. Regs., Part II. and the Staff Manual respectively. Title pages will be prepared in manuscript.

656

Place	Date	Hour	Summary of Events and Information	Remarks and references to Appendices
	Dec. 13th		Movements of units continued in accordance with Div. Orders Nos. 79 and 80 and Tables attached thereto. The 86th Bde. entrained at EDGEHILL during the afternoon for AILLY, PICQUIGNY (H.Q.), BREILLY and SAISSEVAL-SAISSEMONT. 87th Bde. H.Q. proceeded with them to SOUES. Div. H.Q. moved from CORBIE to CAVILLON. A Corps Conference was held at XIV Corps H.Q. near MEAULTE at 10.30 a.m. the G.O.C. was not well enough to attend. The G.S.O.I and A.A. & Q.M.G. attended.	
	Dec. 14th		The 88th Bde. moved to the new area by train from EDGEHILL during the afternoon, thus completing the move of the Division to the Rest Area.	

Army Form C. 2118.

WAR DIARY
GENERAL STAFF
29TH DIVISION.
INTELLIGENCE SUMMARY.
(Erase heading not required.)

Instructions regarding War Diaries and Intelligence Summaries are contained in F. S. Regs., Part II. and the Staff Manual respectively. Title pages will be prepared in manuscript.

657

Place	Date	Hour	Summary of Events and Information	Remarks and references to Appendices
	Dec. 15th		A Division Conference was held at Divl. H.Q. CAVILLON, all Brigadiers, Bde. Majors and Commanding Officers attended, also C.R.E. and A.A. & Q.M.G., the question of training etc. was gone into. (Appendix 3 (a)	App. 3 (a).
	Dec. 16th		The A.A. & Q.M.G. went on leave to England. The G.O.C. rode round some of the billets in the morning. In the afternoon he visited the Corps Commander at Corps H.Q. The G.S.O.I and G.S.O.II visited the rifle ranges at SAISSEVAL and LE MESGE during the afternoon.	

Army Form C. 2118.

WAR DIARY - GENERAL STAFF,
  29TH DIVISION.
or
INTELLIGENCE SUMMARY.

(Erase heading not required.)

Instructions regarding War Diaries and Intelligence
Summaries are contained in F. S. Regs., Part II.
and the Staff Manual respectively. Title pages
will be prepared in manuscript.

658

Place	Date	Hour	Summary of Events and Information	Remarks and references to Appendices
	Dec. 17th		The G.O.C. visited the 87th Brigade billets in the afternoon. A damp foggy day. Dispositions of units were altered as follows, the 2/Hants. Regt. moved from MOLLIENS-VIDAME to RIENCOURT and the 2nd S.W.Bs. from RIENCOURT to LE QUESNOY.	
	Dec. 18th		The G.O.C. and A.D.C. proceeded on leave to England. The G.S.O.I visited the Divisional School at DAOURS in the afternoon. The Royal Fusiliers moved from AILLY-SUR-SOMME to PICQUIGNY and the Border Regiment from PICQUIGNY to HANGEST. G.S.O.II proceeded on leave, and Major Goodliffe temporarily took over his duties. Brig-Gen. Cayley temporarily took over command of the Division.	

Army Form C. 2118.

WAR DIARY
~~INTELLIGENCE~~ SUMMARY

(Erase heading not required.)

Instructions regarding War Diaries and Intelligence Summaries are contained in F. S. Regs., Part II. and the Staff Manual respectively. Title pages will be prepared in manuscript.

Place	Date	Hour	Summary of Events and Information	Remarks and references to Appendices
	Dec. 19th		G.S.O.I visited 88th Brigade Headquarters. The weather turned very cold with a severe frost. G.S.O.II visited the Divisional Gas School at FOURDRINOY and 87th Brigade Headquarters. Instructions regarding matters discussed at Divisional Conference on the 14th were issued (Appendix 3 (b))	App. 3 (b)
	Dec. 20th		G.S.O.I visited the units and training area of the 87th and 88th Brigades with G.S.O.II. The weather remained very cold and frosty. 34 Supply Column moved from MOLLIENS-VIDAME to AILLY-SUR-SOMME.	

659

Army Form C. 2118.

WAR DIARY - GENERAL STAFF,
29TH DIVISION.
INTELLIGENCE SUMMARY.
(Erase heading not required.)

Instructions regarding War Diaries and Intelligence Summaries are contained in F.S. Regs., Part II. and the Staff Manual respectively. Title pages will be prepared in manuscript.

660

Place	Date	Hour	Summary of Events and Information	Remarks and references to Appendices
	Dec. 21st		G.S.O.I accompanied by the Commandant of the Divisional School visited the Cookery School at FLIXECOURT. The 1/2nd Monmouthshire Regiment came into billets at FOURDRINOY. The recent severe frost broke and was followed by heavy rain.	
	Dec. 22nd		Brig-Gen. Williams on return from leave took over the Command of the Division from Brig-Gen. Cayley. K.O.S.B. G.S.O.I visited the South Wales Borderers on their inspection by the Brigade Commander. G.S.O.II visited the Divisional School at DAOURS.	

Army Form C. 2118.

WAR DIARY - GENERAL STAFF,
29TH DIVISION.
INTELLIGENCE SUMMARY.
(Erase heading not required.)

Instructions regarding War Diaries and Intelligence Summaries are contained in F. S. Regs., Part II. and the Staff Manual respectively. Title pages will be prepared in manuscript.

661

Place	Date	Hour	Summary of Events and Information	Remarks and references to Appendices
	Dec. 23rd		G.S.O.I visited the Monmouthshire Regiment, Gas School and R. Dublin Fusrs. G.S.O.II was present at the inspection of the Inniskilling Fusiliers by the Brigade Commander.	
	Dec. 24th		G.S.O.I went to HANGEST and LE QUESNOY to inspect sites for new rifle ranges.	

Army Form C. 2118.

WAR DIARY – GENERAL STAFF, 29TH DIVISION.

~~INTELLIGENCE SUMMARY~~

(Erase heading not required.)

Instructions regarding War Diaries and Intelligence Summaries are contained in F. S. Regs., Part II. and the Staff Manual respectively. Title pages will be prepared in manuscript.

662

Place	Date	Hour	Summary of Events and Information	Remarks and references to Appendices
	Dec. 25th		CHRISTMAS DAY. G.S.O.I motored to PONT REMY to see the 4th Army Musketry School.	
	Dec. 26th		The G.S.O.I visited the Monmouthshire Regiment in the afternoon. G.S.O.II was present at an attack practice of the Monmouthshire Regiment in the morning. The G.S.O.III went to 88th. Brigade Headquarters and the Hampshire Regiment to arrange about training of ~~Monmouthshire~~ bombers.	

T2134. Wt. W708–776. 500000. 4/15. Sir J. C. & S.

Army Form C. 2118.

WAR DIARY
or
INTELLIGENCE SUMMARY

GENERAL STAFF,
29th Division.

(Erase heading not required.)

Instructions regarding War Diaries and Intelligence Summaries are contained in F. S. Regs., Part II. and the Staff Manual respectively. Title pages will be prepared in manuscript.

663

Place	Date	Hour	Summary of Events and Information	Remarks and references to Appendices
	Dec 27th		The G.S.O.1 attended a Company Exercise of the 1st King's Own Scottish Borderers. The G.S.O.2 went to FOURDRINOY to arrange about a Training Area. The G.S.O.3 visited 86th Brigade Headquarters.	
	Dec. 28th		Major General de Lisle returned from leave and resumed command of the Division. The G.S.O.1 and C.R.E. proceeded on leave. The G.S.O.2 and G.S.O.3 were present at an inspection of the 1st Lancashire Fusiliers by the Brigadier General commanding 86th Brigade. The weather was frosty in the morning, but turned to rain in the afternoon. The A.A. & Q.M.G. took over the duties of G.S.O.1 temporarily.	

Army Form C. 2118.

WAR DIARY
or
~~INTELLIGENCE SUMMARY~~
(Erase heading not required.)

GENERAL STAFF,
29th Division.

Instructions regarding War Diaries and Intelligence Summaries are contained in F. S. Regs., Part II. and the Staff Manual respectively. Title pages will be prepared in manuscript.

Place	Date	Hour	Summary of Events and Information	Remarks and references to Appendices
	Dec. 29th		The G.S.O.2 and G.S.O.3 visited the Divisional School at DAOURS.	
	Dec. 30th		The G.S.O.2 accompanied by the C.R.A. and G.S.O.2 held Conferences at all three Brigade Headquarters. These were attended by Battalion Commanders. Training Programmes and improvements of men's billets were discussed. (Appendix 3 (c))	App. 3 (c) 664
	Dec. 31st		The G.O.C. accompanied by A.D.C. visited the 17th Division Headquarters to see G.O.C. 17th Division to make arrangements about relief, and to discuss the state of the trenches etc. WEEKLY OPERATION REPORT from November 30th until 7th December is attached as Appendix 4, DAILY SUMMARIES from 1st to 11th December, are attached as Appendix 5	App. 4 App. 5

G. Fuller
for G.S.O.1.
15th Jany 1917.
for G.O.C.

T2134. Wt. W708—776. 500000. 4/15. Sir J. C. & S.

WAR DIARY, General Staff, 29th Division.

December, 1916.

Appendix I comprises:-

(a) Trench Map, 1/20,000, dated 6th December.

WAR DIARY, General Staff, 29th Division.

December, 1916.

Appendix 2 comprises:-

    (a) Order No. 79, with March and Locations Tables.

    (b) Amendment to Order No. 79.

    (c) Order No. 80 with March Table and Billeting List.

WAR DIARY, General Staff, 29th Division.

December 1916.

Appendix 3 comprises:-

    (a) Agenda of Divisional Conference held on
        December 15th.

    (b) Instructions issued on points disussed
        at Conference.

    (c) Minutes of Conferences held at each
        Brigade on 30th December.

WAR DIARY, General Staff, 29th Division.

December, 1916.

Appendix 4 comprises:-

Weekly Operation Reports.

WAR DIARY, General Staff, 29th Division.

December, 1916.

Appendix 5 comprises:-

Daily Intelligence Summaries.

Appendix 1(A)

TRENCH MAP
29TH DIV. AREA
SCALE = 1:20000
6TH DEC. 1916 N° 6.

Appendix 2(a)

SECRET.   COPY NO. 5

29th DIVISION ORDER NO. 79.

666

Reference.
ALBERT Combined Sheet
1/40,000   6th December 1916.

1.   The 29th Division (less Artillery) will be relieved by the 20th Division (less Artillery) in the front line on the nights of the 11/12th and 12/13th December.

2.   Reliefs will be carried out as follows :-
Right Brigade Group will be relieved by the 59th Brigade in the Right Sector on the 10/11th and 11/12th December.
Left Brigade Group will be relieved by the 60th Brigade in the Left Sector on the 11/12th and 12/13th December.
Details of the relief will be arranged between Brigadiers concerned. Completion of all reliefs will be reported to Divisional Headquarters

3.   The reliefs will be carried out in accordance with the attached March Tables. The times of march will be notified later.

4.   The relief of the rear Battalions of the Brigades in the line will be carried out as far as possible by day, but no relief forward of the FLERS Line will commence before 4.0 pm, All reliefs must be completed before 6.0 am. daily.
                                                except as in para: 6.
5.   (a). Troops will march in file when moving on roads.
East of GUILLEMONT intervals of 300 yards will be kept between platoons.
West of GUILLEMONT intervals of 200 yards between Companies and 500 yards between Battalions will be kept.

     (b). Transport will use the MONTAUBAN- CARNOY - FRICOURT - CEMETERY Road, and intervals of 200 yards will be kept between transport of Units.

6.   The Machine Gun Companies of the 59th and 60th Brigades will as far as possible take over from the Machine Gun Companies of the 86th and 87th Brigades respectively, during the mornings previous to the nights on which their respective Brigades take over the line. This also applies to the personnel of Stokes Mortar Batteries. Stokes Mortars in the line will be exchanged, and receipts taken.

7.   All Defence Schemes, Trench Maps, and Trench Stores, will be handed over and receipts obtained.

8.   The relief of the Field Coys. R.E. will be arranged direct between Cs.R.E.
     The 1/2nd Monmouths (Pioneer Battalion) will remain in its present camp and will take over the work of the Pioneer Battalion 20th Division under the C.E., XIVth Corps, on December 12th.

9.   The relief of the Field Ambulances and Divisional Signal Co. will be arranged direct between the A.Ds.M.S. and Os.C. Signals concerned.

10. The G.O.C., 29th Division, will hand over command of the Left Sector to the G.O.C., 20th Division, at 10. am. on the 13th inst.
     Advanced and Rear Divisional Headquarters will close at A.4.d.6.2. and A.2.d.9.7. respectively, at 10 am. on that day and

                                                          /re-open

(2).

667

~~re-open at CORBIE at the same hour.~~

'11. ACKNOWLEDGE BY WIRE.

C.J. Fuller.
Lieut. Colonel, G.S.
29th Division.

Issued at 8. A.M.

Copies 1 - 5   General Staff.   13 ✓17 A.A.&.Q.M.G.   17*
        6   86th Brigade   ✓18 Guards Division.
       ✓7   87th Brigade   19 - 20 20th Division,
       ✓8   88th Brigade   ✓21 5th Australian Division.
       ✓9   C.R.A. 17th Divn.   ✓22 XIV Corps "Q"
       ✓10   C.R.E. 29*   ✓23 XIV Corps "G"
       ✓11   .... Off i/c Sigs.   ✓24 C.R.A. 29th Divn.
       ✓12   O/C 1/2nd Monmouths

LOCATIONS TABLE.

	Evening of 9th	10th	11th	12th	13th
Right Sector.	Right Group 2 Bns. 86th & 87th Bdes.	Right Group 2 Bns. 86th & 87th Bdes.	59th Bde.x 2 Bns.	59th Bde.x 2 Bns.	59th Bde. 2 Bns.
Left Sector.	Left Group 2 Bns. 88th Bde.	Left Group 2 Bns. 88th Bde.	Left Group 2 Bns. 88th Bde.	60th Bde.∮ 2 Bns.	60th Bde. 2 Bns.
GUILLEMONT CAMP.	Right Group 1 Bn. 86th Bde. Left Group 1 Bn. 88th Bde.	59th Bde.x 1 Bn. Left Group 1 Bn. 88th Bde.	59th Bde.x 1 Bn. 60th Bde.∮ 1 Bn.	59th Bde.x 1 Bn. 60th Bde.∮ 1 Bn.	59th Bde. 1 Bn. 60th Bde. 1 Bn.
GUILLEMONT QUARRY H.Q.	86th Bde. H.Q.	86th Bde. H.Q.	59th Bde. H.Q.	59th Bde. H.Q.	59th Bde. H.Q.
GUILLEMONT STATION H.Q.	87th Bde. H.Q.	87th Bde. H.Q.	87th Bde. H.Q.	60th Bde. H.Q.	60th Bde. H.Q.
BRIQUETERIE.	Left Group 1 Bn. 88th Bde.	59th Bde.x 1 Bn.	60th Bde.∮ 1 Bn.	-----	-----
BRIQUETERIE H.Q.	88th Bde. H.Q.	59th Bde. H.Q.	60th Bde. H.Q.	61st Bde. H.Q.	61st Bde. H.Q.
CARNOY CAMP.	Right Group 1 Bn. 87th Bde. Left Group 2 Bns. 86th Bde. Right Group 2 Bns. 87th Bde.	Left Group 1 Bn. 88th Bde. 2 Bns. 86th Bde. 59th Bde.x 2 Bns.	60th Bde.∮ 1 Bn. Right Group 2 Bns. 86th & 87th Bdes. Left Group 1 Bn. 86th Bde. 59th Bde.x 1 Bn.	Left Group 2 Bns. 88th Bde. 61st Bde.x 1 Bn. 59th Bde.x 1 Bn. 60th Bde.∮ 1 Bn.	59th Bde. 1 Bn. 60th Bde. 1 Bn. 61st Bde. 3 Bns.
MANSEL CAMP.	59th Bde. 1 Bn.	60th Bde. 1 Bn.	61st Bde. 1 Bn.	61st Bde.x 1 Bn.	61st Bde. 1 Bn.
CITADEL.	59th Bde. 1 Bn.	-----	61st Bde. H.Q. Left Group 1 Bn. 88th Bde.	87th Bde. H.Q.	-----
SANDPITS.	-----	60th Bde. 1 Bn.	Left Group 1 Bn. 88th Bde.	61st Bde. 1 Bn.	Left Group 1 Bn. 88th Bde.

669

	Evening of 9th	10th	11th	12th	13th
MEAULTE	61st Bde. 2 Bns. 60th Bde. 2 Bns.	60th Bde. H.Q. 61st Bde. 2 Bns. 60th Bde. 1 Bn. Right Group 1 Bn. 86th Bde.	61st Bde. 1 Bn. 60th Bde. 1 Bn. 86th Bde. H.Q. Left Group 1 Bn. 86th Bde. Right Group 1 Bn. 86th Bde.	Right Group 2 Bns. 86th Bde. Left Group 2 Bns. 86th Bde. 86th Bde. H.Q.	86th Bde. H.Q. 86th Bde. 4 Bns.
VILLE	59th Bde. H.Q. & 1 Bn.	Right Group 1 Bn. 87th Bde. 88th Bde. H.Q.	88th Bde. H.Q. Right Group 1 Bn. 87th Bde.	88th Bde. H.Q. 61st Bde. 1 Bn.	88th Bde. H.Q. & 1 Bn.
MERICOURT	59th Bde. 1 Bn.	Right Group 2 Bns. 87th Bde.	Right Group 2 Bns. 87th Bde.	Left Group 2 Bns. 88th Bde.	88th Bde. 2 Bns.
CORBIE	60th Bde. H.Q. & 2 Bns. 61st Bde. H.Q. & 2 Bns.	60th Bde. 1 Bn. 61st Bde. H.Q. & 2 Bns.	61st Bde. 2 Bns.	Right Group 4 Bns. 87th Bde.	87th Bde. H.Q. & 4 Bns.

Units of 20th Division forming the Right Group are marked with x
"   "   "   "   "   "   "   Left "   "   "   " ɓ

MARCH TABLE.

Date.	Right Brigade Group.	Left Brigade Group.	88th Brigade.
10th Dec.	1 Bn. 86th Bde. GUILLEMONT to MEAULTE. 2 Bns. 87th Bde. CARNOY to MERICOURT. 1 Bn. 87th Bde. CARNOY to VILLE.	1 Bn. 88th Bde. BRIQUETERIE to CARNOY.	H.Q. from BRIQUETERIE to VILLE.
11th Dec.	86th Bde. H.Q. from GUILLEMONT QUARRIES to MEAULTE. 2 Bns. 87th Bde. at MERICOURT. 2 Bns. 86th & 87th Bdes. from Line to CARNOY.	1 Bn. 88th Bde. from GUILLEMONT to CITADEL. 1 Bn. 86th Bde. from CARNOY to MEAULTE. 1 Bn. 88th Bde. from CARNOY to SANDPITS.	
12th Dec.	1 Bn. 87th Bde. VILLE to CORBIE. 2 Bns. 87th Bde. MERICOURT to CORBIE. 1 Bn. 86th Bde. CARNOY to MEAULTE. 1 Bn. 87th Bde. CARNOY to CORBIE (BUS).	87th Bde. H.Q. from GUILLEMONT STATION to CITADEL. 2 Bns. 88th Bde. from Line to CARNOY. 1 Bn. 86th Bde. from CARNOY to MEAULTE. 1 Bn. 88th Bde. from CITADEL to MERICOURT. 1 Bn. 88th Bde. from SANDPITS to MERICOURT.	
13th Dec.		87th Bde. H.Q. from CITADEL to CORBIE (BUS). 2 Bns. 88th Bde. from CARNOY to VILLE (BUS) and SANDPITS.	

59th Brigade.	60th Brigade.	61st Brigade.	Remarks.
H.Q. from VILLE to BRIQUETERIE. 1 Bn. MANSEL to GUILLEMONT. 1 Bn. from CITADEL to BRIQUETERIE. 1 Bn. from MERICOURT to CARNOY. 1 Bn. from VILLE to CARNOY.	H.Q. from CORBIE to MEAULTE. 1 Bn. CORBIE to SANDPITS. 1 Bn. MEAULTE to MANSEL.	H.Q. & 2 Bns. at CORBIE.	59th Bde. becomes Reserve to 29th Division.
Relieves 86th Inf. Bde. in the Right Sector. Bde. H.Q. from BRIQUETERIE to GUILLEMONT QUARRIES. 1 Bn. from GUILLEMONT and 1 Bn. from BRIQUETERIE to the Line. 1 Bn. from CARNOY to GUILLEMONT. 1 Bn. at CARNOY.	H.Q. from MEAULTE to BRIQUETERIE. 1 Bn. from MANSEL to GUILLEMONT. 1 Bn. from MEAULTE to BRIQUETERIE. 1 Bn. from SANDPITS to CARNOY. 1 Bn. from CORBIE to MEAULTE.	H.Q. from CORBIE to CITADEL. 1 Bn. from MEAULTE to MANSEL.	2 Bns. 60th Bde. become Reserve to 29th Division.
	Relieves 87th Inf. Bde. Group in the Left Sector. H.Q. from BRIQUETERIE to GUILLEMONT STATION. 2 Bns. from GUILLEMONT and BRIQUETERIE to the Line. 1 Bn. from CARNOY to GUILLEMONT. 1 Bn. from MEAULTE to CARNOY.	H.Q. from CITADEL to BRIQUETERIE. 1 Bn. MEAULTE to CARNOY. 1 Bn. CORBIE to SANDPITS. 1 Bn. CORBIE to VILLE.	
		1 Bn. VILLE to CARNOY. 1 Bn. SANDPITS to CARNOY.	

N.B. 1 Bn. 59th Bde. moves from MERICOURT to CITADEL on the 9th inst.

Appendix 2(b).

HEADQUARTERS,
29th DIVISION.
GENERAL STAFF.
No. C.G.S.125
Date 7-12-16.

672

S E C R E T.

Amendment to 29th Division Order No. 79.
----

1. The relief will now take place one day earlier. All dates and times referred to in 29th Division Order No.79 and attached March and Locations Tables will, therefore, be amended to read 24 hours earlier.

2. For para. 2 of 29th Division Order No.79 substitute the following :-

    "Reliefs will be carried out as follows :-
    Right Brigade Group will be relieved by two Battalions of the 59th Brigade on the 9th/10th and 10th/11th December. The G.O.C. 59th Brigade will take over command of the Right Brigade Group on completion of relief on the 10th/11th December.
    Left Brigade Group will be relieved by the remaining two Battalions 59th Brigade on the 10th/11th and 11th/12th December. The G.O.C. 60th Brigade will take over command of the Left Group on completion of relief on the 11th/12th December.
    Details of the relief will be arranged between Brigadiers concerned.
    Completion of all reliefs will be reported to Divisional Headquarters."

3. In accordance with the above amendment the Locations Table attached to 29th Division Order No. 79 will be amended to read as follows :-

	Evening of 10th	11th	12th
LEFT SECTOR		59th Bde. 2 Bns.	59th Bde. 2 Bns.
GUILLEMONT CAMP		61st Bde. 1 Bn. 60th Bde. 1 Bn.	61st Bde. 1 Bn. 60th Bde. 1 Bn.
BRIQUETERIE	59th Bde. 1 Bn.		
CARNOY CAMP	60th Bde. 2 Bns. Right Group 2 Bns. 86th & 87th Bdes. Left Group 1 Bn. 86th Bde.	Left Group 2 Bns. 88th Bde. 60th Bde. 3 Bns.	60th Bde. 3 Bns. 61st Bde. 2 Bns.

Delete the note at the end of the Locations Table. The following alterations will also be made in the

/ March

- 2 -

March Table attached to 29th Division Order No. 79 :-

(a) The notes in the column of remarks on 9th and 10th December are cancelled; attention is drawn to para. 4.

(b) Dec. 10th. Cancel "1 Bn. 59th Bde. CARNOY" and substitute "1 Bn. 59th Bde. from CARNOY to BRIQUETERIE".

(c) Dec. 10th. Amend "1 Bn. 60th Bde. from MEAULTE to BRIQUETERIE" to read "1 Bn. 60th Bde. from MEAULTE to CARNOY".

(d) Dec. 11th. Insert in column under 59th Bde. "Relieves 87th Bde. Group in the Left Sector, 2 Bns. from GUILLEMONT and the BRIQUETERIE to LINE"

(e) Dec. 11th. For column under 60th Bde. substitute "H.Q. from BRIQUETERIE to GUILLEMONT STATION 1 Bn. from MEAULTE to CARNOY".

(f) Dec. 11th. For column under 61st Bde. substitute "H.Q. from CITADEL to BRIQUETERIE, 1 Bn. MEAULTE to MANSEL, 1 Bn. CORBIE to SANDPITS, 1 Bn. CORBIE to VILLE, 1 Bn. MANSEL CAMP to GUILLEMONT".

4. Reference para. 3 of 29th Division Order No. 79, the times of march will be as follows :-

9th Dec. 1 Bn. 87th Bde. Right Group will leave CARNOY at 8.30 a.m. for MERICOURT.
   1 Bn. " " " " " " " at 9.30 a.m. for MERICOURT.
   1 Bn. " " " " " " " at 10.30 a.m. for VILLE.

10th Dec.
   1 Bn. 86th Bde. Left Group " " " at 9 a.m. for MEAULTE.
   1 Bn. 88th Bde. " " " " at 10 a.m. for SANDPITS.

11th Dec.
   1 Bn. 86th Bde. Right Group " " " at 8.30 a.m. for MEAULTE.
   1 Bn. 86th Bde. Left Group " " " at 9.30 a.m. for MEAULTE.
   1 Bn. 87th Bde. Right Group " " " at 10.30 a.m. for CORBIE (by BUS)
   1 Bn. " " " " " " MERICOURT at 9 a.m. for CORBIE.
   1 Bn. " " " " " " " at 10 a.m. for CORBIE.

12th Dec.
   1 Bn. 88th Bde. Left Group " " CARNOY at 9 a.m. for SANDPITS.
   1 Bn. " " " " " " at 10 a.m. for VILLE (by BUS)

All units not mentioned above must be clear of their respective Camps by 12 noon daily.

5. Units of the 20th Division on arrival in Camps at or forward of MANSEL CAMP will come under the command of the

/ G.O.C.

- 3 -

G.O.C. 29th Division until 10 a.m. on the 12th instant.

6. The relief of parties attached to the 255th Tunnelling Company will be arranged direct between the Group Commanders concerned.

7. ACKNOWLEDGE.

                                                            C.F. Fuller.
                                            Lieut-Colonel, G.S.,
                                                   29th Division.

7th December, 1916.

To all recipients of 29th Division Order No. 79.

Appendix 2(a)

E. 695

S E C R E T.   Copy No............

29TH DIVISION ORDER NO. 80.

                                    10th December, 1916.

1.   The 29th Division (less Artillery and Pioneer Battalion) will move on December 12th, 13th and 14th from the area CORBIE - VILLE - AFRICOURT - MEAULTE - SANDPITS to XIV Corps Back Area (Area 3) for rest, replacing the 17th Division, who move into Corps Reserve.

2.   Entrainment will be carried out by Brigade Groups in accordance with the attached table A. All further instructions regarding the move by train will be issued by the A.A. & Q.M.G. The Composition of the Brigade Groups is given in Table B.

3.   Billeting parties of units will be sent forward by motor lorries under arrangements to be made by the A.A. & Q.M.G. The destinations of units are shewn in Table C.

4.   Troops will entrain with rations for the day of detrainment. Instructions regarding rations for the day following the day of detrainment will be issued by the A.A. & Q.M.G.

5.   All motor vehicles, except motor cars, will move to the new area by road in convoys under orders to be issued by the A.A. & Q.M.G.

6.   An Officer from the Headquarters of each Brigade will be detailed for duty at each entraining and detraining station. The detraining officers will proceed in the first train of their respective Brigade Groups.

7.   Divisional Headquarters will close at CORBIE and reopen at CAVILLON on a date and time to be notified later. at 4 p.m on Dec 13th.

8.   ACKNOWLEDGE.

                                        J P Fuller.
                                        Lieut-Colonel, G.S.,
                                        29th Division.

Issued at 9 p.m.

        Copies 1 - 5 General Staff.   11.   Off. i/c Sigs.
              6   86th Brigade.   12.   O.C. 1/2nd Monmouths.
              7   87th Brigade.   13-17. A.A. & Q.M.G.
              8   88th Brigade.   18.   17th Division.
              9   C.R.A. 29th Divn.   19.   XIV Corps "G".
              10   C.R.E.   20.   XIV Corps "Q".

TABLE "A".

Unit	Date	Road or train.	From	To.	Route.	Remarks.
(A) Transport 87th Bde.Group	Dec. 12th	Road.	CORBIE	Area 3	VECQUEMONT-AMIENS - N. of SOMME - Cross to S. of SOMME at LONGPRE	Not to enter AMIENS before 11.15 a.m.
(B) Personnel 87th Bde Group	13th	Train	CORBIE	Area 3		Entrain at CORBIE at a time to be notified later. To start at 9 a.m.
(C) Transport 86th Bde.Group	13th	Road	MEAULTE	DAOURS		No restrictions as to time. Head of transport to pass VECQUEMONT at 9.20 am
(D) Transport 86th Bde Group	13th	Road	DAOURS	Area 3	VECQUEMONT-AMIENS - N. of SOMME - Cross to S. of SOMME at LONGPRE	
(E) Personnel 86th Bde Group	13th	Train	MEAULTE	Area 3		Entrain at EDGEHILL at a time to be notified later.
(F) Transport 88th Bde Group	13th	Road	VILLE MERICOURT & SANDPITS	DAOURS		No restrictions as to time.
(G) Transport 88th Bde Group	14th	Road	DAOURS	Area 3	VECQUEMONT-AMIENS - N. of SOMME - Cross to S. of SOMME at LONGPRE.	No restrictions as to time. Head of transport to pass VECQUEMONT at 9.20 am.
(H) Personnel 88th Bde Group	14th	Train	VILLE MERICOURT & SANDPITS	Area 3		Entrain at MERICOURT at a time to be notified later.

TABLE "B".

Composition of Brigade Groups
(for the march only).

86th Brigade Group.

    86th Brigade.

    3/Kent Field Co. R.E. (less 1 section MEAULTE).

    89th Field Ambulance.

    No. 2 Co. A.S.C.

87th Brigade Group.

    87th Brigade.

    2/London Field Co. R.E. (less 1 section at DAOURS).

    87th Field Ambulance.

    No. 3 Co. A.S.C.

88th Brigade Group.

    88th Brigade.

    1/W. Riding Field Co. R.E.

    88th Field Ambulance.

    No. 4 Co. A.S.C.

TABLE "C".

BILLETING LIST.

Divisional Headquarters (less as detailed below)	CAVILLON.
C.R.A. Headquarters	CAVILLON.
C.R.E. Headquarters	PICQUIGNY.
86th Brigade H.Q. (less M.G.Coy)	PICQUIGNY
2nd Royal Fusiliers	AILLY-sur-SOMME.
1st Lancashire Fusiliers	AILLY-sur-SOMME.
1st R.Dublin Fusiliers	SAISSEVAL & SAISSEMONT.
16th Middlesex Regt.	BREILLY.
86th M.G.Coy.	SAISSEMONT.
3/Kent Field Co.R.E.	PICQUIGNY.
89th Field Ambulance	PICQUIGNY.
No. 2 Co. A.S.C.	FOURDRINOY.
87th Brigade H.Q.	SOUES
2nd South Wales Borderers	RIENCOURT.
1st K.O.S. Borderers	LE MESGE.
1st R.Inniskilling Fus.	PICQUIGNY.
1st Border Regt.	PICQUIGNY.
2/London Field Co. R.E.	RIENCOURT.
87th Field Ambulance.	SOUES.
No. 3 Co.A.S.C.	PICQUIGNY.
88th Bde. H.Q.	MOLLIENS-VIDAME.
4th Worcester Regt.	MOLLIENS-VIDAME
2nd Hants. Regt.	MOLLIENS-VIDAME.
1st Essex Regt.	MONTAGNE.
1st Newfoundland Regt.	CAMPS-en-AMIENOIS.
1/W.Riding Field Co.R.E.	BREUIL.
88th Field Ambulance.	MOLLIENS-VIDAME.
No. 4 Co. A.S.C.	MOLLIENS-VIDAME.
A.D.M.S., A.D.V.S., D.A.D.O.S.	OISSY.
Reserve Co.	OISSY.
Divisional Train H.Q.	OISSY.
Mobile Vet. Section.	OISSY
Supply Column	MOLLIENS-VIDAME.
Sanitary Section	RIENCOURT.

Appendix 3(a).

Divisional Conference No.14 held at CAVILLON, December 15th, 1916, Brigadiers and Battalion Commanders attending.

679

(A) <u>Points of general interest.</u>

(B) <u>Interior Economy.</u>

    (1) Company Orderly Officers.

    (2) Daily Inspection of Billets.

    (3) Comfort of the troops.

    (4) Amusements.

(C) <u>Transport.</u>

    (1) Care of horses, harness and vehicles.

    (2) First Line Transport on the march.

    (3) Order of march.

    (4) Distance to be maintained between Units.

    (5) Position of Officers.

    (6) Riding on Wagons.

    (7) Details to march in formed bodies.

    (8) Wearing equipment.

    (9) Overloading Wagons.

(D) <u>Training.</u>

    <u>Trench Warfare</u> :-

    (1) Attention drawn to 4th Army No. G.S.360 and Divisional Memorandum No. 62 issued herewith.

    (2) Musketry - Every officer and man to fire a modified course. Those who do not reach a reasonable standard to repeat.

    (3) Drill - Drills must be short, their object being more for officers to acquire powers of command than for the instruction of the men.

    (4) Organisation of work for the following day by Commanding Officers by means of daily conferences, to decide on what is to be done and how to do it.

    <u>Open Warfare</u> :-

    (1) Skirmishing.

    (2) Fire and Movement.

    (3) Villages - Barricades.

    (4) Protection - Advanced, Flank and Rear Guards - Outposts.

    (5) Digging in.

Appendix 3(6)

C.R.A.
C.R.E.
Officer i/c Signals.
86th Brigade.
87th Brigade.
88th Brigade.
O.C. 1/2nd Monmouths.
A.D.M.S.
A.A. & Q.M.G.
A.D.V.S.
O.C. Divl. Train.

With reference to the Agenda of the Divl. Conference No. 14 held at CAVILLON on the 14th inst., units are reminded of the following instructions, which were issued verbally by the G.O.C.

B. Interior Economy.

(2) Billets should be inspected by platoon, Company, Battalion and Brigade Commanders. Two 4-inch nails on which to hang his equipment should be issued to every man. A uniform method of storing equipment and clothing should be adopted throughout each Battalion or other unit.

(3) The following is the order of precedence for the improvements to existing accommodation in billets :-
- Cookhouses
- Latrines
- Urinals
- Bunks for officers and men
- Washhouses.

The A.D.M.S. will investigate and report on the water supply arrangements, with a view to their improvement.

(4) As far as possible, canteens will be opened in each area. The Divisional Band will be placed at the disposal of Brigades in turn, and where possible arrangements will be made for cinemas to visit the billets in turn.

C. Transport.

A memorandum on the "March Discipline of Transport" No. A.45/4 has been prepared, and three copies of it will be issued to each Battalion or other unit.
The transport of Brigades, Battalions and other units should be inspected on the march.
Units, who have not got in their possession copies of Field Service Regulations or other manuals, should apply for them direct to Divisional Headquarters (G.S.).

D. Training.

Copies of G.S. Memorandum 62, regarding "Trench Warfare", and G.S. Memorandum 63 re "Open Warfare" have been issued to all concerned.
(2) Every man should be exercised in firing his rifle and in throwing a Mills Grenade. Those who do not attain a reasonable standard in these respects, should repeat the practises.

19th December, 1916.

Lieut-Colonel, G.S.,
29th Division.

Appendix 3(c)

68

Minutes of Conferences held at each Brigade
Commanding Officers attending, on 30th December, 1916.

G.O.C. Division read out notes of the last Conference, again emphasising the necessity for the recovery of barrack discipline, by uniformity of system in battalions.

Battalion commanders reported good progress had been made with straw mattresses and latrine seats, but material for bunks was still lacking, this will be further expedited.

G.O.C. Division inquired what training had been done. Satisfactory progress appeared to have been made in the training of Companies and Battalions for the attack, of Lewis Guns and rank and file in musketry. Further efforts must be made in the training of grenadiers, who still appear to be short of the numbers required.

It was pointed out that officers require to be taught the meaning of contours, use of the compass, and finding their way across country. The best way of doing this is to take officers out for a ride in the afternoon, stopping and asking them to locate themselves on the map, and similar questions.

The point that must not be overlooked is to the training of flanking bombing parties, including the use of stokes guns and snipers. At least one such party per Battalion is to be trained on the lines of G.S. Memorandum No. 62 dated 15th December, 1916, already sent out.

With reference to G.S. Memo. 26 dated 19th December, 1916 :-

(1) Lewis Guns should be employed on the outer flanks of platoons instead of in the centre as shown on the diagram

with

- 2 -

with this memo., the object being to cover gaps caused by men closing inwards during an advance.

(2) Grenadiers should be 5 yards in front of platoons, to prevent their throwing being hampered by the men in the ranks coming up behind them.

(3) Mopping-up parties (which will always be at least 25% of the attacking party) should be found from a reserve battalion and provided with rifles, grenades, "P" bombs, and one stokes bomb, the latter for clearing dug-outs.

(4) One Blocking party per Company must be trained for use where required, and provided with Stokes guns and snipers, which will be employed as a general rule on the flank.

Tactical schemes in which the G.O.C. Division will see Commanding Officers, will be prepared by Brigades and submitted early to Divisional Headquarters for G.O.C. Division's approval.

The foot exercises for prevention of trench feet, recently published, form an important part of training and must receive particular attention.

G.O.C. Division will inspect 2 Battalions at a time together with their transport. It is important that march discipline of transport should be attended to now, if we want to see our transport up on the march when we move forward.

First line transport will be placed at the disposal of Battalions for training and march discipline, under Brigade arrangements. Any extra transport required to effect this to be applied for to D.A.Q.M.G.

The G.O.C. Division will see the two battalions together, who will normally attack together.

Employed men and grooms now being trained are to

/ be

be included on the G.O.C's inspection parades which will begin on Tuesday 2nd January, 1917. Programme will be issued separately.

Each Brigade will select ground for their two Battalions in the attack and write orders for the attack, the Battalions writing their orders on the Brigade orders. The Battalion orders will not, however, be issued to Company Commanders till the troops are in position to attack.

Attention was called to the French pamphlet on the offensive, para. 5 as to what Battalion and Company Commanders should include in orders.

L.H. Abbott

30th December, 1916.

Lieut-Colonel,
for G.S.O.1, 29th Division.

Appendix (4)

HEADQUARTERS.
W.R.28.
INTELLIGENCE.

684

29TH DIVISION WEEKLY OPERATION REPORT.

From 8.30 a.m. 30th November to 8.30 a.m. 7th December, 1916.

ARTILLERY. Enemy artillery activity was on the whole normal with periods of increased intensity, during the period under review.
About 5.30 p.m. on the 1st December White flares bursting into red stars were fired from the enemy's lines, and an artillery barrage on support lines followed immediately. The area covered by this fire extended from the left of SLUSH TRENCH for a distance of 600 yards to the right. The barrage extended in a less degree to the support trenches of the Left Brigade. The average depth appeared to be about 400 yards.
On the 2nd December several high velocity naval shells fell in GUILLEMONT but did little damage.
On the 3rd December our Trenches T.6.1 - T.6.12 were heavily bombarded with 77 mm. and 5.9" howitzer shells. A good deal of damage was done to these trenches.
There has been the usual intermittent shelling of LES BOEUFS and the approaches to the line during the week.
Our own Artillery have maintained their continuous shelling of the enemy lines. Our reply to the enemy barrage on the night of 1st December was most effective.

INFANTRY. The enemy infantry have been far more lively during the week, and it has required every effort on the part of our snipers etc. to subdue them.

SNIPING. On the 30th November a party of the enemy were observed about 150 yards from ZENITH TRENCH. They were fired on, and three seen to fall.
On the 4th December we accounted for three more of the enemy near the gun pits at T.5.b.9.9.
Several other parties have been dispersed with probably good results.
The enemy have been active from the vicinity of ORION TRENCH and SLEET TRENCH, also from T.6.a.,
During the bombardment on the 3rd December, but they were rapidly silenced by our own snipers and Lewis guns.

MACHINE GUNS. We continue to worry the enemy with Machine gun and Lewis gun fire; yet draw little fire in reply.
On the night of the 6th December, enemy machine gun activity was more pronounced. A gun fired on one of our wiring parties evidently from a sap at N.35.a.3.5.

RIFLE GRENADES. Rifle grenades were fired for the first time against our line on the night of the 2nd December, in reply to a volley fired by us from Trench N.35.4.
The enemy fired two grenades only which burst 50 yards short. A further volley from us silenced them.

PATROLS. Our patrols maintain complete mastery in NO MAN'S LAND, and every night bring back important information as to the enemy's wire, new trenches, etc.
No enemy patrols have been encountered.
As no recent aeroplane photographs have been taken of the greater part of our line, this information has been doubly necessary.
An enemy patrol approached our trench N.35.7 and were dispersed by our fire, on the night of 5th December.

/ IDENTIFICATIONS.

IDENTIFICATIONS.

(1) Just before dawn on the 30th November two Germans approached our sap head in N.35.3. They were called to come in but both turned round and ran away. One was shot and his body found. He was identified as belonging to the 81st Reserve Regiment (normal).

(2) Three prisoners were taken on the 1st December on the new front taken over from the French. Two of these belonged to the 193rd Reserve Regiment and the other to the 397th Regiment.

(3) Another prisoner of the 397th Regiment was taken by our Right Battalion on the morning of the 6th December.

TAKING OVER FROM FRENCH.

On the night of the 1st/2nd December we completed the taking over of the French line as far as T.6.b.85.40.

8th December, 1916.

Lieut-Colonel, G.S.,
29th Division.

Appendix 5

29TH DIVISION DAILY SUMMARY.

From 8.30 a.m. 30.11.15. to 8.30 a.m. 1...

OPERATIONS.

Artillery. Enemy shelled intermittently during the day; little damage was done.
A portion of LA GRAHR Trench was enfiladed last night by a few field gun shells.

Infantry. Just before dawn two Germans approached our sap head in PALL Trench. They were called to come in, but both hesitated, turned round, and made off. One man was shot and his body found. He had 81 on his shoulder strap, and the enclosed pocket book was the only other identification on him. He was unarmed. It is presumed he belongs to the 81st Reserve Regiment (normal).

At dawn enemy were observed about 150 yards in front of TRINITY Trench by the wire. They were fired on, and three seen to fall.

INTELLIGENCE.

Enemy Movements. From our Observation Post in the trench in front of HUSSAR Trench, enemy parties were fired at, coming along the SUNKEN Road in front of LE GRANTAIN, and stretcher parties were seen moving along the same road (H.29.d.).

Signals. Red flares were fired opposite our line at 8.15 p.m. last night. It is reported that they were sent up when the Germans appeared to be firing short and hitting their own trench.

WORK DONE.

Clearing and draining trenches. Many trench boards have been put down in GLOBE Avenue and in ULSTER Trench. Owing to the soil being in harder condition, much improvement has been made in all trenches.

A sketch is enclosed showing the approximate position of enemy line in front of PALL Trench, as reported by patrol on the 30th November.

Captain, G.S.,
29th Division.

1st December, 1915.

29TH DIVISION DAILY SUMMARY.

From 8.30 a.m. 3.12.16. to 8.30 a.m. 4.12.16.

OPERATIONS.

Artillery. Enemy artillery were more active than usual throughout the day and night on most of the forward area. Between 10 a.m. and 1 p.m. the right of our line was heavily bombarded. Shells fired were mostly 5.9's and 77 mm. shells. (H.E.) A good deal of damage was done to our trenches.
T.6.9 and T.6.8 were both blown in, also the communication trenches forward.
Most of the shells fell on the support line, and two machine guns were put out of action.
The left of our line was shelled heavily during the night. Early this morning LES BOEUFS, THISTLE and WINDY TRENCHES, were shelled with 77 mm and 105 mm H.E.

Snipers. Hostile snipers were active after the above bombardment, opposite the right of our line, but were quietened by our snipers and Lewis guns.

Rifle grenades. A certain amount of rifle grenade fire was also directed against this portion of our line.

INTELLIGENCE.

Enemy Movements. It is reported that the enemy opposite our right does not show himself nearly as freely as when we first took over this portion of the line from the French.

About 10 a.m. a party of 20 of the enemy were observed to be working N.N.E. of the strong point in BENNETT TRENCH (T.5.1). Fire was opened on the party and they dispersed rapidly, evidently suffering several casualties.

Enemy Defences. Enemy wire opposite the right of our line consists of broken lengths of French barbed wire and trip wire. This wire is very thin and only of a depth of about 4 feet (patrol report).

Signals. The enemy put up flares during the night opposite our Left Brigade, which burst into 4 red lights.
Single red flares were also observed and it appeared that these were sent up when the enemy artillery was firing short. (This seems to confirm previous information on this subject.)

It is reported that a shell which fell just E. of MORVAL, threw out a green rocket which burnt for a few seconds after reaching the ground.

WORK DONE.

Work has been continued on clearing Communication Trench between SUMMER and AUTUMN TRENCHES; also the trench between ZENITH TRENCH and OZONE AVENUE.
Improvements have been made to shelters in DEWDROP and THISTLE TRENCHES.
Wire has been erected in front of T.6.9 to T.6.11.
T's have been deepened in front of T.5.2 and ANTELOPE TRENCH.

4th December, 1916.

Captain, G.S.,
29th Division.

29TH DIVISION DAILY SUMMARY.

From 8.30 a.m. 4.12.16. to 8.30 a.m. 5.12.16.

OPERATIONS.

Artillery. Enemy artillery activity normal. The area chiefly shelled was that around LES BOEUFS. Our own artillery were very active especially during the night.

Machine Guns. A machine gun fired several bursts opposite our Left Brigade during the night, but could not be located.

Snipers. Our snipers claim to have disposed of three of the enemy near the gun pits at T.5.b.9.9. There was considerable hostile sniping opposite our centre throughout the day. Attempts have been made to deal with this also.

INTELLIGENCE.

Hostile aircraft. From 8.30 a.m. yesterday and onwards, there was considerable aeroplane activity on both sides. A hostile plane was heavily engaged by anti-aircraft guns on the GUILLEMONT - GINCHY road at 9 a.m. Between 2 p.m. and 4 p.m. a hostile plane reconnoitred our front lines from a low elevation. This aeroplane carried streamers (possibly this denotes a contact patrol machine). It was engaged by rifle and machine gun fire from the trenches, and driven off though apparently not hit. When our anti-aircraft guns opened fire, the machine was observed to drop white, red and green flares in quick succession. Later six more hostile machines flew over LES BOEUFS and MORVAL, and were engaged by our anti-aircraft guns.

Enemy Defences.(1)There is a row of French concertina wire in front of the German line at the gun pits at T.5.b.9.9, and in front of the trench from these gun pits to the gun pits at N.36.c.6.0.
(2) A new sap appears to have been dug to a point about 50 or 60 yards in front of N.35.7.

Method of holding the line. A patrol of one officer and 2 other ranks left N.35.7 at midnight, and proceeded N.E. for 30 yards. There they discovered a line of sentries in groups of 2 or 3. It was noticed that all lights sent up, were sent up from behind this line. The patrol returned at 12.45 a.m., and went out again from trench N.34.2 and found a similar line of sentries about 120 yards from our lines.

WORK.

Work Done. Trench boards laid in BENNETT TRENCH. 45 yards of berm constructed. Trench commenced to join MARBURG TRENCH to SLUSH TRENCH. Fire step commenced in MARBURG TRENCH. Work continued on clearing of FLANK AVENUE. OZONE TRENCH further cleared and more trench boards laid. Communications between ZENITH and SUMMER, WINTER, THISTLE and DEWDROP, are all being improved. Artillery boards have been placed in position by the right battalion of the Left Brigade.

ENEMY NEW DOCUMENTS.

Some documents taken off enemy dead are forwarded herewith.

5th December, 1916.

Captain, G.S.,
29th Division.

29TH DIVISION DAILY SUMMARY.

From 8.30 a.m. 5.12.16. to 8.30 a.m. 6.12.16.

OPERATIONS.

Artillery.   The enemy shelled principally our support and reserve trenches.
THISTLE TRENCH was heavily shelled in the afternoon about 2 p.m. and LES BOEUFS as well, but on the whole the period was quieter than the average.
Our own artillery were active between 11 a.m. and dusk.

Rifle Grenades.   Six rifle grenades were fired into N.35.9. Our bombers retaliated in kind.
The right battalion of the left Brigade also fired Rifle grenades into shell holes in front of their line which it is suspected the enemy are occupying.

Snipers.   Between 8.30 a.m. and 9.30 a.m. enemy sniping was very heavy in front of N.35.4.   Our snipers engaged the enemy snipers and effectively silenced them, as there was no more sniping on this part of the line for the remainder of the day.

Patrols.   An enemy patrol of 5 men approached our trench N.35.7 from a direction N.N.E.   They were fired on and dispersed.

INTELLIGENCE.

Enemy Defences.   Our Bombing Post in N.35.8. report that the enemy was wiring immediately in front of them during the night. The rise in the ground prevents the ground wired being observed by daylight from our left O.P., so the extent of the work is not yet known.

Identifications.   A prisoner of the 397th Regiment, 222nd Division, was captured by our right battalion this morning (normal).

N.B.   No Intelligence Summary has yet been received from the Right Brigade.   Any information of importance will be wired to XIV Corps "I".

WORK DONE.

The gap between T.5.7. and T.5.6. is linked up, a communication trench having been dug.
Communication trenches between FALL and AUTUMN have been cleared out.
50 yards of wire has been placed in front of N.35.2, and 50 yards in front of N.35.9.
Fire steps have been made in SUMMER and MENDETT TRENCHES.
OZONE TRENCH.
Trench has been improved and more duck-boards laid.
Work has also been done on other important Communication trenches.

6th December, 1916.

Captain, G.S.,
29th Division.

29TH DIVISION DAILY SUMMARY.

From 8.30 a.m. 8.12.16. to 8.30 a.m. 9.12.16.

OPERATIONS.

Artillery. Enemy artillery activity was below normal during the day.
The chief areas shelled were LES BOEUFS, S.W. of ZENITH TRENCH and in the vicinity of COW TRENCH.
In reply to our artillery bombardment at 10 p.m. the enemy opened a heavy fire against our lines. Trenches which suffered the most were as follows :- ANTELOPE TRENCH, Front Line from T.6.1. to T.6.4., FLANK AVENUE, OZONE AVENUE, SUMMER and DEWDROP TRENCHES.
A direct hit was obtained on left battalion headquarters at N.34.c.1½.8. One of the entrances was completely blown in, but luckily no casualties were caused.
FROSTY, AUTUMN and COW TRENCHES were also shelled but not with the same effect.
Quiet was restored by 11.30 p.m.
There was a certain amount of shelling this morning after dawn mostly W. and N.W. of LES BOEUFS.

Sniping. Enemy snipers were considerably less active than usual throughout the day.

Patrols. A patrol which went out from our line from our new trench at about T.5.b.9.6. after proceeding 40 yards from our trench, saw 3 of the enemy. Our patrol attempted to follow them but a machine gun opened fire from a point very close and they were obliged to return (probably from the gun pits at T.5.b.9.9).

Lewis Guns. Several enemy working parties were heard during the night and were dealt with by our Lewis Guns.

INTELLIGENCE.

Enemy Signals. It is reported from both Brigades that when our artillery opened fire last night, numerous green rockets were fired from the enemy lines, whereupon their artillery immediately opened fire.

Machine Gun Positions. A machine gun traversed our lines yesterday, evidently firing from detached post at N.36.c.8.2. Men have frequently been seen moving towards this point over the open. This agrees with information given by aeroplane photographs.

Enemy Tracks. A much used track can be seen leading down the slope fronting FALL TRENCH at approximately N.35.d.9.9.

WORK DONE.

New trench in front of T.5.2. etc. deepened and broadened.
FLANK AVENUE cleared for distance of 100 yards.
SUMMER TRENCH revetted with sandbags and trench boards laid.
FALL TRENCH improved and fire stepped.
Sumps constructed in OZONE AVENUE and trench boards relaid.
Six strong points constructed in new Intermediate Line.

Captain, G.S.,

9th December, 1916.   29th Division.

29TH DIVISION DAILY SUMMARY.
From 8.30 a.m. 9.12.16. to 8.30 a.m. 10.12.16.

OPERATIONS.

Artillery. Enemy artillery activity was below normal. About 10.30 a.m. the Headquarters of the Left Battalion at N.34.c.1½.8. were again shelled with 105 mm. H.E. shells at the rate of about 10 rounds per minute. Our own artillery fired intermittently throughout the night; our heavies being particularly active between 8 p.m. and 11 p.m.

INTELLIGENCE.

Enemy Defences.
(a) An officer's patrol reconnoitred the enemy lines from N.35.d.8.3 to N.35.d.0.7 approximately. They brought back the following information :-
(1) The enemy trench is lightly held but has two Machine Guns in it about 35 yards apart.
(2) Wire extends along the whole of the area examined and is 6 ft. deep and lightly staked.
(3) A sniper was at work firing from approximately N.35.d.0.7.
(b) Another patrol went out from T.5.b.7.6. and report that the enemy were wiring their line about the gun pits at T.5.b.9.9.

Signals.
Yesterday when enemy artillery was firing short red flares were sent up by the infantry, apparently from a house in LE TRANSLOY about N.30.c.8.3.

R.E.

All available men were engaged in maintaining trenches where they had fallen in owing to heavy rain.
Work was done making a fire step in COW TRENCH.
A considerable amount of salvage was brought back by the Left Brigade.

Documents.
Papers recovered from the body of a dead German, are forwarded herewith.

L. Carden Roe
Captain, G.S.,
10th December, 1916.   29th Division.

D.S.201.

29TH DIVISION DAILY SUMMARY.
From 8.30 a.m. 10.12.16 to 8.30 a.m. 11.12.16.

OPERATIONS.

Artillery. Enemy artillery was active during the day; MORVAL and vicinity of T.10.b. were shelled heavily with 15 cm. and 10.5 cm. shells. T.8.10 and T.9.3. shelled all day with 77 m. T.13.b. and T.14.a. intermittently shelled. Railway at T.13.d.9.4., one direct hit.

During the night the enemy artillery activity was much below normal. There was practically no shelling at all on front line and support line.

SNIPING.

Intermittent sniping with machine guns firing from about N.35.d.5.3. and also from about N.36.d.5.3.

INTELLIGENCE. **Movements.** No enemy movements or signals observed.

Aircraft. Hostile aeroplane passed over our front line from West to East about 1.30 a.m.

Owing to relief little intelligence has been collected.

L. Carden Roe

Captain, G.S.,
29th Division.

11th December, 1916.